Lessons from an Unconventional War

Pergamon Titles of Related Interest

Daniel   STRATEGIC MILITARY DECEPTION
Kronenberg   PLANNING U.S. SECURITY
Sarkesian   BEYOND THE BATTLEFIELD:
  The New Military Professionalism
Taylor   DEFENSE MANPOWER PLANNING:
  Issues for the 1980s

Related Journals*

BULLETIN OF SCIENCE, TECHNOLOGY AND SOCIETY
PROGRESS IN AEROSPACE SCIENCES
UNDERGROUND SPACE SYSTEM

*Free specimen copies available upon request.

PERGAMON
POLICY
STUDIES

ON INTERNATIONAL POLITICS

Lessons from an Unconventional War

Reassessing U.S. Strategies for Future Conflicts

Edited by
Richard A. Hunt
Richard H. Shultz, Jr.,

Pergamon Press

NEW YORK • OXFORD • TORONTO • SYDNEY • PARIS • FRANKFURT

Pergamon Press Offices:

U.S.A.   Pergamon Press Inc., Maxwell House, Fairview Park,
                             Elmsford, New York 10523, U.S.A.

U.K.   Pergamon Press Ltd., Headington Hill Hall,
                             Oxford OX3 0BW, England

CANADA   Pergamon Press Canada Ltd., Suite 104, 150 Consumers Road,
                             Willowdale, Ontario M2J 1P9, Canada

AUSTRALIA   Pergamon Press (Aust.) Pty. Ltd., P.O. Box 544,
                             Potts Point, NSW 2011, Australia

FRANCE   Pergamon Press SARL, 24 rue des Ecoles,
                             75240 Paris, Cedex 05, France

FEDERAL REPUBLIC   Pergamon Press GmbH, Hammerweg 6
OF GERMANY   6242 Kronberg/Taunus, Federal Republic of Germany

Library of Congress Cataloging in Publication Data
Main entry under title:

Lessons from an unconventional war.

   (Pergamon policy studies on international
politics)

   1. Vietnamese Conflict, 1961-1975. I. Hunt,
Richard A., 1942-   . II. Shultz, Richard H.,
1947-   . III. Series.
U742.L47   1981   959.704′31   81-10648
ISBN 0-08-027186-3   AACR2

Printed in the United States of America

We respectfully dedicate this book to our parents

Contents

CHAPTER

List of Acronyms

AID	Agency for International Development (U.S.)
ARVN	Army of the Republic of Vietnam (South Vietnam)
AVF	All Volunteer Force (U.S.)
CG	Civil Guard
CIA	Central Intelligence Agency (U.S.)
CMH	(U.S. Army) Center of Military History
CORDS	Civil Operations and Revolutionary Development Support (U.S.)
COSVN	Hanoi's Field Command for the Southern Part of South Vietnam
CPSU/ID	International Department of the Committee of the Communist Party (USSR)
CTZ	Corps Tactical Zone (a military designation for the four corps areas of South Vietnam. Also called military region).
DMZ	Demilitarized Zone
DOD	Department of Defense (U.S.)
DRV	Democratic Republic of Vietnam (North Vietnam)
DSA	District Senior Adviser (U.S.)
FNLA	National Liberation Front for Angola
GRU	Chief Intelligence Directorate of the Soviet General Staff
GVN	Government of Vietnam (South Vietnam)
HES	Hamlet Evaluation System
KGB	Soviet Commission of State Security (USSR)
LIC	Low Intensity Conflict
LOC	Lines of Communication
MAAG	Military Assistance Advisory Group (U.S.)
MACV	Military Assistance Command, Vietnam
MATA	Military Assistance Training Adviser
MPLA	Popular Movement for the Liberation of Angola
MR	Military region, same as CTZ or corps

NATO	North Atlantic Treaty Organization
NCO	Noncommissioned Officer
NLF	National Liberation Front
NVA	North Vietnamese Army
OCO	Office of Civil Operations, Saigon (predecessor of CORDS)
OPEC	Organization of Petroleum Exporting Countries
PAAS	Pacification Attitude Analysis Survey
PACES	Pacification Evaluation System
PF	Popular Forces (South Vietnam)
PROVN	Program for the Pacification and Long-Term Development of South Vietnam
PSA	Province Senior Adviser (U.S.)
PSG	Pacification Studies Group, CORDS
RAD	Research and Development Division of CORDS
RDF	Rapid Development Force (U.S.)
RF	Regional Forces (South Vietnam)
RVN	Republic of Vietnam (South Vietnam)
RVNAF	Republic of Vietnam Armed Forces (South Vietnam)
SDC	Self-Defense Corps
SEATO	South East Asia Treaty Organization
SF	Special Forces (U.S.)
UNITA	National Union for the Total Independence of Angola
USIA	United States Information Agency
USOM	United States Operations Mission
VC	Viet Cong
VCI	Viet Cong Infrastructure
VNAF	Republic of Vietnam Air Force
VSSG	Vietnam Special Studies Group (U.S.)

Introduction
Richard A. Hunt

This book contains a collection of essays on Vietnam by authors of diverse backgrounds, each with his own viewpoint.
It is the work of historians, political scientists, and war-
participants turned writers. Each writes on a different aspect
or period of the longest war in U.S. history. No attempt has
been made to smooth the sharp edges of individual interpretation or to reach a homogeneous perspective or conclusion
about the war. Each interpretation is the author's own. What
unifies the collection is a common concern with pacification or
counterinsurgency.
 Of all the components of the Vietnam war, the pacification
program has become perhaps the most encrusted with miscon-
ceptions and the most in need of clarification. Pacification encompassed military and civil functions. It sought to secure
inhabited villages and hamlets with paramilitary forces; it also
sought to provide police forces both to maintain law and order
and to uncover and uproot the clandestine Viet Cong political
apparatus, often called the infrastructure, that directed the
rural insurgency. Pacification included such political actions
as propaganda and psychological operations aimed at inducing
the Viet Cong to desert and at winning the allegiance of villagers. It also attempted to mobilize popular support through
local and national elections, economic development, and sorely
needed social changes. Pacification was, thus, conceived as a
counterstrategy to Wars of National Liberation.
 It cannot be stressed too much that South Vietnamese
political officials and military and police forces administered
and carried out the pacification program; the Americans served
only as bankers and advisers. Despite charges that the Saigon
government was a puppet regime, U.S. policy, especially in
regard to pacification, respected the sovereignty of the fledg-
ing Republic of Vietnam, a deference that sharply limited the

influence or leverage that United States officials could exert. In no facet of the war did Americans command South Vietnamese; at best, U.S. advisers exhorted, cajoled, or sought to persuade. Whether the government of South Vietnam won the political support of the people, whether the villagers felt secure from the taxation or terrorism of the infrastructure or from the raids of guerrillas, whether local officials were responsive to local problems were tasks that the South Vietnamese alone could accomplish. How well the Saigon regime performed those tasks indicated how well they were doing in the countryside.

Other factors circumscribed U.S. influence. Withholding U.S. aid from the South Vietnamese in exchange for reform or a purge of corrupt officials pointed to an inherent dilemma of leverage and pacification. Withholding aid could be self-defeating because it would give the communists an opportunity to strike at our weakened ally. Forcing the South Vietnamese government to reform could jeopardize its own interests, because swiftly and vigorously pursuing social justice might undermine the very political and social structure supporting the government. If U.S. policy was to promote security before reform, there was a danger that the government elite would have no incentive to reform. If the United States insisted on reform first, it was possible that the government might fall from internal conflict.

In theory and practice, pacification was never self-sufficient or autonomous. It was dependent on the provision of military protection to keep large, unfriendly units from the villages undergoing pacification. The program was intended to counter Viet Cong propaganda, terrorism, and guerrilla forays, not to cope with battalions and regiments, tanks and artillery. The success of pacification at the province and national levels also depended on the cooperation and coordination of civil and military authorities. Without support from U.S. or South Vietnamese military engineers, for example, building or clearing roads in contested areas might prove impossible. On the other hand, fighting in the villages undoubtedly set the process of pacification back, whether the Viet Cong started the action or whether American or South Vietnamese units overreacted with excessive firepower.

Pacification was an appropriate strategy in Vietnam in a relative sense only. Before American and North Vietnamese troops entered the war, pacification was, at least in official rhetoric, the centerpiece of the attack against the Viet Cong's political/military insurgency. This is the period about which James Dunn writes in chapter 1. When the North Vietnamese sent conventional military forces to finish off a floundering Saigon government and the Americans responded in 1965 with combat forces to prop up the South Vietnamese, the on going political struggle and the advisory effort were soon over-

Robert W. Komer, believed success would remain beyond the grasp of the United States if the South Vietnamese government was unable to protect its own people.

Pacification involved the South Vietnamese government in the dual tasks of developing the countryside and protecting its people from the Viet Cong. Yet, by nearly all accounts, progress in pacification was disappointing, and not merely because the conventional war deprived it of attention and resources. The diffuse and cumbersome way in which U.S. agencies were organized to advise and support Vietnamese pacification efforts also hampered progress. There was no focal point for U.S. support of pacification which was carried out by military as well as civilian agencies. The State Department and the Agency for International Development, which managed U.S. support for the civilian aspects of the program, had neither the assignment nor the ability to assist the Vietnamese in halting terrorism; the U.S. Army had no mandate for fostering political development or economic growth.

In 1966 and 1967, American support of pacification expanded in size and was unified in direction. After a series of interim reorganizations, President Johnson decided in May 1967 to make his military commander, General William Westmoreland, responsible for both civil and military support of pacification. His decision took account of the army's success against enemy main force units and the inescapable fact that the army had the most people and facilities in Vietnam and was the best qualified agency to manage an expanded effort in support of pacification. The President appointed Komer as Westmoreland's deputy for pacification and directed him to run a new pacification support organization named Civil Operations and Revolutionary Development Support (CORDS).

CORDS integrated the duties and personnel of the military and civilian agencies at all levels so that neither was dominant. For example, Komer was subordinate to Westmoreland, held the rank of ambassador, and had a general officer (Maj. Gen. George Forsythe) as his deputy.

As an advisory and support organization, CORDS had the mission of helping the South Vietnamese achieve security for contested territory and gain the support of the rural population. All members of CORDS from the district to the national level exhorted and pressed the South Vietnamese to perform better and to build and develop a sense of national political community. Since CORDS had more people and funds than had been previously available, it could theoretically exert greater influence on the South Vietnamese. Moreover, giving pacification an organizational focus in command councils showed the South Vietnamese that pacification was important to the United States and that it would receive more American support.

Other events in mid-1967 also indicated that the reorganization of pacification was part of a new direction in U.S.

policy. Ellsworth Bunker, who replaced Henry Cabot Lodge as the U.S. Ambassador to South Vietnam in May 1967, rejected the term "other war" to describe the isolation of pacification from other aspects of U.S. strategy. "To me this is all one war," Bunker declared. "Everything we do is an aspect of the total effort to achieve our objective here." Also in May, the President appointed General Creighton Abrams as Westmoreland's military deputy, and Westmoreland gave him the specific responsibility of helping to improve South Vietnamese military forces. These events demonstrated how the balance of U.S. strategy was shifting: greater attention from that point would be paid both to pacification and to upgrading South Vietnamese military efforts. If the military effort had become "Americanized" from 1965 to 1967, the announcements of May 1967 demonstrated a belated awareness that U.S. policy again had to devote more attention to programs designed to bolster the government and military forces of South Vietnam.

James Dunn's chapter assesses the early advisory effort (1962-1965) when U.S. Army advisers were sent to the provinces and districts of Vietnam to help devise a workable counterinsurgency strategy. Dunn analyzes the various plans that were enacted to put down the Viet Cong movement and extend government control in the countryside. He shows a large organization, the U.S. Army, attempting to come to grips with the unfamiliar milieu of a political war in Asia.

Chapter 2 deals with some of the inherent conflicts between a pacification strategy and the military strategy of attrition. Richard Hunt chooses to explore this conflict from the perspective of two important provinces where the U.S. Army operated conventional fighting units and, simultaneously, attempted to support the pacification program. His chapter focuses on the period from 1965-1968.

Richard Shultz's analysis deals with the question of whether pacification and the attendant effort to improve and modernize the armed forces of South Vietnam succeeded. He concentrates on the halcyon days of 1969-1972 when the Nixon administration and officials in MACV believed pacification was extending Saigon's political control and weakening the Viet Cong. He makes extensive use of archival material, some of which has not been previously available for public use.

Lawrence E. Grinter, in chapter 4, introduces a shift from the historical/political analysis of the first three chapters to a set of interpretative essays that range broadly across the war. Grinter puts the war in the context of the larger struggle in Indochina, although his focus is on Vietnam. The question he addresses explicitly (the other chapters less so) is whether a population security strategy (pacification) could have succeeded in Vietnam and avoided the financial and political costs of attrition. He is convinced the answer is yes.

Douglas Blaufarb recapitulates the arguments of the preceding chapters and in chapter 5 raises an important issue he
feels they fail to address fully: the structural weaknesses of
the political and social system of Vietnam. That defect
severely crippled the government's conduct of the war and, in
1975, the regime miserably failed.

Donald Vought's chapter treats the question of why the
U.S. Army "failed" in Vietnam from a novel perspective. He
seeks the answer to that question by examining the interplay
of American cultural values and the U.S. style of war as it
was expressed in Vietnam. His broadly stated criticisms,
resembling in some respects those of the recently published
book by Cincinnatus, are bound to be controversial.

The concluding chapter, more than the others, explicitly
raises policy issues for the coming decade. Alan Sabrosky and
Richard Shultz analyze the role of low intensity conflicts in
America's military and policy arsenal. They find the United
States unprepared to meet the security threats of the 1980s
which are more likely to resemble the insurgency environment
of Vietnam than the conventional theaters of World War II or
Korea. They argue that the nation must reassess its economic
and security interests in the Third World to be able to deal
with the threat of low intensity conflict better than it did in
Vietnam.

1 Province Advisers in Vietnam, 1962-1965*

James W. Dunn

Among the decisions made by the Kennedy administration in late 1961 concerning the insurgency in South Vietnam was one to put advisory teams at the regiment, battalion, and province levels. Prior to that time, American advisers had been working with the South Vietnamese at high military and governmental levels, believing that decisions made at those levels, with American advice, would filter down to the working levels in the countryside. With Kennedy's decision, the United States Army became involved in the largest, most concentrated effort ever attempted at advising a foreign army engaged in armed combat with an aggressor. The advisory effort was an attempt to buy time for South Vietnam. While not stated in so many words, inherent in the decision to send more advisers was the suggestion that, if the increased effort was not successful, consideration would be given to sending U.S. combat forces.

The military advisers - who, for the most part, were trained for or had experience in conventional warfare in the European and Korean war theaters - would be required to provide advice of an unconventional nature to forces engaged in a counterinsurgency war. For the advisers at province level, this meant that they would not only be advising paramilitary forces in counterinsurgency warfare but also that they would become involved in such nonmilitary matters as the politics, economics, and social customs of Vietnam. The Army trained advisers to prepare them for this endeavor but,

---

*The views expressed in this chapter are those of the author and not necessarily those of the Department of Defense, the Department of the Army, or the U.S. Army Center of Military History.

at least initially, the preparatory program was limited by a lack of experience not only in Vietnamese life but also in the type of unconventional warfare being practiced in 1962 in Vietnam.(1)

The insurgency in South Vietnam was so serious by October 1961 that President Ngo Dinh Diem asked the U.S. government for a bilateral defense treaty. President Kennedy's reaction was to send a survey team headed by General Maxwell Taylor, his military adviser, and Dr. Walt W. Rostow of the State Department to South Vietnam on a fact-finding mission. General Taylor was to determine if the situation in South Vietnam warranted direct U.S. military intervention consisting of combat forces, or if an increase of advisers with more equipment would be sufficient.(2)

General Taylor found that there was a lack of intelligence at the national level about the situation in the countryside, governmental administrative procedures were poor, and the army lacked initiative and was content to sit in defensive positions rather than take the offensive against the Viet Cong. Although General Taylor thought that the situation required a limited U.S. military force to buy time for the South Vietnamese government, the Kennedy administration decided not to commit troop units but to increase the advisory effort and to provide more military equipment to the South Vietnamese.(3)

President Diem was concerned about the deteriorating situation in South Vietnam, which was a result of the resurgence of the Vietnamese communist, Viet Cong, insurgency throughout the country but, most particularly, in the area around Saigon and in the delta provinces to the south. Although historians differ as to when the Viet Cong began the military struggle against the South Vietnamese government, a Viet Cong defector stated that the attack on a South Vietnamese army unit in Tay Ninh province on January 25, 1960 marked the beginning of the campaign.(4) During the next two years, the situation continued to deteriorate to the point where, finally in late 1961, President Diem had to ask the U.S. government for an increase in assistance.

Prior to the Viet Cong-initiated military campaign, the Diem government had some success in confronting the insurgency. From 1956 to 1959, the Viet Cong had all but succumbed to the increasing and effective antiinsurgency measures of the South Vietnamese government. By 1959, the government was able to collect more than 80 percent of the land tax in Long An province whereas, in 1955, less than 6 percent was collectable. A senior U.S. military adviser thought that the Viet Cong had ceased to be a major menace to the South Vietnamese government by 1959.(5)

The Diem government's success against the Viet Cong came as a result of a combination of political and military actions against an insurgent movement that was primarily political. The terrorist actions of the Viet Cong in the late 1950s, such as the assassinations of local government officials, the Diem government was able to absorb. Diem's national police force, protected by the South Vietnamese army, penetrated deeply into the countryside to weaken the insurgent movement which did not counter with any military measures of its own. By late 1959, Diem's success forced the Viet Cong either to act militarily or see their insurgency fail. As their terror attacks increased throughout South Vietnam, the Viet Cong added a military effort to their political struggle and the Diem government no longer had a military advantage. Diem's national police became less and less effective as the South Vietnamese army became progressively more embroiled in its campaign against the Viet Cong military effort.(6)

The American advisers presented "The Counterinsurgency Plan for Viet-Nam" to the Diem government in late 1960. The plan was an administrative blueprint for reorganization within Diem's government rather than a strategy for confronting the Viet Cong. Diem insisted upon dividing responsibility for security between the paramilitary forces of the province chief, who reported directly to him, and the South Vietnamese army, which operated through the military chain of command. Diem was reluctant to establish unity of command and give all authority to the military because of his fear of an army-supported coup.(7) The advisers, ignoring the realities of Diem's fears, believed that a reorganized effort would be sufficient to regain the initiative against the Viet Cong. They suggested that a weak chain of command was the issue and that the South Vietnamese army should reinforce the paramilitary effort against the Viet Cong to control the counterinsurgency campaign.(8)

As the Viet Cong military campaign intensified through 1961, U.S. military advisers felt that the uncoordinated counterinsurgency effort being mounted by the Diem government was at fault. A coordinated effort between paramilitary forces and the South Vietnamese army, under a single chain of command, would allow the army to concentrate mobile military forces against the Viet Cong while the government's paramilitary forces provided the static security effort.(9) The advisers believed at that time that the army was both strong enough to confront the threat of invasion from the north by conventional forces and mobile enough to handle the threat of the Viet Cong insurgency.

The September 1961 "Geographically Phased National Level Operations Plan for Counterinsurgency" outlined a coordinated effort against the insurgency under a single chain of command. The South Vietnamese army would control and coordinate the geographically organized effort. Concentrating on one area at a time, the territory around Saigon first, the army would take the offensive to clear the area and then turn it over to the paramilitary forces which would hold the area against any local guerrilla effort. The army would then move to the next priority area to take the offensive, and in successive movements all of South Vietnam would eventually be secured.(10)

Both of these plans were American-generated, and, while both provided advice, neither plan required an increase in advisory personnel or military equipment. The Diem government was confronting a growing insurgency with an uncoordinated effort, but was searching for a solution that would not place it too deeply in debt to the United States. Diem wanted American help, but did not believe the United States really understood the problem so they could not provide worthwhile advice.(11) Diem wanted a plan that he could use together with increased U.S. financial aid. He did not want to place South Vietnam in a position of indebtedness to the United States from which it could not eventually escape. Increased American financial assistance, which Diem badly needed, would give the Americans more influence; therefore, to offset that, Diem had to have a non-American plan.

STRATEGIC HAMLET ERA

When General Taylor discussed the need for detailed prior planning with him, President Diem indicated that he had a new strategic plan of his own. A British Advisory Mission was visiting South Vietnam in response to Diem's request for third country nationals to assist him in counterinsurgency planning, and the head of the mission, R.K.G. Thompson, provided Diem with a plan that concentrated on separating the people from the Viet Cong rather than on confronting the Viet Cong with a direct military effort.

Thompson's approach was based on a belief that the insurgency was of a political as well as a military nature and, therefore, countermeasures should be both political and military. Thompson further felt that the insurgency threatened the political stability of the populated rural areas and that the most effective countermeasure was to separate the people from the Viet Cong and to provide security in populated areas. Other specific objectives of Thompson's Strategic Hamlet Program were to unite the people in support of Diem's government and to develop social, economic, and political programs for them.(12)

Thompson's plan was to be initiated in the delta region south of Saigon where the army and paramilitary forces were to conduct clear and hold operations with the army being responsible to work in support of the paramilitary forces. Thompson believed that protecting the people was the offensive aspect of the war against the insurgent, while pure military operations were of a defensive nature since they should be undertaken only when necessary to enhance the security of the population. The idea was to secure a firm base and then to expand into territory held by the insurgents, thereby becoming an offense to seize the initiative from the insurgent. Large sweeping operations were to cease, and the army was to concentrate on acting as a reaction force to guarantee the people in the hamlets and villages protection from the Viet Cong military threat.(13)

Thompson's plan ran counter to the U.S. military advisers' counterinsurgency plans. There was disagreement as to area priority, with Thompson recommending the delta while the Americans wanted to start in a Viet Cong base area, War Zone D, northwest of Saigon. The primary point of disagreement, however, was in the role of the South Vietnamese army. Thompson wanted the army to react to Viet Cong military threats against the protected hamlets which were beyond the capability of the paramilitary forces, while the U.S. military advisers wanted the army to take the offensive against the Viet Cong main force military units and, in that manner, protect the people from the insurgent threat.(14)

While Thompson and the U.S. military advisers were reaching an amicable agreement on how to counter the Viet Cong threat, Thompson's plan was being well received at the presidential level in both Saigon and Washington, D.C. The United States envisioned the government undertaking civic action programs in the strategic hamlets that were being protected by the South Vietnamese paramilitary forces. The South Vietnamese added another aspect: the attempt to unite the people and to win them, with positive action, to the side of the government. As understood by President Diem's brother, Ngo Dinh Nhu, who was in charge of the program, if this third aspect of the program were successful, it would be possible for the Diem regime to build a base of political power in the countryside. In Saigon, the basic concept of Thompson's plan was accepted with one significant adjustment; rather than initiating the program in the delta region south of Saigon, as recommended by his U.S. military advisers, Diem selected a Viet Cong base area in Binh Duong province northwest of Saigon.(15)

Thus, as the first province-level advisory teams were being trained and organized, a strategy to confront the growing insurgency had been agreed upon by both the advisers and the advisees. The Strategic Hamlet Program was a strategy designed not only to confront the Viet Cong but also to develop support among the rural people, the peasants, for Diem's government in Saigon.

Although the Americans and Vietnamese agreed on the basic strategic concept of the program, the method of operation and the expectations for the program were matters of differing views. The U.S. military advisers continued to press for a more aggressive, offensive-oriented South Vietnamese army and were not content with using the army as simply a reaction force to ensure the security of the hamlets. No one, least of all the South Vietnamese, thought that that was anything but a logical way to use an American advised and trained conventional army. But high casualties from offensive operations caused Diem to reconsider this position. President Diem saw the program not only as a means to build a political base in the countryside but also as a way to get the United States firmly committed to South Vietnam. Since the program was a product of British advisers and was centrally controlled from Saigon, he did not fear a loss of his independence to the United States. The United States, for its part, saw a chance to gain more influence in South Vietnamese affairs by placing advisory teams at the province level, even if those teams had to advise a program that was not exclusively American.

The provincial advisory teams that went to work in 1962 found that the Strategic Hamlet Program was the accepted strategy, and it was within that program that their advice was used. In the beginning, the province teams were small; the senior adviser was either a lieutenant colonel or a major. The staff consisted of an intelligence adviser, a lieutenant or captain, and two enlisted men - one an intelligence specialist and the other a radio operator. The paramilitary advisory team, consisting of one officer, lieutenant or captain, and one enlisted man, also worked at province level. The relationship between this team and the province senior adviser varied from province to province; in some, the paramilitary advisers worked for the province senior adviser while in others they worked for the adviser to the South Vietnamese army unit in the area. (16)

The United States Operations Mission (USOM) also began in 1962 to place representatives at the province level. The USOM representative and his assistant, together with other technical specialists, advised the South Vietnamese in areas such as agriculture, health, and education. The USOM representative, the province senior adviser, and the South Vietnamese province chief formed the Provincial Coordinating Committee, which had among its many responsibilities coordination of the execution of the province Strategic Hamlet Program. (17)

The senior adviser's job was the most challenging duty in the U.S. Army at that time. He was responsible for advising the province chief on the best method of using military assets to execute the Strategic Hamlet Program. The specific areas of advice included training and use of paramilitary forces, care and use of military equipment and weapons, acquiring and disseminating intelligence, and observing and providing advice during military operations. The senior adviser also became responsible, as time went on, for providing advice on civic action programs in coordination with the USOM representative. As such, he had responsibility for advising in such nonmilitary areas as public safety, finance, public works, education, and labor practices.(18)

The best method of providing advice and getting the South Vietnamese to accept that advice was to use a plan. The adviser usually wrote out the plan and suggested it to his South Vietnamese counterpart who, in turn, could then act upon the plan, if he so desired, and issue it in the form of an order after it had been rewritten to conform to South Vietnamese procedure. If the plan was unacceptable to the South Vietnamese, it at least served as a matter of discussion between the adviser and his counterpart. The senior adviser had to be very careful when carrying on his activity not to usurp the position of the province chief. He had to enhance the prestige of that individual by making it obvious that he worked with and for the province chief as a member of his staff and that he was an adviser only, not a commander.(19)

Most advisers received some special training before going to South Vietnam. The Military Assistance Training Adviser (MATA) course was established at the U.S. Army Special Warfare Center, Ft. Bragg, North Carolina, in early 1962; and the first class of 184 officers and 171 enlisted men graduated on March 24, 1962. In a four-week course, the students were given training in physical conditioning, Vietnamese language and area study, weapons and radio procedure, and counterinsurgency operations.(20) The counterinsurgency training in the initial courses was not specifically oriented to South Vietnam, but drew on experiences of military and paramilitary operations in the Philippines Huk campaign, the French Algerian campaign, and the German campaign in the Ukraine during World War II.(21)

Apart from language training and the area study classes, which concentrated on geography and some history, little if anything was available in the way of instructional material on the South Vietnamese people, their customs, traditions, or way of life. The academic community in the early 1960s could boast of only one true expert on South Vietnam, Professor Bernard Fall of Howard University.(22) His writings were available for study and he did some lecturing. There was nothing in the training program to prepare the province senior adviser and members of his staff to offer the civic action advice which they would be responsible for providing to the province chief. The last week of the MATA course was set aside for specialized instruction for specific advisers, but the province senior adviser was not included.(23) Experience had yet to illustrate the importance of that position to the counterinsurgency program in South Vietnam.

In the training courses, there was a noteworthy absence of significant information on the enemy in South Vietnam, the Viet Cong, or the organization of the National Liberation Front (NLF). The NLF was a highly structured organization from the central committee down to the village level. It was at the province level that their operations, both political and military, were conducted. It would have proven most beneficial if the training provided province advisers some detailed instruction concerning the Viet Cong and the NLF system; but, at the time, our knowledge was rudimentary and neither experts nor materials abounded.

By 1962, the Viet Cong army consisted of both paramilitary and main force units. The paramilitary units were of the village guerrilla variety and usually operated in either squad or platoon size with a platoon averaging approximately 20 men. These local forces were usually armed with rifles and light machine guns and generally limited their operations to the area from which recruited. The main force units were of company size; but, for large-scale operations, the Viet Cong were capable of operating at the battalion level. Main force units were similarly armed and, in addition, had heavier weapons such as crew served machine guns and mortars. The main force units could be and were deployed anywhere they were needed. In addition to these military forces, the NLF system contained a government structure which shadowed the South Vietnamese government: the Viet Cong Infrastructure (VCI). The VCI supported and controlled the military arm of the NLF in keeping with the principle that military efforts should only be undertaken in support of political objectives.(24)

It was such an enemy that the province advisers confronted in attempting to advise on the execution of the Strategic Hamlet Program. While U.S. advisers continued to recommend that the South Vietnamese army be used in offensive operations, the Viet Cong successfully targeted the peasants in the hamlets. The province advisers were neither trained nor experienced enough in the methodology of the Viet Cong to be able to recommend reassigning the South Vietnamese army and paramilitary forces to provide security to the Strategic Hamlet Program. Since the advisers to the army dominated the advisory effort in the beginning, it is doubtful if the province advisers would have had the clout to change U.S. policy.

The paramilitary forces available for providing security to the hamlets were the Civil Guard (CG), a regional type force ultimately controlled by Diem from Saigon but under the operational control of the province chief, and the Self-Defense Corps (SDC), part-time soldiers controlled by the village and district chiefs who performed guard duty in the villages and hamlets. Although a team of one officer and one enlisted man from the province senior adviser's staff advised these forces, the paramilitary effort as such was a much neglected aspect of the Strategic Hamlet Program.

Training programs were hampered because there were no replacements to assume the duties of units that were attending a training center. The weapons of the paramilitary were few and outmoded; the Diem government was fearful that they would surrender or even sell them to the Viet Cong. Finally, too often were forces placed in Beau Geste type forts - static defensive positions susceptible to being overrun by Viet Cong attackers which did not have to worry about any South Vietnamese army reaction efforts. The paramilitary forces were intended to provide security to the hamlets in relatively secure areas after the South Vietnamese army had cleared away main force Viet Cong units. Since many of the strategic hamlets were organized in insecure areas, the paramilitary forces were hard-pressed to defend against Viet Cong main force units. Under the U.S. concept, the South Vietnamese army was to be used in offensive operations against these Viet Cong main force units. All too often, when conducting these large-scale offensive operations, the army did not remain in an area long enough to make sure that the Viet Cong main force units had either been eliminated or forced out of the area. The result was that, in most cases, when the strategic hamlets were attacked, usually at night, the paramilitary forces were overmatched and at the mercy of the Viet Cong which had eluded the army to attack an area of South Vietnamese weakness - the paramilitary forces.(25) All too often the army units were tired from their daytime offensive operations or were reluctant to undertake unfamiliar night operations. In that way, the darkness gradually came to belong to the Viet Cong, who used the daytime to evade the groping efforts of its enemy.(26)

The Viet Cong strategy was to have the main force units confront the South Vietnamese army only as necessary to support the political struggle, i.e., only when the Viet Cong was certain of a victory which could reinforce its propaganda campaign. The South Vietnamese army thus usually conducted futile sweeping operations against an enemy who chose to fight only on his own terms, for example, ambushing army units that ventured to help a paramilitary force under attack.(27) By December 1963, one USOM provincial representative reported the almost total collapse of the Strategic Hamlet Program in his province. The basic problem, as he saw it, was the inability or unwillingness of the South Vietnamese army to provide timely reaction forces to the hamlets under attack by the Viet Cong.(28)

There was more to the failure of the Strategic Hamlet Program than simply a lack of support by the South Vietnamese army. A major problem was the overexpansion of the program without consideration for some consolidation. In 1962, the initial efforts of the program had caused problems for the Viet Cong whose immediate reaction was to back off. However, once the Viet Cong determined that it could infiltrate vulner-

able hamlets, the program became susceptible to decay from
within as well as to attack from without. Many of the hamlets
such as the first one in Binh Duong province had been constructed in unsecured areas, partly through pressure on the
Diem government by U.S. military advisers. Part of the failure of the program was attributable to the lack of expertise of
the province advisers. They were not experienced nor were
they properly prepared for many of their advisory responsibilities. Because they were not experienced and were operating in an unfamiliar environment, they did not recognize
many of the failures of the program. Even if they had, it is
doubtful if the advisory effort could have been reoriented
according to their views. The U.S. advisers to the South
Vietnamese army, rather than the province advisers, dominated
the advisory effort; and they were convinced - as prescribed
by U.S. doctrine - that the solution remained large-scale
confrontations between the army and Viet Cong main force
units. (29)

POST COUP

During the period immediately following the fall of the Diem
government, the United States adopted an attitude of cautious
optimism. The end of the Diem regime resulted in the elimination of such unwise Saigon-generated pressures as the drive to
rapidly expand the Strategic Hamlet Program. By November
1963, after almost two years of trial and error, U.S. advisers
were gaining valuable experience even though the lessons had
to be relearned annually owing to the military's yearly personnel rotation policy. As reports from the countryside
reached Washington optimism quickly turned to despair. The
number of villages and the population under South Vietnamese
control dropped, defections from the Viet Cong declined, and
South Vietnamese army and paramilitary desertions increased.
The provinces in the southern part of III Corps and northern
IV Corps were critical because of their proximity to Saigon and
the presence of established enemy supply routes from Cambodia
and the open sea. In some of these provinces, the situation
in early 1964 was much worse than it had been before the
Strategic Hamlet Program. In Hau Nghia, a province west of
Saigon on the Cambodian border that was created in October
1963 to prevent the Viet Cong from sending supplies along the
waterways which ran through that area, the Viet Cong was
gaining the advantage. Duc Hue district, bordering Cambodia,
had been evacuated by government forces and declared a free
strike zone, meaning that unlimited use of air and artillery was
authorized. The Viet Cong was in virtual control of the entire
province. In Binh Duong province the situation was critical,

with the morale of both the South Vietnamese and their U.S. advisers rated as low. Although the military adviser in Long An province believed that "pacification was proceeding satisfactorily," the province USOM representative argued otherwise. The lack of South Vietnamese army support for the village militia forces had resulted in the sharply declining morale of those forces. The VCI was so strong within the province that a concentrated and capable counterintelligence effort was absolutely needed to help restore government control and root out Viet Cong cadres. The government administrators, the USOM representative argued, were poorly motivated.(30)

Adviser reports from other provinces noted additional problem areas. South Vietnamese army support of paramilitary forces was either untimely or nonexistent. Defense systems for the protected hamlets were poorly constructed. Civic action projects were nonexistent due mainly to a lack of security. Command was a problem since paramilitary forces were under the control of the province chief while South Vietnamese army units had their own separate chain of command. The advisers further noted that plans were plentiful but that South Vietnamese organization and execution was a problem.(31)

Adviser recommendations to counter the deteriorating situation centered on simplifying the chain of command. There should be only one command chain, argued the advisers, who recommended the elimination of that chain which reached the provinces directly from central offices in Saigon. The advisers wanted the army to become more directly involved in pacification and to dominate the chain of command. They also believed that the paramilitary forces, which had often been left on their own without strong reaction efforts from the army, would benefit if the army concentrated on providing security rather than taking the offensive against the main force Viet Cong units.(32)

The plan to guide this renewed effort, the National Pacification Plan 1964, officially replaced the Strategic Hamlet Plan. This plan had two phases. During phase I, all efforts in support of pacification, both military and civilian, were to be controlled by the military. The aim was to confront the Viet Cong in the densely populated and prosperous centers of South Vietnam. The government would attempt to destroy the Viet Cong administrative organization and replace it with the administration of the government of South Vietnam. Then the Viet Cong main force units were to be forced from these areas to their bases in the more remote parts of the country. During phase II, military operations were to be undertaken against these Viet Cong units in their base areas with the intention of destroying them and ending the insurgency in the country.(33)

The plan was analogous to dropping some oil on a surface and watching the rings spread out from the center where the oil hit: a spreading oil spot concept. From the center, which was to be a secure population area (such as a city, town, or village) the rings were to move out to the less secure, low population areas, the countryside where the Viet Cong was in control. Before the next ring could be started, the inside ring had to be declared secure; and before a ring could be declared secure, a census had to be taken, the Viet Cong organization had to be destroyed, a South Vietnamese intelligence organization had to be constructed, paramilitary forces supported by the local population had to be organized, and the Viet Cong main force units had to be forced out of the ring. The South Vietnamese military forces used in executing the plan included the army, which was to be responsible for the initial clearing of the ring, and the paramilitary forces, which were to provide security for the cleared rings. The army also provided reaction forces to the paramilitary forces in the event that Viet Cong main force units made an attempt to reenter a cleared ring.(34)

Security of the population centers was very important under the new plan. Target hamlets were called "new life hamlets" in this new plan. The basic concept remained the same: the peasant was to be separated from the Viet Cong, security was to be provided, and the peasant was hopefully to carry on a productive way of life in support of the central government in Saigon. Significant changes were that the peasant was not be to forcibly moved to a new location, the government was to provide the resources for security construction, and the emphasis was to be on qualitative rather than on quantitative criteria.(35)

With the recognition of the importance of pacification came the added recognition that the South Vietnamese programs to support that aspect of the conflict needed to be more efficient in direction and execution. The paramilitary forces which functioned at the village and hamlet levels had always been a problem. They were underpaid, poorly motivated, ill-used, and took very high casualties. Believing that the time was past when these problems could be solved by an increased training effort at existing central facilities, the senior U.S. advisers recommended that the advisory effort associated with the pacification program - and, in particular, with the paramilitary forces - be expanded at the province and district levels.(36)

In March and April 1964, teams consisting of one officer and one enlisted man were assigned to thirteen critical districts. This was a pilot program to determine the feasibility of stationing district advisers throughout the remainder of the country. The South Vietnamese were not particularly enamored of the program, feeling that it was a further infringement on their sovereignty. Recognizing the military need for the teams but not wanting to allow the United States too deep a penetration into other governmental areas, the South Vietnamese insisted that the teams be given the military designation of subsector rather than the civilian designation of district.(37)

No matter what they were called, the teams had a variety of responsibilities and tasks, not all military. Their military tasks were to accompany the paramilitary forces on combat operations, provide advice, evaluate effectiveness, and recommend areas for additional training. Nonmilitary areas of responsibility included developing and maintaining a data base on the district population and on the agricultural, educational, and health situation in the district. Additionally, the adviser was to provide advice on the use of U.S. funds, evaluate projects constructed with those funds, and expedite the flow of U.S. and South Vietnamese resources to the village and hamlet levels. The district adviser was assisted in all these areas by a province advisory staff which, by the spring of 1964, had expanded to include an operations and training adviser, a civil affairs adviser, and a weapons adviser.(38)

In 1964, the American training to support this expanded advisory effort was in a state of flux. Some officers assigned as advisers, to South Vietnam were trained during the regular year-long course of instruction at the Command and General Staff College, Ft. Leavenworth, Kansas, or at the one of the war colleges. Selected senior officers were given instruction at a one week course at the JFK Special Warfare School, Ft. Bragg, North Carolina. The Special Warfare School provided an expanded six week course of instruction, Military Assistance Training Adviser (MATA) for most officers and enlisted men assigned as advisers to South Vietnam.

The MATA course, which provided the largest number of trained advisers was most affected by changes to Army doctrine concerning counterinsurgency. Senior advisory positions in South Vietnam were not being filled by properly trained officers. To overcome their deficiencies, advisers at corps and division levels would be taught such subjects as the current situation in South Vietnam, organization and missions of national level South Vietnamese headquarters, and national level pacification planning. Junior officer advisers (captains and majors) would receive similar training except that it was to be focused at the province and district levels.(39)

These training adjustments were based on almost two years' experience with the advisory effort in South Vietnam and included many of the subjects in which better preparation was required for counterinsurgency advisers. It is noteworthy that the province and district senior advisers were not singled out for specialized training but, rather, received the same training available to all junior officer advisers. It is equally noteworthy that specialized training in specific regional orientation or ethnic and religious customs and traditions was not provided to any of the advisers. In view of their military background, which was reinforced by the refresher subjects of the MATA course, the advisers were competent to deal with their military problems. But the training adjustments of 1964 did nothing to strengthen their weakest area, their unfamiliarity with life in South Vietnam.

While the districts with the new advisory teams were showing some limited signs of improvement by midsummer, the pacification effort in general was stagnant. There were no significant military achievements and the new life hamlets were seen as nothing more than new names for the old strategic hamlets. The South Vietnamese government and military, disorganized and poorly motivated owing to the unstable political situation in Saigon, were not providing security for the peasants. Province administration was poor and civic action programs were nonexistent.(40)

Something was needed to accelerate the pacification effort before events doomed any possibility of corrective actions. The advisers felt that the U.S. goods and services were available but that the South Vietnamese were still not making proper use of them. Problems in leadership, organization, and administration had to be resolved first in the critical provinces and then throughout the country. The senior adviser to the III Corps suggested that capable military officers be appointed as province and district chiefs. He also believed that better coordination between the military and nonmilitary aspects of pacification was needed and qualified administrators at the province and district level were required to supervise the numerous pacification programs.(41)

HOP TAC

The place to get started, so thought the American advisers, was in the area surrounding South Vietnam's capital, Saigon. Believing that the South Vietnamese were not making proper use of Saigon in the oil spot concept of the National Pacification Plan, the advisers recommended that a special effort be made in the provinces surrounding the capital. The Hop Tac (Cooperation) plan would profit from the presence of the district level advisory teams and adding one officer and two enlisted men to make five-man teams was seen as having a better chance for further success. The idea was to clear and hold the critical provinces around Saigon, prove that it could be done and, then, focusing on other major cities in South Vietnam, to use the oil spot strategy to force the Viet Cong back to a base area.(42)

The Hop Tac plan had the highest priority in the National Pacification Program in the second half of 1964. Initially, the III Corps, the area surrounding the capital, was given the responsibility to carry it out; but, because III Corps' area of responsibility infringed on the territorial jurisdiction of the Capital Military District, the advisers recommended that a special council be organized at the national level to oversee the plan. The Hop Tac council, organized in August 1964, consisted of a chairman; the commanding generals of the III Corps, the Capital Military District, and of a special zone encompassing the Saigon River approach to the capital's port facilities; as well as representatives from the Ministry of the Interior, National Police, and the Vietnamese Central Intelligence Organization. The U.S. adviser counterparts to all these were also members of the council. (43)

The abiding principle of the Hop Tac plan was the oil spot concept. Using Saigon as the secure center of the spot, the idea was to extend the zone of security in ever-widening rings around the capital. Beginning with the inside ring, a concentrated effort was to be made using the South Vietnamese army to clear and the paramilitary forces to hold. The newly-expanded district teams would not only provide their expertise but also would help to motivate the South Vietnamese to support the plan. To keep track of how the plan was proceeding, the expanding rings were color-coded to indicate the degree of pacification success. Saigon, the center, was colored blue indicating that pacification was complete. Extending out from the secure center, the next ring was light blue, indicating that pacification efforts were being conducted in that area, i.e., the South Vietnamese army had finished clearing the area of Viet Cong but the paramilitary forces were still in the process of holding the area against incursions of Viet Cong guerrilla forces. The next ring was colored green to indicate that the South Vietnamese army was still in the process of clearing the area of Viet Cong main force units. The outer ring was colored red to indicate that that area was in the control of the Viet Cong, and that the South Vietnamese had not yet initiated any pacification efforts there. A whole ring or parts of a ring might be colored white to indicate that neither the Viet Cong nor the South Vietnamese where interested in the area; it was uncontested. (44)

It very quickly became apparent that there were problems with both the concept and the execution of the plan. The most significant problem was not so much that it was a product of the U.S. advisers, as had usually been the case in the previous two-year history of the advisory program, but that the plan had been hurried into execution before the South Vietnamese really accepted it. The South Vietnamese, therefore, were lukewarm at best toward the Hop Tac plan. The council chairman was the former commanding general of the III

Corps, from which post he had been relieved.   By February 1965, funds to support the plan had not been released to the provinces by the central government in Saigon.(45)   Beyond the internal problems that the South Vietnamese had with the plan were the problems of execution.   The notion that pacification could proceed in ever-widening rings from a secure center was not realistic.   There were problems with geography, in that rivers and swamps got in the way, and with secure Viet Cong base areas, where the insurgents got in the way.   So, rather than a nice, neat oil spot expanding evenly from the center, the Hop Tac program experienced broken rings and blots in its color codes.

The most serious and continuing problem with Hop Tac, however, was the incapability and unwillingness of the South Vietnamese to believe in and carry out the program.   No matter what the qualities of the advisers or the willingness of the United States to increase their numbers, the answer to the insurgency continued to lie with the South Vietnamese.

In August 1964, the South Vietnamese army 25th Infantry Division was moved from the II Corps area to the III Corps area and given the mission to support the Hop Tac program in the provinces of Long An and Hau Nghia.   The mission of the 50th Regiment of that division was to operate in an area of 130 square kilometers containing approximately 150,000 of the population living in Long An province.   The regiment had three battalions and was supported by the paramilitary forces available to the province chief.   The Viet Cong in the area consisted of the normal village guerrilla forces up to company strength reinforced by the Viet Cong 506th Battalion, a main force unit with a long and distinguished record.   The South Vietnamese regiment gave each battalion a zone of responsibility where clearing operations were to be conducted by day; outposting and ambushes were to be used at night.   As the villages and hamlets were declared cleared, paramilitary forces and civic action teams were to begin holding operations.

The area of responsibility was rather large for one regiment and, since under the New Life Hamlet Program families could not be forceably moved to provide security, the South Vietnamese forces were overextended.   In November 1964, the Viet Cong attacked one of the South Vietnamese battalions operating along Highway #4 in northeastern Long An province. The battle was a draw, with losses about equal, the South Vietnamese considered it a victory because security had been preserved.

Since the Viet Cong had initiated the action, the South Vietnamese, to prevent such activity in the future, moved one of their battalions in December 1964 west toward the Plain of Reeds, long a Viet Cong secure base area and colored red on the Hop Tac maps.   Pacification efforts were then begun with the South Vietnamese army clearing villages and then turning them over to the paramilitary forces and civic action teams for holding operations. In January 1965, the Viet Cong 506th Battalion attacked one company from a South Vietnamese battalion conducting these clearing operations. Before reaction forces could intervene, the Viet Cong dealt the company a devastating defeat and withdrew.(46) The Viet Cong gained a significant victory. Not only did the paramilitary forces lose confidence in the army's ability to provide support but, more important, the peasants lost confidence in the government's ability to provide security. In spite of the South Vietnamese army's inability to rid the area of Viet Cong main force units, the government declared the area secure and the 50th Regiment moved further west into the Plain of Reeds to continue operations against the Viet Cong 506th Battalion.(47)

By the summer of 1965, the Hop Tac program had been defeated. Security in Long An province was worse than it had been in 1964 when the program was started. Bao Trai, the capital of Hau Nghia province, was virtually isolated; no roads were usable, even by day. The province was so dominated by the Viet Cong that they staged a victory parade in Cu Chi district in August 1965. There were numerous reasons for this defeat, including the failure of the paramilitary forces to meet expectations even with the addition of advisory teams at the district level. Recruiting for paramilitary forces was particularly difficult in Hau Nghia province because many of the young men were serving with Viet Cong units. Some Hoa Hao units were recruited for short periods of time from their IV Corps native area. Some few Cao Dai recruits were also hired from Tay Ninh province. The South Vietnamese army was overextended and, when it concentrated on attacking Viet Cong main force units rather than providing reaction forces to the paramilitary units, the peasants in the villages and hamlets were denied the security so necessary to the success of the pacification effort. In addition, because of the lack of paramilitary forces, the Viet Cong could and did concentrate on defeating the South Vietnamese army. In April 1965, two ranger battalions suffered heavy casualties when they crossed the Oriental River into Duc Hue district, a free strike zone since the summer of 1964. With the capital, Bao Trai, the only declared pacified village in the province in the summer of 1965, Hau Nghia belonged to the Viet Cong.(48)

As the Hop Tac program faltered and the South Vietnamese army suffered a series of near catastrophic defeats in the spring and summer of 1965, the spotlight shifted from the advisory effort to the commitment of U.S. combat forces. Serving as an adviser had been the most challenging assignment in the U.S. Army but, as U.S. combat forces entered South Vietnam, assignments to those units were sought and the adviser became more of a liaison officer than an adviser.(49)

CONCLUSION

The first U.S. advisory teams at province level resulted from General Taylor's visit to South Vietnam in October 1961. His mission had been to determine if U.S. combat forces were necessary to reverse the deteriorating situation, or if an increased advisory effort would suffice. President Kennedy decided to increase the advisory effort.

When the first U.S. province advisers arrived in Vietnam the Strategic Hamlet Program was the accepted strategy to counter the growing insurgency throughout the country. U.S. advisers at the national level had been seeking to have Diem execute the Counterinsurgency Plan based on a strategy of geographically phased goals. The South Vietnamese army would seek out and destroy the Viet Cong main force units in successive geographical areas while the paramilitary forces provided local security to the villages and hamlets. President Diem, not wishing to mortgage South Vietnam to the United States, sought help from other nations and accepted the plan of the British Advisory Mission, headed by Robert Thompson. Thompson's Strategic Hamlet Plan concentrated on providing security to the peasant and separating him from the Viet Cong. That step would make it easier for the South Vietnamese army to eliminate the insurgents. Upon arrival in Vietnam, the American province advisers found themselves at the heart of the conflict, but they were advising in areas and on subjects for which they had little if any expertise. Experienced and trained in the particulars of conventional warfare, they were neither experienced nor properly trained in counterinsurgency, or in the nonmilitary aspects of pacification. What limited training they did receive to function as advisers was not specialized enough to overcome their lack of experience. The U.S. advisers contributed what they knew best, conventional offensive military operations. Meanwhile, the Strategic Hamlet Program, which failed for many additional reasons, suffered because of the unwillingness and the inability of the South Vietnamese army to provide military support. That army was more interested in conventional operations than in helping provide security to the hamlets. The advisers were unable to cope with the causes of this failure.

The failure of the Strategic Hamlet Program and the fall of the Diem administration resulted in a stagnant, confused period in the early months of 1964. Strategic hamlets were now called "New Life Hamlets," a name change only. The South Vietnamese devised a National Pacification Plan which relied upon the oil spot concept as the method of pacifying the country. The United States seemed to believe that quantity could substitute for quality in the advisory effort. In June 1964, a pilot program for putting advisory teams at several critical districts around Saigon was initiated; and, after almost two years' experience in the field, the U.S. Army restructured the training program for advisers to provide more specialized training that emphasized pacification training. Oddly, the province and district advisers were not included in the revised program; they continued to receive the same training available to all advisers assigned to South Vietnam.

As the pacification effort continued to lag in the summer of 1964, senior U.S. advisers sought a stimulant. The Hop Tac plan, which incorporated the oil spot concept of the National Pacification Plan, put Saigon in the center of the spot. The plan was intended to prove to the South Vietnamese that pacification would work if a sufficient effort was made. In the late summer of 1964, Hop Tac began in the critical provinces surrounding Saigon, and the new district advisory teams were deeply involved. There was immediate trouble with Hop Tac. The plan did not take into consideration the varied geography of the area and the degree to which the Viet Cong would resist. Although the South Vietnamese army did move an infantry division into the Hop Tac area, that division failed to work with or support the paramilitary forces. The ultimate defeat of Hop Tac was due to a combination of problems built into the plan, the ineffectiveness of the South Vietnamese army and paramilitary forces involved, and the aggressiveness of the Viet Cong.

The defeat of Hop Tac and the arrival of American combat units signaled the end of the first advisory effort. That initial effort, the largest, most concentrated ever attempted during a period of armed combat, was an attempt to buy time. The advisers found themselves in a counterinsurgency environment for which they were ill-prepared. Providing advice in what they knew best - conventional warfare - and unfamiliar with the subtleties of Vietnamese life, they were unable to cope with the causes for the failures of the pacification programs attempted between 1962 and 1964. By 1965 troops were needed. The arrival of U.S. combat forces in South Vietnam changed the advisers into liaison officers. The first U.S. advisory effort in South Vietnam was over.

NOTES

(1) General Cao Van Vien, ARVN, The U.S. Adviser, "Indochina Refugee Authored Monograph Program," (McLean, Va., General Research Corporation, 1977), p. 6.

(2) The Pentagon Papers, Gravel edition, Vol. II (Boston: Beacon Press, 1971), p. 447, (hereafter PPG II).

(3) Ibid., p. 439.

(4)   Jeffrey Race, War Comes to Long An (Berkeley: University of California Press, 1972), p. 107.

(5)   Ibid., pp. 101-04.

(6)   Ibid., p. 183.

(7)   Douglas S. Blaufarb, The Counterinsurgency Era (New York: The Free Press, 1977), p. 90.

(8)   Ronald H. Spector, Advice and Support: The Early Involvement, 1940-1961, "US Army in Vietnam Series," (Washington: Government Printing Office, to be published in 1982), Chapter 25, p. 15.

(9)   PPG II, p. 437.

(10)   Ibid.

(11)   Weldon A. Brown, Prelude to Disaster (Port Washington, N.Y.: Kennikat Press, 1975), p. 156.

(12)   Sir Robert Thompson, Defeating Communist Insurgency (New York: Praeger, 1966), p. 123.

(13)   Interview, Sir Robert Thompson with Center of Military History (CMH) historian, September 1969; Thompson, Defeating Communist Insurgency, p. 126.

(14)   PPG II, p. 141.

(15)   Thompson interview.

(16)   William A. Nighswonger, Rural Pacification in Vietnam (New York: Praeger Publishers, 1966), p. 83.

(17)   Ibid., p. 89.

(18)   Wilson Papers, III Corps Mission Folder, August 1, 1963 (CMH).

(19)   Ibid.

(20)   Memo, Stromberg to Office, Chief of Staff, United States Army, Feb. 13, 1962, sub: Requirements for Vietnam (CMH).

(21)   Advance Sheet, Fundamentals of Counterguerrilla Tactics, U.S. Army Special Warfare School (CMH).

(22)   Letter, Professor Vincent Davis, University of Kentucky to Edward Mayer, BDM Corporation; May 15, 1979, sub: BDM Corporation Oral History Program (CMH). BDM completed a study of the Vietnam War for the U.S. Army.

(23)   Memo, Stromberg to Chief of Staff, Feb. 13, 1962.

(24)   Douglas Pike, Viet Cong (Cambridge: M.I.T. Press, 1966), p. 239.

(25)   David Halberstam, The Making of a Quagmire (New York: Random House, 1964), p. 143.

(26) Report, Senior Adviser Final Report of LTC John P. Vann, April 1, 1963 (CMH).

(27) Pike, Viet Cong, p. 86.

(28) The Pentagon Papers, Gravel edition, Vol. III (Boston: Beacon Press, 1971), p. 7 (hereafter PPG III).

(29) Col. Carl W. Schaad, The Strategic Hamlet Program in South Vietnam (U.S. Army War College Student Thesis, 1964), p. 79. Vien, The U.S. Adviser, p. 151.

(30) Adviser Reports, III and IV Corps, January-June 1964. USOM Report, Long An Province, July 1964 (CMH).

(31) Province Senior Adviser Reports, III Corps, January-March 1964 (CMH).

(32) Memo, Col. Wilson to Commanding General, III Corps, February 15, 1964, sub: Chain of Command (Wilson Papers, CMH).

(33) Msg., Westmoreland to CINCPAC, January 9, 1964, sub: National Pacification Plan 1964 (CMH).

(34) PPG III, p. 44; MACV Command History 1964, pp. 60-65, (CMH).

(35) Msg., Office of Prime Minister, Government of (South) Vietnam, to Province Chiefs, January 23, 1964, sub: New Life Hamlets (CMH).

(36) PPG II, p. 457.

(37) MACV Command History 1964, p. 59; PPG II, p. 282.

(38) G.C. Hickey, The American Military Adviser and His Foreign Counterpart: The Case of Vietnam (Santa Monica: The Rand Corporation, 1965), pp. 59-62.

(39) Memo, Johnson to Assistant Chief of Staff for Force Development, June 29, 1964, sub: Doctrine, Training and Organization for Counterinsurgency (CMH).

(40) Memo, Wilson to Chief, Military Assistance Advisory Group, Vietnam, April 10, 1964, sub: Situation in III Corps (CMH).

(41) Memo, Wilson to Westmoreland, May 25, 1964, sub: Concept to Accelerate the Pacification Effort in Vietnam (CMH).

(42) Talking paper, Westmoreland, June 1964.

(43) MACV Command History 1964, p. 68.

(44) Status Report, MACV, May 30, 1964.

(45) Memo, MACV J3 to COMUSMACV, February 1965, sub: Hop Tac Funds, (CMH).

(46) LTC Edwin W. Chamberlain, Jr., USA, "Pacification," Infantry (Nov.-Dec. 1968), pp. 32-39.

(47) Ibid.

(48) Hau Nghia Province Reports; February, March, April 1965; and personal observations of the author as operations adviser, Hau Nghia Province, summer 1965.

(49) Vien, The U.S. Adviser, p. 7.

2 Strategies at War: Pacification and Attrition in Vietnam*

Richard A. Hunt

The introduction of U.S. ground forces in South Vietnam in 1965 did more than involve the United States Army in land combat in Southeast Asia. U.S. troops, relying on lavish use of artillery, tactical air support, and sweeps by heavily armed and mechanized units, changed the style and scale of combat in the area. The U.S. strategy of attrition by actively seeking out and destroying enemy formations was at odds with the tactics and philosophy of South Vietnam's pacification program - Saigon's effort to bring security, economic development and responsive government to the countryside. Attrition offered a convenient way to measure success in the short run by counting the number of enemy who were put out of action. Hence, the dynamics of attrition mitigated against static, population control missions and encouraged American commanders to actively pursue their adversary. Attrition was not designed to achieve an outright military victory, nor to resolve the political issues of the war. It had two basic purposes: (1) to prevent South Vietnam's military defeat at the hands of the Viet Cong and North Vietnamese; and (2) to convince the communists that they could not afford to win, to diminish their warmaking capacity, and thus make the cost of their continuing the war against South Vietnam prohibitive.

The focus on attrition of the Viet Cong through conventional combat operations meant the underlying political issues of the war were overlooked. The struggle in South Vietnam

---

*The views expressed in this chapter are those of the author and not necessarily those of the Department of Defense, the Department of the Army, or the U.S. Army Center of Military History.

was between rival groups of Vietnamese, and the principal
enemy goal was to subvert the authority of the government in
the settlements of the countryside and to supplant Saigon's
officials with persons loyal to or members of the Viet Cong - a
broad term that encompassed both political and military
communist elements. The contrasts between the two strategies
- pacification and attrition - were seen very clearly at the
province level: in this chapter two provinces, Long An and
Hau Nghia, located near Saigon. The problems that emerged
in those provinces were similar in nature, although not
necessarily in intensity, to other provinces where U.S.
soldiers fought in the midst of the South Vietnamese people.

Before U.S. and North Vietnamese combat troops entered
the war, pacification was, at least in official rhetoric, the
centerpiece of the attack against the Viet Cong (VC)
insurgency. The South Vietnamese - from the army (ARVN)
to the regional and popular forces (RF/PF) to police and militia
- had, with U.S. advice and materiel support, the full burden
of fighting Viet Cong guerrilla units, countering insurgent
political and terrorist activity, and trying to displace the
enemy's politico-military command structure, known as the
infrastructure, that directed and supported the insurgency
and constituted a rival government in the countryside. U.S.
army officers served as advisers to the South Vietnamese
army, supplying them with weapons, munitions, uniforms, and
technical know-how, as well as good intentions. Officials from
U.S. civilian government agencies such as the Agency for
International Development (AID), advised the South Vietnamese
on programs of political and economic development. AID was
involved, as was the CIA, with programs to improve South
Vietnam's police forces. The United States Information
Agency, (USIA) helped the government set up information
programs at the national and provincial levels. It was publicly
understood before the infusion of American fighting forces
that, in spite of growing U.S. advisory strength, the war was
a test of the strength and will of South Vietnam both as a
government and as a military power. No other nation could
win this test by proxy; the war was South Vietnam's to win or
lose.

That fundamental point was obscured during 1965. The
U.S. Army and Marines entered the fray in growing numbers
to prevent South Vietnam's defeat at the hands of the VC
guerrillas increasingly reinforced by the conventional forces
Hanoi was sending into South Vietnam. The pacification
program had fallen into disarray following the overthrow of
President Diem in 1963. In late 1964 and early 1965, the
communists changed the nature of the war and threatened to
defeat the armed forces of South Vietnam. By late spring of
1965, ARVN was reportedly losing almost an infantry battalion
a week to enemy action, and the government a district capital

a week.(1)   Hanoi, sensing the political and military weakness of the Saigon government, decided to conduct a conventional war in addition to promoting the insurgency. It upgraded Viet Cong forces and brought in regular North Vietnamese units to fight against poorly led and poorly motivated South Vietnamese soldiers. The communists seemed on the verge of moving into the final phase of Mao and Giap's doctrine of revolutionary warfare - open, mobile, and large-scale fighting - to bring down the Saigon regime.

According to captured documents and intercepts, Hanoi was also exercising an increasing degree of control of the war against the Saigon government. The number of cadres from North Vietnam was expanding; many of them were moving into leadership positions. Hanoi was also, through its chain of command and communication, impressing its views on the communists and nationalists who comprised the National Liberation Front of South Vietnam and opposed the Saigon regime.(2)

The patent weakness of ARVN in coping with the combined North Vietnamese and VC forces was the basis of a joint U.S. and South Vietnamese agreement, codified in the annual campaign plans, to have U.S. troops engage the enemy's regular main forces, battalions and regiments; ARVN would protect populated areas and support the pacification program. General William Westmoreland, the commander of the U.S. forces in South Vietnam, believed that ARVN was better suited to work among its own people than foreign forces and this would not arouse the xenophobia that prolonged contact between the South Vietnamese people and American soldiers might easily provoke. The small numbers of U.S. combat troops in the country in 1965 and early 1966 ruled out American military assistance to the South Vietnamese pacification effort. In any event, since Washington perceived the enemy as truly menacing and the ARVN as demoralized, there was little choice but to have the Americans assume the militarily more demanding assignment - fighting the main force war. And, as more U.S. troops arrived, their role in that aspect of the war continued to expand. The conventional military contest quickly overshadowed the on going political struggle in the villages and the provinces, and absorbed the bulk of American war resources and the largest share of attention from the news media. Pacification in the jargon of the 1960s became "the other war."

Even if General Westmoreland had wanted the Americans to support pacification, U.S. Army and Marine units were less well-equipped by doctrine, organization, and training to support a civil/military operation, such as pacification, requiring the use of small, lightly armed forces, than to pursue their foe and overwhelm him with firepower. Using small unit patrols to protect settlements against guerrilla raids or to root out the enemy's infrastructure was not a central part of the U.S. Army's standard repertoire, nor that of the U.S. Marines'. From the beginning of their involvement, the Marines were generally deployed in heavily populated parts of I Corps, the northern part of South Vietnam, where they had less room for maneuver and less opportunity to bring to bear the full panoply of their firepower than the U.S. Army units located in the thinly populated central highlands. Accordingly, the Marines tended to conduct smaller-scale operations, more attuned to the political nature of the war. Still, Lieutenant General Walt, commander of the U.S. Marines in South Vietnam, later confessed that when he arrived in the country he had to learn how to fight the VC, since the combat environment, with its melding of combatants and civilians, was so unlike his previous experience.(3)

Even after two years of fighting and many more of advising in Vietnam, the U.S. Army made no fundamental changes in its counterinsurgency doctrine when it published a new Field Manual (FM 31-16) on Counterguerrilla Operations in March 1967. Counterinsurgency was a duty added to the regular combat mission of divisions and brigades; the Army prescribed no changes in organization nor any scaling down of the firepower to be used in fighting an insurgency. Although the verbal strictures of the manual ordained that firepower be used "discriminatingly" and that the customs, activities, and well-being of the people be disturbed as little as possible, the manual enjoined the brigade, the basic military unit of counterinsurgency, to use all weapons and equipment - even tanks, heavy artillery, armored personnel carriers, chemical weapons, and aircraft. There was no substantive or doctrinal adaptation to the requirements of counterinsurgency, a simpler form of warfare, for increased mobility, lighter weapons, and smaller units. MACV did issue a directive in September 1965 advising commanders to avoid "unnecessary force" in populated areas and that "free strike zones should be configured to eliminate populated areas." The directive did not attempt to define "unnecessary force," allowing the commander wide discretion in interpreting the directive and employing his forces on the battlefield.(4)

At the end of the war, General Westmoreland conceded the U.S. Army was less than ideally prepared for fighting an insurgency. Noting that insurgents preferred to deploy in small, highly mobile units and that counterinsurgency put a premium on small unit leadership, patrolling, night fighting, and counterambush techniques, he stated that the Army "had failed to pay sufficient attention to [fighting] a combination of guerrillas, local forces, and invading regular troops." Most of the unique problems of insurgency had to be learned in the field. Yet, even after the war, he did not rule out the use of artillery or tanks as being inappropriate in Vietnam or in the case of another insurgency elsewhere.(5)

General Westmoreland enjoyed the traditional prerogatives of a theater commander. Neither President Johnson nor the Joint Chiefs of Staff issued any directives on how he should deploy ground forces or what tactics to use in pursuit of the U.S. policy of preserving a free, independent South Vietnam. There was one considerable restriction, however: U.S. Army and Marine forces could operate only within the territorial boundaries of South Vietnam. That prohibition prevented Westmoreland from conducting conventional ground operations against known enemy sanctuaries in Laos and Cambodia or against North Vietnam, which was sending men, munitions, and other supplies into South Vietnam.

Westmoreland accepted, albeit with private reservation, the political restrictions. He devised in the summer of 1965 a three-phase concept of operations that fit within the restrictions and was attuned to the traditional role and capabilities of U.S. forces. The first phase was defensive: to build up a logistical base, protect military installations, avert defeat at the hand of the North Vietnamese and Viet Cong, and secure heavily populated areas from enemy attack. In the second phase, Westmoreland expected to take the offensive against enemy main forces as well as help ARVN "resume and expand pacification operations" in important areas. (Pacification was not mentioned in phase one.) In the third phase, Westmoreland expected to defeat his foe at some unspecified point in the future. Attrition was the operating principle of each phase. Air operations against North Vietnam and in South Vietnam were corollaries of attrition; it was hoped this would help to reduce the flow of men and supplies to enemy forces in the south. The air war complemented the efforts of U.S. Army and Marine units in seeking out and destroying the enemy and his bases inside South Vietnam. (6)

In practice, the attrition strategy was merely a framework for operating that allowed subordinate commanders wide latitude in how they chose to wear down the enemy. That concept, in turn, was posited on the traditional U.S. Army doctrine of mass and firepower and encouraged subordinate commanders to act according to military convention, even though there were no front lines in South Vietnam from which to launch operations and measure progress as there had been in World War II and Korea. Certainly, any military action or strategy that weakened the enemy was bound, at least indirectly, to improve security; yet, pursuing large enemy units or capturing territory had in themselves less meaning in a political war than controlling or protecting the people of South Vietnam. Once the imminent military threat to South Vietnam ended in 1966, Westmoreland's concept still encouraged his commanders to keep their units on the move rather than in positions that provided continuous security for the population. Activity as reflected by body counts and prisoners taken came to be the measures of operational success by which commanders were judged.

The arrival of U.S. Army divisions in Vietnam relying on helicopters to transport troops facilitated search and destroy operations, a key tactic of the attrition strategy. The ubiquitous helicopter lessened, to a degree, the need for extensive small unit patrolling on foot and gave U.S. commanders a new means to employ the doctrine of mass and take advantage of superior mobility and firepower. With a full complement of 400 helicopters, a division could conduct operations within a large radius of its base camp, for example, moving a battalion several times a day.(7) The mobility fostered by the helicopter encouraged an illusory feeling of mastery of the territory of South Vietnam, since commanders could literally place soldiers almost anywhere they wanted. The helicopter and helicopter-gunship gave a new dimension to the phrase "search and destroy" that had been used in other wars.

Despite the constant movement of U.S. units, the strategy of attrition did not alter the underlying battlefield dynamics: the other side kept the initiative on the battlefield and chose when and where to fight, or when to husband resources. The communists could do this despite inferiority in mobility and weaponry because they could retreat to their cross-border sanctuaries, because they enjoyed the sympathy if not the support of a considerable segment of the population, and because there were large tracts of sparsely inhabited land through which they could maneuver or in which they could disperse their forces. Moreover, throughout the war, ARVN tended not to pursue its foe with vigor; and shortcomings in collecting timely, accurate intelligence contributed to the difficulty of closing with the insurgents. The tendency to use artillery fire to "soften" landing zones gave the VC the opportunity to run and hide, if they so chose.

Westmoreland himself was aware of the communists' ability to set the pace of the fighting.(8) Attrition under those cir-cumstances depended heavily on accurate, timely intelligence to locate enemy formations while they were massed or before they endangered populated areas. The American commander was confident the mobility and firepower of his forces would allow them to find, fix, and defeat the enemy.

Throughout the war, the North Vietnamese and Viet Cong concentrated on fighting the weaker, less well equipped and armed components of South Vietnam's military: the police, the Regional and Popular Forces, and militia. The combat death rate in South Vietnam 1967-1971 was higher, for example, for territorial forces (RF/PF) than for regulars. The exception was 1968 when the Tet offensive intensified the conventional fighting (see table 2.1). From 1967 to 1971, the RF/PF suffered more than half of all South Vietnamese military casualties (see table 2.2). The territorial forces operated in rural areas, often distant from friendly supporting units, where they were vulnerable to attack. Most assaults occurred at night when the RF/PF's handicaps of poor leadership, training, and weaponry were exaggerated.

If the nonregulars bore the brunt of enemy operations, it was also true that those forces were more effective in terms of relative cost, desertions, and casualties inflicted on the enemy than the ARVN. Data collected from Long An province in 1968 illustrated that (see table 2.3). Data for the rest of South Vietnam confirmed the thrust of the findings in Long An. Since support costs (uniforms, salaries, and equipment) for RF/PF were lower than for ARVN, the territorial forces were the more cost effective.(9)

The enemy practice of evading large, heavily armed American units and attacking weaker South Vietnamese units took advantage of the dispersal of U.S. forces across the breadth of South Vietnam, generally in sparsely populated areas. While North Vietnamese and VC main force units sought to defeat and demoralize opposing armed forces through military engagements and through such subversive means as proselyting and propaganda, those same enemy forces also supported actions by local guerrillas against villages and hamlets to enable VC political cadres to organize the local populace. The guerrilla units that threatened the villages and the government's outposts and supported the main force units, along with the VCI that controlled the local guerrillas, were the most serious threats to the government's control of the rural population. U.S. troops by strategy, composition, and deployment were ill- suited to counteract that threat.

The common objective of the Vietnamese antagonists was political control of the countryside, but each side placed different connotations on the related concepts of control and security. In conventional military thinking, the South Vietnamese and Americans equated control with local security and predicated both concepts on the absence or expulsion of hostile forces, or the presence of friendly ones. Thus, a secure village was in government eyes one that the other side could not attack militarily because government forces protected it. Often, security and control were a matter of military occupation.(10)

Friendly military operations in populated areas, whether in support of pacification or not, tended to fall into the pattern of occupation. County Fair operations, in which South Vietnamese or U.S. forces cordoned off a village so that local police could interrogate and hopefully arrest the local infrastructure, were an attempt to bring a more pervasive sense of local security. Yet, poor intelligence on enemy guerrillas and political cadres and the brief time allotted for operations in any village (usually a few days) meant all too frequently that

Table 2.1.　Combat Deaths per 1,000

Year	1967	1968	1969	1970	1971
RF/PF	22	29	22	22	25
Regular Forces	18	30	17	16	17

Source:　Thomas C. Thayer, "How to Analyze a War Without Fronts," Journal of Denfese Research, Series B, vol. 7B (Fall 1975): 887.

Table 2.2.　Yearly RF/PF Deaths as a Percentage of Total South Vietnamese Deaths

Year	1967	1968	1969	1970	1971	1972*
Percent	60	55	55	66	65	45

*The year 1972 saw unusually heavy conventional fighting during the communist invasion of South Vietnam.

Source:　Thomas C. Thayer, "How to Analyze a War Without Fronts," Journal of Defense Research, Series B, vol. 7B (Fall 1975): 887.

Table 2.3.　Comparative Effectiveness of GVN Forces in Long An Province (1968)

	Strength	Rate of Desertions (Percent)	Enemy/Friendly Deaths
ARVN	5,500	66*	2.5
RF	4,000	29	3.2
PF	2,700	18	3.1

*Only one regiment

Source:　Jeffrey Race, War Comes to Long An (Berkeley: University of California Press, 1973), p. 231.

members of the VCI disappeared during the operation and
reappeared when government forces and cadres had moved to
another location. Large-scale sweeps through enemy controlled
territory were also often too brief. At the end of Operation
Cedar Falls-Junction City, in which U.S. and South Vietnamese
forces penetrated and disrupted a hitherto inviolate enemy
stronghold, the Iron Triangle, one of the U.S. Army
commanders, General Bernard Rogers, remarked in frustration
that within a period of weeks the Iron Triangle was again
"literally crawling with what appeared to be VC."(11)

   There was an important difference between what the
Americans and South Vietnamese could do to provide control.
Since the United States respected South Vietnam's sovereignty
and made no effort to command indigenous troops or govern
the country, the only control the U.S. Army could exercise
vis-a-vis the enemy was military and rudimentary, namely, to
keep his forces at bay so that the government of South
Vietnam would have the opportunity to win the political war.
It was up to the South Vietnamese to develop the political
institutions and provide the local security - police,
paramilitary forces, and militia - that would enable the
government to consolidate its hold on the villages rather than
merely to station its officials in them.

   The VC concept of control, based on the presence of a
sympathetic or at least neutral population, encompassed more
than military occupation. There were varying degrees of VC
control to be sure, ranging from outright political domination
of settlements beyond the reach of government forces or their
influence to operating shadow governments in the villages the
Saigon government considered contested or relatively secure.
In a village where the population actively supported or merely
tolerated the communists, government control was likely to be
superficial or ephemeral. Viet Cong agents or sympathizers
undermined the government's efforts in a number of ways - by
killing or kidnapping officials, by betraying military plans
and government programs to communist cadre, and by planting
VC agents in RF/PF units. Under those conditions, there was
no need for the VC to try to spread its forces everywhere,
or to assign soldiers to protect the people. The VC could
concentrate its military forces where their foe was vulnerable.(12)

   The VC sought political control; U.S. troops were in
South Vietnam to prevent the military defeat of South Vietnam.
Viewed from the perspective of provinces like Hau Nghia and
Long An, what could U.S. soldiers do to help resolve the
political issues of the war?

   The experience of the U.S. 25th Division in Long An
and Hau Nghia was a mirror reflecting the opportunities and
problems U.S. ground forces both encountered and created
in South Vietnam.   There were obvious, frequently reported

incidents involving the misuse of U.S. troops that were
detrimental to the goal of gaining the sympathy of the people
in the countryside. Forcing peasants to move from their
homes because the VC was suspected to be in a village or
because relocation made it easier to mount an operation had
unmistakable drawbacks for pacification, as did using
firepower and heavy machinery to level homes and damage rice
crops and fruit trees.(13) There were other issues, less
publicized, that revealed the limits to what foreign military
power could accomplish when applied to a contest between
Vietnamese rivals for the political control of South Vietnam.
These limits were clearly visible when seen from the context of
U.S. military operations in heavily populated provinces.

HAU NGHIA

Hau Nghia, situated on the Cambodian border and adjacent to
Long An, became a separate province in 1963 when it was
created from parts of neighboring Long An, Tay Ninh, and
Binh Duong. From the days of French rule in Indochina, the
authorities in Saigon exercised little control over the Hau
Nghia area. The Communist party had been active there since
the 1930s and many families had, over several generations,
served with first the Viet Minh and then the Viet Cong. The
Communist movement in the province thus predated the birth
of the national government in Saigon and had enormous influence in shaping local political and social beliefs. Historically,
the Hau Nghia area supplied rice to the VC and was the site
of enemy supply and liaison routes from Cambodia to VC bases
in the Mekong Delta and the Plain of Reeds. As a sign of the
area's military significance, the government designated Hau
Nghia a special tactical zone to coordinate ARVN activities
against VC units before it made the area a separate province.
Its population in 1965 was estimated at 220,000.
        Government control of Hau Nghia was tenuous - even the
province capital of Bao Trai, a former VC hamlet, was located
in enemy-controlled territory. The ill-fated strategic hamlet
program, begun in Cu Chi district in 1961, improved security
only temporarily. After the coup against President Diem in
1963, the situation deteriorated further and prompted the government to move the ARVN 25th Division to Duc Hoa district.
That step and the inclusion of parts of the province in the
Hop Tac priority pacification program failed to halt Hau
Nghia's slide.(14)
        Apart from the district and province capitals, there was a
near total lack of security through 1964 and 1965, even though
Saigon singled out Hau Nghia in 1964 as one of fourteen provinces deserving priority. According to U.S. advisers, the VC

could interdict or close at will any road in Hau Nghia, and overwhelm any government outpost or many towns. The VC mortared and assaulted the district capitals and even the province capital. Road blocks were not uncommon. In October 1965, the communists staged a multibattalion operation against Duc Lap, a settlement two and a half kilometers from the province capital, causing the government to withdraw the defending South Vietnamese rangers stationed there. Lacking protection and fearing further destruction, many townspeople left Duc Lap.(15)

Poor public administration had long plagued the province. Not only did the government have few able public officials, but VC kidnappings and assassinations dissuaded some qualified South Vietnamese from taking government assignments in Hau Nghia. Poor living conditions in the capital, which was too small to house a provincial government, also made duty in the province unattractive. Hau Nghia was an undesirable assignment in itself, a kind of administrative exile for South Vietnamese officials. For two months in 1965 the province had no province chief. As a result, pacification programs languished, government cadres were inactive, and the ARVN battalion in Trang Bang sat idly guarding its base camp. The U.S. province adviser remarked sarcastically that the absence of a province chief did more to harm the government's position in Hau Nghia than the VC.(16) Given Hau Nghia's history and the absence of a strong pacification program, winning the allegiance of the people of the province loomed as a long-term task that required extraordinary effort to end the political and military domination of the VC. The U.S. 25th Division initially went to Hau Nghia primarily to facilitate that task and help protect Saigon's western flank. In January 1966, the division's 2d brigade arrived in the province; and the division established its headquarters in late March at Cu Chi, in one of the least pacified districts in South Vietnam.

The U.S. division's operations disrupted the VC's normal military activity, kept them on the move, and inflicted heavy although by no means irreparable losses on the communists. The emphasis was on search and destroy operations. According to one of the battalion commanders in the U.S. 25th Division, the division's firepower gave it an advantage over the VC. Engaging the enemy with small units, rifle versus rifle, would take away that advantage. His conclusion was that the Americans needed to employ all available artillery, tanks, and aircraft, and to mount operations only within their range. In the first six months of 1966, the security of Hau Nghia improved markedly, but progress began to taper off in the second half of the year. According to the Hamlet Evaluation System (HES) reports that were one measure of population security, the government's control over Cu Chi district actually declined in 1967.(17)

There were several reasons. The VC adapted its own tactics to cope with superior American firepower by either avoiding contact or moving into "pacified" hamlets and inviting armed retaliation, in which case the hamlet bore the brunt of the destruction. The VC was able to move into those hamlets because defending South Vietnamese forces were unable to keep it out. The Regional Forces tended to confine themselves to defending their own bastions. VC local force battalions also operated in company or smaller size units which made it harder for the Americans and South Vietnamese to locate enemy units and engage them in combat. The U.S. 25th Division was unable to eliminate the VC main forces in the province or prevent them from infiltrating through the province in preparation for the enemy's offensive at Tet in 1968. American operations were generally sporadic brigade or battalion-size sweeps lasting several days in an area, thus allowing the VC to recuperate if hurt or to return once the U.S. troops moved on. A brigade's tactical area of operations encompassed several districts, making it difficult for U.S. troops to provide continuous security for any single location. Moreover, during the first three years of its operation in South Vietnam, many of the division's units operated in neighboring Tay Ninh or Binh Duong province, further reducing the number of U.S. forces available for operations in Hau Nghia.

That type of deployment changed in the fall of 1968 when Major General Ellis Williamson, the commander of the U.S. 25th Division, instructed his brigades to support a special short-term pacification effort, the Accelerated Pacification Campaign, by devoting more attention to protecting the population. Accordingly, Williamson assigned a battalion to each of Hau Nghia's districts and established liaison teams so the battalions could work closely with district police and military officials in helping defeat guerrilla forces and uproot the VCI. Having the U.S. combat units work closely with the South Vietnamese in smaller size units was a welcome change from the search and destroy sweeps of the attrition strategy, but closer contact between allies uncovered points of contention among the division command, U.S. advisers, and South Vietnamese officials, each of whom had a distinctly different perspective about the nature of the enemy and how security, and hence pacification, should be defined and measured.(18)

The division tended to equate its presence in Cu Chi district with local security on the assumption that if it occupied a village or an area the other side was, or could, not be there. Accordingly, division reports generally gave higher security ratings to hamlets in its area of operations than either the HES or the monthly reports of the Hau Nghia Province Senior Adviser. The difference in security ratings was important to the division since its effectiveness in supporting pacification was measured by changes in local security. The 25th Division worked hard to support pacification in an especially difficult province; and pacification advisers, thankful for the division's presence in Hau Nghia, firmly believed its actions had improved security. But the division commander was dissatisfied. Acknowledgments of help and progress meant little from his perspective if widely accepted indices of progress such as HES (and that was how HES was used) failed to show improvement. He interpreted declining security ratings in effect as an indictment of his efforts - even if the local officials and U.S. advisers that were most familiar with Hau Nghia knew that continued improvement depended on the continued presence and operations of the division in the province and that the underlying reasons for poor security were beyond the remedy of U.S. arms. Pressure within the division for good results was so severe the news of the disagreement reached the press. There were newspaper accounts relating the efforts of U.S. unit commanders to have district advisers upgrade HES scores and of an unnamed general in the 25th Division who allegedly wanted to gerrymander the boundaries of three hostile hamlets to create one that could be rated as relatively secure. The province adviser was eventually reassigned because of repeated differences with the division over security ratings.(19)

Nor was friction over reporting the only issue pitting the 25th Division against the Hau Nghia advisory team. Some brigade and battalion commanders, according to a newspaper story, viewed pacification as a charade and the time and effort spent supporting pacification as diluting the combat effectiveness of the division by reducing its mobility. Rather than spending time on show of force operations in pacified hamlets, many of the division's officers wanted to undertake a greater number of traditional offensive operations.(20)

The division met frustration from another quarter: the South Vietnamese military and government. The frequency of friendly military operations among ARVN, RF/PF, and the U.S. Army, while it kept the VC off balance and on the defensive, forced a degree of intimacy between U.S. and South Vietnamese forces that, in the words of the province adviser, "produced some friction and disillusionment." U.S. commanders, distressed at the number of U.S. casualties, resented ARVN's less than all-out military effort in the province. ARVN's seeming casualness in American eyes was matched by the apparently sluggish performance on the part of local government officials who failed to take advantage of the relatively better population security U.S. forces provided by quickly starting follow-up development and assistance programs. One reason was a scarcity of funds and cadre for all the areas that were cleared of VC forces. Without competent and well paid officials, pacification programs were unlikely to take hold, much less flourish, in Hau Nghia.(21)

For their part, the South Vietnamese came to resent American impatience and feelings of superiority. Lieutenant Colonel Ma San Nhon, province chief of Hau Nghia, manifested that. A strong-willed man, he often ignored American demands, and at times was a focal point of anti-American feeling in the province. Some Americans wanted to replace him with a more cooperative South Vietnamese; others defended him as a dedicated leader with the kind of talent, perception, and drive all too rare in South Vietnamese officials. The province adviser staunchly supported his counterpart, because he believed the province chief knew better than any American how to approach the people of his province.(22)

Here was the key. The war was essentially between competing Vietnamese groups for control of South Vietnam. Ideally, the government had to win the people to its side; as a practical matter, it had to at least be able to protect them. Although the Americans could help, it was up to Saigon to gain popular support and control through the services its officials provided and the security its police and military afforded. Without the sustained efforts of the South Vietnamese, the pacification support of the 25th Division amounted to a temporary occupation. At the end of 1968, the province adviser fittingly described the people of Hau Nghia as atten-tiste, and doubted that South Vietnamese forces could maintain, let alone improve, security without the continued presence of the U.S. division.(23) (Chapter 3 assesses the impact of the strategy of Vietnamization, of replacing departing American soldiers with South Vietnamese.)

During 1969, security as measured by the HES and province adviser reports increased. The VC military threat diminished because of the heavy losses suffered in the Tet offensive of 1968 and because of the frequent operations of U.S. and South Vietnamese troops. VC terrorism and attacks by fire (random mortaring or rocketing) were reminders of the enemy's continued presence. With easy access to the Cambodian sanctuaries, the VC remained capable of mounting guerrilla raids or even confronting the South Vietnamese with main force units.

The fundamental problem was unchanged. What was the staying power of the Saigon government? Could it develop roots in the harsh political soil of Hau Nghia? The government needed more civil servants and police officers to establish even the most rudimentary form of linkage between the province and Saigon. There were not enough local officials in early 1969, and the government began a major effort to train additional local officials and police. Although there were fewer unfilled positions in the civil service and local political offices at the end of the year, the quality of those officials was not uniformly high, nor was there firm assurance that government security forces would be able to protect them from VC terrorism, which was specifically targeted against local government officials. With the campaign against the infrastructure lagging in Hau Nghia, the VC retained the capability to continue to exercise some political influence over the people of the province as well as to tax, recruit, and assassinate. Despite evidence that the military struggle was abating in 1969, the VC was able to continue the political struggle.(24)

Long An

A province of 838 square miles, Long An had an estimated population of 350,000-400,000 in 1965. It was largely ethnic Vietnamese and predominantly Buddhist. Most people earned their livelihood tilling the fertile rice fields which, despite the fighting, continued to produce enough for local needs as well as for the markets in Saigon. At one time, the province extended from the edge of Saigon to the Cambodian border. Long An ceded one district to the new province of Kien Tuong which was formed in 1957 and two additional districts to the newly formed province of Hau Nghia in 1963. The Rung Sat area, largely rivers and mangrove swamps and a Viet Cong base area, was also removed from Long An's jurisdiction and made part of the Capital Military District, the area surrounding Saigon. The reason for making Long An smaller and creating new provinces was to increase the number of political units, thereby allowing the government to bring additional men and funds to bear on an insecure area. Changing the boundaries was a way of identifying and isolating particularly troublesome spots.

In spite of these changes, security remained poor throughout 1965. The government estimated it controlled one-fourth to one half of the land in Long An and one-third to one half of its people, mainly those living in large towns or along major roads. Those were the only parts of the province that local military forces could defend. In three of the province's six districts, the roads were unusable owing to the enemy's presence. Supplies could be brought to those district towns only by helicopter, armed boats, or military convoys. In the other districts, the authorities considered the roads as only generally passable. In many sections of the province, there was not even a token government presence. A key government program, land reform, was at a standstill. The Viet Cong recruited manpower for military units freely and collected taxes. The American Military Command (MACV) estimated enemy military strength in the province, excluding overt or covert political cadre, at 2,200. Government strength, including police, paramilitary, and ARVN, was much higher.(25)

Poor security bred apathy toward the Saigon government - even in the areas more or less under its control. A 1965 government survey of some 6,000 people living in the "safe areas" of Long An concluded that most people cared less about who might win the war than about ending it. Other findings were equally disheartening from Saigon's perspective. People were naturally unlikely to support the government as long as they lived under the very credible threat of VC retaliation and intimidation against government supporters and officials. The survey reported a "gross lack of communication" between local government and the people, who tended to view Saigon's officials as aloof, corrupt, and incompetent. VC propaganda exploited the feeling of alienation with promises of reform and tracts discrediting government officials and their promises and exacerbating popular grievances.(26)

The government was losing to the VC in Long An and not because the other side had more soldiers. Local government was not credible. Official programs and promises had accomplished little in improving conditions in the areas under Saigon's control, and most of the people surveyed viewed the Saigon regime as alien and disinterested. Nor was the protection offered by the police and paramilitary forces credible. The problems the survey revealed in 1965 were ones only the South Vietnamese could resolve.

The government's forces were unable to make any headway against the VC or in protecting the population. Long An had a panoply of forces from regular soldiers to police that outnumbered the VC, yet the South Vietnamese remained on the defensive, giving their foe great operational leeway. The territorial forces, responsible for providing close-in population security, were under strength and hampered by deficient logistical support from Saigon, province, and district officials. VC banners were frequently spotted flying over villages, particularly those near district headquarters. The communists blocked the same stretch of Highway 4 at regular intervals and even mortared the outskirts of the province capital, Tan An, on Christmas day 1965.(27)

In response to the province chief's request, General Westmoreland decided to deploy one battalion of the U.S. 25th Division to Long An, the northernmost delta province, as an experiment to see how well U.S. troops could fight in a populated area as well as to gain experience in case additional troops were needed in the delta later. Westmoreland's decision represented a basic change in the pattern of deployment of the U.S. Army, since it hitherto operated mainly in unpopulated or sparsely populated areas. The only U.S. soldiers in the delta up until then were advisers. Westmoreland thought a battalion of Americans would enhance security and support the pacification program by helping keep the enemy away from the people, and opening roads and canals so that more rice could reach the markets in Saigon and the province. He also expected the presence of U.S. soldiers to boost the morale of the South Vietnamese 25th Division. The battalion went to Long An in the fall of 1966; its stated mission seemed to encompass features of pacification and attrition.

Moving a battalion to Long An involved the U.S. Army in direct support of South Vietnamese pacification efforts and offensive operations against main VC base areas for the purposes of destroying VC forces and disrupting their communication and liaison networks in the province. Westmoreland and Ambassador Lodge hoped the U.S. division would weaken the infrastructure as well. Accordingly, the division commander, Major General Frederick Weyand, planned to integrate South Vietnamese forces - from police to ARVN - into his operations, to exploit all intelligence jointly by establishing intelligence coordinating centers, and to fire artillery only in daylight hours into nonsettled areas after obtaining permission from the province chief. Weyand also pledged to deploy forces in company and platoon formations and refrain as much as possible from larger size sweeps in order to minimize the number of civilians displaced by the fighting. Between September 21 and November 5 two companies from the U.S. 25th Division operated in Long An with mixed results. Handicapped by unfamiliar and sometimes flooded terrain, the small number of soldiers involved, and some restrictions on the use of firepower, the companies' raids into contested and enemy controlled hamlets did not appreciably quicken the pace of pacification. The number of persons defecting from VC ranks under the Chieu Hoi program, which offered amnesty and job training to ralliers, increased, but there was no evidence of greater vigor on the part of ARVN in pursuing the VC. The ARVN regiment and two ranger battalions stationed in Long An avoided combat and claimed to have killed six enemy soldiers between February and November 1966.

After a month in Long An, Ambassador Lodge felt the United States had to do more to boost pacification than move troops to the delta. He assigned the Mission Council Coordinator, Colonel Samuel V. Wilson, as the leader of the U.S. advisory team to test the concept of unified direction and management of U.S. civil and military activities in one province. In that capacity, Wilson reported to Deputy Ambassador William Porter on pacification, to Westmoreland on military issues, and to Lodge on the general situation of the province. Lodge hoped Wilson's appointment would improve the coordination of the activities of the battalion and the U.S. civilian agencies, such as AID and the CIA, who were supporting Saigon's local development and security programs.

The Long An single manager experiment was possible because pacification support from disparate U.S. civilian agencies had already been centered for the first time at the

Saigon level in one place, the Office of Civil Operations (OCO), and put under a high ranking officer, Deputy Ambassador Porter. That step provided a framework for the Long An trial. The point of setting up OCO and of making Colonel Wilson head of the U.S. advisory effort in the province was to unify U.S. support, try to eliminate waste and redundant programs, and increase the scale of resources and command attention devoted to the political side of the war. Although Colonel Wilson had direct authority over nearly all American civilian elements (save intelligence operatives) and operational direction of U.S. military advisers, he did not have operational control of U.S. Army forces or write the efficiency reports of advisers from civilian agencies. The scope of his authority was vaguely stated; something that restricted his ability to coordinate and manage both the civilian and military efforts in Long An.

Less than a month after Wilson went to Long An, stories about the province appeared in the press. The gist of the articles was that, if pacification did not make headway in Long An, where U.S. resources were more closely coordinated than elsewhere, then it was unlikely that pacification could succeed anywhere in Vietnam. Although such accounts were dismissed out of hand by mission officials and, in any case, overlooked the central role of the South Vietnamese in pacification, they were a clear indication of the significance of the Long An single manager concept.

Colonel Wilson's best known action as province team leader was the widely publicized pacification campaign in Long Huu village, a settlement of 11,000 people situated on a triangular island in the southeastern corner of the province in Can Douc district. Although Long Huu was far from the primary land routes to Saigon, it was located between two rivers that flowed to the capital. The French recognized the island's strategic importance and, in 1916, built a substantial fort at its extreme northeastern end to defend the river approaches to Saigon. The villagers supported themselves by rice farming and fishing. Long Huu fell under VC control in 1965 when the communists overran the last government outpost. The VC used the village as a logistic support base and transit point for units operating out of the Rung Sat. The island's rice and fish provided food for VC soldiers and the dense population gave the communists a ready source for taxation and recruitment. The VC never established a strong military hold on the island, because they knew it would be hard to defend against a large invading force. However, their control was secure.

Colonel Wilson and the district chief, Major Tran Troung Nghia, felt Long Huu could be taken easily. Major Nghia - who had clandestine contact with the people of the village, 60 percent of whom belonged to the anticommunist Cao Dai sect - reported that most villagers wanted the government to return.

Since the village was lightly defended, Wilson felt friendly units could hold onto it with no difficulty once they retook Long Huu. He envisioned Long Huu as a springboard from which to pacify other areas, even though the land directly north of the village was an extensive and entrenched VC base.(28)

On March 7, 1967, the operation began and Long Huu reverted to government control. The landings went smoothly and ARVN and U.S. soldiers occupied the island literally without fighting. Following the invasion, one U.S. Army company remained and it, along with the ARVN unit, patrolled the island. Government workers from various agencies - Social Welfare, Information, Refugees, Health, Psychological Warfare, Police, Public Administration, Agriculture, Education and Chieu Hoi - started programs to help the villagers and, it was hoped, to win their loyalty. Premier Nguyen Cao Ky and Ambassador Porter visited the newly pacified village and, as a result of the attendant media publicity, Long Huu became a showcase of pacification.

With time, however, Long Huu was a less glittering success. Forewarned of the operation, most VC cadre slipped away beforehand but gradually reappeared in the village to reassert their authority. The VCI remained part of life in Long Huu. The operation failed to disrupt it. The American unit stayed for a short time and then left the island's defense in the care of two ARVN, one RF, and one PF companies. When ARVN departed during the summer, the RF/PF withdrew to the vicinity of the village seat, Ap Cho, conceding the rest of the island to the VC who, without hesitation, reestablished control. In September, some South Vietnamese civilians moved to Ap Cho from VC areas hoping to avoid the continuing air strikes, artillery barrages, and combat operations directed against the enemy-held parts of the island.

The island's people welcomed the government's cadre in March, but soon they were complaining. Agricultural cadres were not implementing the developmental plan they drafted, and most government cadres soon moved on to other villages. The misbehavior of the Regional Forces angered many villagers. Thefts of fruit and chickens did little to win popular support. ARVN soldiers were openly hostile to the 32 members of the local VC who had defected. The political training course for the ralliers was shorter than promised and the new village government was composed of Diem-era appointees or wealthy landlords, who looked to the PF to help collect back rents and taxes. Clearly, the government did little to win popular support or protect the people of Long Huu.

The Long Huu operation resulted in temporarily displacing the VC with U.S. and South Vietnamese soldiers, not in pacifying the island. A survey of households in Long Huu, conducted by the South Vietnamese in December 1969, found the

respondents disappointed in the quality of village government
officials.   The capable people in the village did not run for
election because wages were low and they feared VC retaliation. (29)

Colonel Wilson departed from Long An in the spring of
1967 in the aftermath of a cause célèbre, the Chinh-Hunnicutt
affair.   General Chinh, the commander of the ARVN 25th Division, accused the U.S. adviser to the division, Colonel
Hunnicutt, of trying to have Chinh removed and attempting to
dismiss other officers.   According to the MACV Command History, an official annual report, Chinh was regarded as a weak
commander and Hunnicutt as an energetic adviser; but Hunnicutt, not Chinh, was reassigned.   The story broke in the
press.   The significance of the affair, from Colonel Wilson's
perspective, was that MACV's reluctance to pressure Chinh, or
in more general terms to work for the removal of incapable
leaders, undermined the adviser's influence.   Perhaps the most
important means of improving a province or unit was getting
rid of corrupt or incompetent South Vietnamese officials.   The
Chinh-Hunnicutt affair thus weakened that important form of
leverage.   And it could be crucial, for the success or failure
of the government ultimately rested as much on good officials
as on good programs. (30)

With the weakening of VC military forces as a result of
the Tet 1968 offensive, the Saigon regime had an opportunity
to consolidate its position in Long An.   During 1969, the government improved the procedures for disbursing funds for
development projects and training programs for local officials.
Yet the U.S. province adviser reported in May 1969 that progress was below expectations because of an insufficient number
of government security forces and a continued failure to attack
VC forces and the VCI aggressively.   Although the government claimed by mid-1970 that the VC overtly controlled a mere
4 percent of the population of Long An, the VCI, the covert
political arm of the communists, was considered to be largely
intact.   The VCI still recruited, proselyted, and taxed about
half the people in the province; government political activity
and local leaders were ineffective in countering the VC political
threat. (31)

The province adviser and U.S. military still had differences of view.   Tactical commanders continued to equate the
presence of their units with secure HES ratings and viewed
the destruction of enemy military forces as their primary
mission.   Pacification support was considered, along with road
security, as a secondary mission.   Lieutenant General Julian
Ewell, commander of the U.S. II Field Force which encompassed Long An and other provinces in the III Corps area, remained sceptical of the utility of search and clear operations in
support of pacification, because they yielded lower body
counts than large-scale or search and destroy sweeps.   To the

U.S. Army commander, who was trained in conventional warfare and who gained his battlefield experience in World War II and Korea where massive firepower was widely used, deploying troops in small formations in order to support pacification continued to have less appeal than operations that offered a higher return as measured by the number of enemy killed, captured, or wounded.(32)

CONCLUSION

Viewed from the perspective of the village and the province, the attrition strategy of the United States was not the most effective or appropriate response to the insurgency rending South Vietnam in the 1960s.   General Westmoreland developed attrition to prevent by conventional military means the defeat of South Vietnam in 1965.   Given the communists' access to sanctuaries, attrition as employed in Vietnam was not designed to secure a military victory in the conventional sense, but rather to make it impossible for the other side to win and thus deter them from continuing. If the North Vietnamese and Viet Cong had intended in 1965 to cut South Vietnam in half, defeat Saigon's forces, and capture the cities, then attrition succeeded, for none of those things happened as long as U.S. air and ground forces fought in South Vietnam.   However, if the other side's intentions were political and more modest, namely, to set in place a communist infrastructure while undermining the local government nominally in charge and weakening South Vietnam's military, then attrition was ill-suited.   There is another possibility.   The introduction of U.S. ground forces might have caused the communists to modify their immediate objectives and postpone the completion of their timetable.

Although the exact intentions of the communists in 1965-1966 are still far from clear, their conduct of the war, save for the major, conventional offensives they set in motion in 1968, 1972, and 1975, was consistent.   They fought a war without frontlines and deliberately concentrated their attacks on their weakest foe, the territorial forces.   That pattern held true not just for the war against the Americans but for the Viet Minh's struggle against the French as well.(33)

The consistency of that pattern underscores the weakness of attrition in a political war.   It points as well to a more appropriate response on the part of the U.S. government: devoting more funds and materiel to arming, equipping, and training South Vietnamese forces to fight a war unlike any that the U.S. Army had in its recent past fought - a war without fronts.   In other words, the so-called "Vietnamization" program that began in 1967 and received wide publicity during the tenure of Westmoreland's successor, General Creighton W.

Abrams, should have started even earlier. In addition, Washington should have devoted more resources and better management in support of the pacification program; it was both vital and a uniquely Vietnamese responsibility. Unified management of U.S. support and a buildup of manpower and money for pacification came in 1967; not until early 1969 was their effect visible. According to HES reports, which are useful mainly as indicators of aggregate, long-term trends, the percentage of the South Vietnamese population living in secure or relatively secure settlements improved from 42 percent in December 1967 to over 79 percent in January 1969.(34)   That change also reflected a decline in VC capability over that period.   Nevertheless, it is not clear if Washington had begun the Vietnamization program and improved support of pacification earlier than it did that South Vietnam's fate would have been different. After all, it was up to the South Vietnamese to build a cohesive political community, subdue its foe on the battlefield and in the villages, and protect its people from terrorism.   U.S. arms, equipment, economic assistance, and technical advice (military as well as nonmilitary) could not serve indefinitely as proxies for the Saigon government's own achievements in providing security and a better life for its citizens and establishing a bulwark against the North Vietnamese.

Certainly, Long An and Hau Nghia were more hostile to the Saigon government and more difficult to pacify than most provinces in the country, but the very severity of the situation in those troubled areas starkly illuminated the central issue of the war for the South Vietnamese side: the performance of the government and its forces.   The danger to Hau Nghia, Long An, and the rest of South Vietnam in the 1960s was less a military defeat at the hands of the North Vietnamese, however real that possibility was in 1965, than a continuation of internal political and military problems.   Why the South Vietnamese government failed to improve and reform despite serious threats to its existence and the repeated efforts of American officials is perhaps the basic question of the war and one that cannot be explored fully in a short essay.   Part of the answer was Washington's concern for South Vietnam's sovereignty.   In no aspect of the war did U.S. officials command or control the South Vietnamese military or government, however strong or pervasive American influence was.   For the United States to take charge of South Vietnam's affairs would have most likely resulted in greater efficiency, but would have exposed Washington to well-founded charges of neocolonialism.   Another part of the answer stems from the decision in 1965 to use U.S. soldiers to keep the Saigon government afloat.   The United States' commitment of forces to fight the North Vietnamese and Viet Cong and money to support the economy of South Vietnam had a profound effect. Because we were so deeply involved, we could not afford to leave and let our allies fail. Because we could not let them fail, we lost leverage in forcing them to improve. American-izing the war lowered the incentives for the South Vietnamese to make fundamental political changes or prosecute the war with vigor. Sending U.S. forces also diverted attention from the village political war to the sparsely populated areas of South Vietnam where most of the search and destroy operations of the attrition strategy took place.

The gravest danger to the Republic of Vietnam in the long run was the unabated spread of unresponsive and corrupt government administration, poor civilian and military lead-ership, and lackluster indigenous forces. Those factors directly contributed to the inability of successive governments in Saigon to gain the political commitment of the peasantry, or to preempt the appeal or loosen the hold of the Viet Cong on the villagers. Without solving its internal problems, the Saigon government was apt to last as long as U.S. forces remained in South Vietnam and thus made it unlikely that the North Vietnamese would win a military victory.

NOTES

(1)   William C. Westmoreland, "Report on Operations in South Vietnam, January 1964-1968," in Report on the War in Vietnam (Washington, DC: U.S. Government Printing Office, 1969), pp. 97-98.

(2)   The following documents are reproduced in The Pentagon Papers, Gravel edition, (hereafter PPG), 4 vols, (Boston: Beacon Press, 1971): Department of State Research Memoran-dum, December 3, 1962, sub: The Situation and Short Term Prospects in South Vietnam, PPG II-693; NSC Working Group on Vietnam Intelligence Assessment: The Situation in Vietnam, November 24, 1964, PPG III-652-53; Draft, Courses of Action in Southeast Asia, November 26, 1964, PPG III-656; Briefing, Maxwell Taylor, sub: The Current Situation in South Vietnam November 1964, November 27, 1964, PPG III-668, 670; Docu-ment 262, November 30, 1965, PPG IV-622. See also PPG IV-304-05. Westmoreland, Report on the War, pp. 84, 97-98.

(3)   Lewis Walt, Strange War, Strange Strategy (New York: Funk and Wagnalls, 1970), pp. 26-27, 32-33.

(4)   Douglas S. Blaufarb, The Counterinsurgency Era (New York: The Free Press, 1977), p. 81; Headquarters, Depart-ment of the Army, Field Manual 31-16, Counterguerrilla Opera-tions, March 1967; MACV Directive 525-33, September 7, 1965.

(5)   William Westmoreland, A Soldier Reports (Garden City: Doubleday, 1976), pp. 58, 149, 414-15.

(6)   Westmoreland relates the development of his strategy and concept of operations in his "Report on Operations," Chapter 2-3, and in his autobiography, A Soldier Reports, especially Chapter 8.   This analysis of his strategy is based largely on Westmoreland's writing.

(7)   Lieutenant General John Tolson, Airmobility, 1961-1971 (Washington, DC: Department of the Army, 1973), p. 3; Richard K. Betts, Soldiers, Statesmen, and Cold War Crises (Cambridge: Harvard University Press, 1977), pp. 136-37.

(8)   A Soldier Reports, pp. 147, 194.

(9)   Jeffrey Race, War Comes to Long An (Berkeley: University of California Press, 1973), p. 232; Thomas C. Thayer, "How to Analyze a War Without Fronts," Journal of Defense Research Series B, vol. 7B (Fall 1975): 885-90.

(10)   Race, War Comes to Long An, pp. 146-55.

(11)   Lieutenant General Bernard W. Rogers, Cedar Falls-Junction City: A Turning Point (Washington, DC: Department of the Army, 1974), p. 158.   The County Fair Operation is described in Lieutenant General John H. Hay, Jr., Tactical and Materiel Innovations (Washington, DC: Department of the Army, 1974), Ch. 12.

(12)   Race, War Comes to Long An, p. 146.

(13)   See, for example, the article by Roger Williams, "Pacification in Vietnam: The Destruction of An Thinh," Ramparts (May 1969), pp. 21-24.

(14)   Information Briefing Hau Nghia Province, 1969, copy in U.S. Army Center of Military History files (CMH), Washington, DC.

(15)   Reports, Hau Nghia Province Adviser, 1965 (CMH).

(16)   Ibid.

(17)   Dale B. Pfeiffer, "Evaluation of Pacification Techniques of the 2d Brigade, US 25th Infantry Division," December 20, 1968 (CMH).   Pfeiffer was a field evaluator for MACV.   LTC Boyd Bashore, "The Name of the Game is Search and Destroy," Army (February 1967), pp. 56-59.   Bashore commanded the 2d Battalion, 27th Infantry, 25th Division in late 1966.

(18)   Pfeiffer, ibid.

(19)   Bud Collins, ". . . In the 89th Month," Boston Globe Sunday Magazine, May 18, 1969, pp. 8-20; David Hoffman, "Pacification: Merely a 'Numbers Game'?" Washington Post, January 28, 1969, p. A12.

(20)   Hoffman, ibid.

(21)   Reports, Hau Nghia Province Adviser, November 1968 - February 1969 (CMH).

(22) Ibid.

(23) Report, Hau Nghia Province Adviser, January 1969.

(24) Report, Hau Nghia Province Adviser, January 1969–February 1970.

(25) Information Briefing Long An Province, 1969 (CMH).

(26) Survey, sub: Facts and Attitudes: Long An Province, February 1965 (CMH).

(27) Reports, Long An Province Adviser, November–December 1965 (CMH).

(28) The story of the Long Huu operation is based on the unclassified reports of an American adviser assigned to III Corps (CMH).

(29) Local Survey Detachment Report, sub: Long Huu Village, December 1969 (CMH). These detachments were teams of South Vietnamese who visited rural areas to sample popular attitudes.

(30) PPG-II, pp. 392-95.

(31) Report, Long An Province Adviser, January 1969–February 1970.

(32) Ibid. For a full statement of Ewell's position see his Sharpening the Combat Edge (Washington, DC: Department of the Army, 1974).

(33) Thayer, Ch. 2.

(34) MACV, Monthly Pacification Status Report, January 14, 1968, and February 15, 1969 (CMH).

3 The Vietnamization-Pacification Strategy of 1969-1972: A Quantitative and Qualitative Reassessment

Richard H. Shultz, Jr.

Between the first week of March and the last week of April 1975, an unexpectant world witnessed the rapid disintegration and surrender of the government of South Vietnam (GVN) to the North Vietnamese/Viet Cong (VC) forces. What made the debacle even more astonishing was the fact that, as late as the end of February 1975, there was little evidence of the looming tragedy. Furthermore, just two years earlier, in the aftermath of the Paris accords, members of the U.S. intelligence community were confidently stating that the GVN had won the war in the countryside against the VC, and that the regime was stronger, more stable, better defended, and more ably led than at any time since its 1954 inception. On the other hand, it was estimated that due to the failure of its Easter offensive of 1972 and the almost total destruction of its logistic, distribution, and communication systems by U.S. bombing, North Vietnam was "in danger of internal collapse."(1)

Given such assessments, how can the rapid collapse of South Vietnam be explained? While the answers have been diverse, two explanations predominate: (1) a superior North Vietnamese Army (NVA), in a straight-forward conventional invasion, overwhelmed a South Vietnamese force that was desperately short on military supplies due to severe U.S. cutbacks and unable to rely on the awesome U.S. air support that had saved it in 1972; and (2) President Thieu, jolted by early defeats during the Easter offensive, panicked the army and population with his decision to abandon the Central Highlands, and this set in motion a series of crises that resulted in the unnecessary collapse of April 30, 1975. While various aspects of each of these explanations contributed to the collapse, it will be the position of this chapter that such explanations do not address the fundamental cause - the failure of the regime to successfully implement the strategy of Vietnamization-

48

Pacification during the 1969-1972 period. This policy emerged as a result of the devastating political and psychological impact of the Tet offensive of 1968 on the U.S. strategy for fighting the war in Vietnam. For the three years prior to Tet, the United States followed a dual strategy that sought: (1) through a reliance on U.S. forces and military capabilities to reduce the flow and/or increase the costs of the continued infiltration of men and supplies from North Vietnam and break the will of the Hanoi leadership to continue the war; and (2) through the attrition tactics of "search and destroy," to separate the VC from its population base in the south and destroy its political infrastructure and military forces. The aim was to take the war to the enemy to deny their freedom of movement and, through superior firepower, to deal them the heaviest possible blows. The Tet offensive signaled the failure of this 1965-1968 strategy (these efforts did continue for awhile after 1968),(2) even though from a military perspective the enemy suffered a tactical defeat.(3)

In the aftermath of Tet, the Nixon administration introduced the Vietnamization-Pacification strategy, the goal of which was the deescalation and gradual withdrawal of U.S. forces as the GVN was transformed into an effective politico-military system that could legitimate itself with the populace and maintain a favorable balance of forces vis-a-vis the VC/NVA. Conceptually, this new strategy was reflective of the counterinsurgency programs of 1961-1963. It consisted of programs designed to ameliorate the instability and tension that had characterized South Vietnam since early after its inception. Its advocates reasoned that the loyalty and support of the populace must be won if the insurgents were to be defeated. To achieve this, they devised a combination of interrelated social, economic, political, civic action, and military programs. While there were certain tactical military differences between the strategy of 1969-1972 and the earlier counterinsurgency strategy, both focused on the "other war," taking the position that such conflicts are "20 percent military action and 80 percent political."(4) This is signified by the importance placed on the pacification program.

In terms of scope, this chapter will proceed along the following lines. First, a brief review of the insurgent strategy and tactics of revolutionary warfare will be undertaken. In order to reassess the strategy of 1969-1972 conceptually and operationally, an accurate understanding of the enemy is essential. As the French strategist Andre Beaufre adroitly points out, a military strategy must reflect the situational context into which it is to be introduced. Second, the Vietnamization-Pacification strategy will be delineated along with the computer-based evaluation system that was designed to measure strategy effectiveness. With these preliminaries completed, the reassessment of the 1969-1972 strategy will be undertaken.

With respect to the data utilized in this reassessment, they are drawn from a number of declassified, war-related materials. Much of the textual data are contained in the Military Assistance Command-Vietnam (MACV) records. This collection includes all the textual files of the different military branches and other governmental agencies that were involved in military and nonmilitary programs.(5) Other primary textual materials are drawn from private research firms such as Rand, which conducted extensive contract research for the Defense Department during the war. In terms of quantified-computer-filed data, the Vietnam War Records from the Office of Secretary Defense for Systems Analysis are utilized.(6)

INSURGENT STRATEGY

The insurgent strategy employed by the communist organization in the Vietnam conflict closely parallels Mao's doctrine of "Revolutionary Warfare."(7) Robert Thompson, the British insurgency expert, succinctly defines this form of conflict:

> Revolutionary war was designed both to be immune to the application of conventional military power and, unlike guerrilla or resistance campaigns in support of conventional armies, to be decisive on its own. It is total war in that it involves everyone within the threatened country and embraces every aspect of human endeavor and thought - military, political, economic, social, and psychological. It is also total in the sense of Mao Tse-tung's dictum that there should be no concern for "stupid scruples about benevolence, righteousness and morality in war."(8)

While Thompson is quite correct in terming this form of conflict as total war, it is also a protracted form of conflict in which the insurgents can, with minimal manpower and logistics, maintain the insurgency for an extended period of time. In fact, the irregular tactics of the insurgent provide him with potential for controlling the level of military engagement with the government.(9) Given that victory in such conflicts does not necessarily result from conclusive military engagements but from the moral isolation and disintegration of the regime, the ability to protract the conflict can be an important element of an insurgent victory. To again quote Thompson, "A conclusive military victory is not essential. If a stalement can be achieved, the dominant factor becomes will, and will can be politically or psychologically collapsed or eroded."(10)

In light of these observations, a more exact illustration of the process of revolutionary war is presented by the French strategist, Colonel Georges Bonnet, in the following equation: (11)

$$RW \text{ (Revolutionary War)} = \frac{G \text{ (Guerrilla Tactics)}}{P \text{ (Political Activity)}}$$

This equation reflects Mao's division of this strategy into the two interrelated parts of general military stages and political measures. (12)   The former is subdivided into three distinct phases.   The initial defensive or organizational stage is marked by the establishment of a communist party cellular network (infrastructure) within the population.   Political propaganda teams are employed during this period to win popular support, while terrorist units are trained to intimidate government officials and recalcitrant individuals.   The length of this stage is dependent on the appeal of the party to the population and the effectiveness of the regime in its response to such tactics. The second period of rough balance is marked by initiation of guerrilla warfare.   This begins with low-level attacks in remote areas, but gradually rises in scale.   These tactics buttress the subversion and infiltration techniques developed in phase one, in order to detach elements of the population from the government.   The insurgents fill out the regional organizational machinery, both civil and military, that was established in embryonic form during phase one in those areas showing the greatest promise.   Finally, in the third stage - the insurgents' victorious offensive - the insurgency moves into the civil war. At this point, the guerrilla units are converted for deployment in mobile-conventional warfare, as they actively seek military confrontation with the enemy's heaviest units.   The goal is to collapse the government forces and seize power.

While this form of warfare has been conceptualized in terms of these three military phases, it is important to note the flexibility that exists in employing this strategy.   In the first place, it is not necessary for the insurgents to complete all three phases to achieve victory.   Secondly, the insurgents can move back and forth within the three stages in order to protract the conflict.   If we examine the Vietnam case, we can identify certain cyclical patterns in the insurgent conduct of this strategy.   For instance, in the period 1950-1975, we can identify a pattern of periodic major offensives that employed level three tactics, followed by extended periods of more protracted level one and two tactics.   During the French period, these major offensives occurred in 1950 and 1954, while during the U.S. involvement they took place in 1964, 1968, and 1972 (all U.S. election years).   Finally, the GVN was toppled by such a thrust in 1975.   Additionally, there was an annual cycle of combat continuing year after year during the interims between these periods of major combat.   This cycle was characterized by varying degrees of phase one and two tactics during the spring and early fall months, with lulls in between. In the following data from the Vietnam conflict, the pattern of periodic major offensives can be discerned (see table 3.1).

Table 3.1 Enemy Initiated Actions, 1965-1972

VC/NVA Ground Assaults	1965	1966	1967	1968	1969	1970	1971	1972
Battalion or Larger Units	73	44	54	126	34	13	2	106
Smaller Units	612	862	1,484	1,374	1,581	1,757	1,613	2,323
Total Ground Assaults	685	906	1,538	1,500	1,615	1,770	1,615	2,429
VC/NVA Harassment								
Harassment By Fire			15,502	13,434	13,812	12,927	7,682	8,939
Other Harassment			7,566	9,716	10,638	12,056	9,973	8,906
Political & Coercion			1,756	3,237	2,776	3,844	3,552	5,658
Anti-Aircraft Fire			12,066	12,646	9,706	8,081	6,794	774
Terrorism								
Killed	1,900	1,732	3,706	5,389	6,202	5,947	3,771	4,405
Kidnapped	8,315	3,810	5,369	8,759	6,289	6,931	5,378	13,119

Source: Summary of data reported by Thomas Thayer "How to Analyze a War Without Fronts," Journal of Defense Research (Fall 1975), pp. 800-05.

While certain questions can be raised about the accuracy of the figures in table 3.1, especially the acts of a political and coercive nature which often went unreported, the data nevertheless substantiate these two VC/NVA cycles. This is particularly true of the tactics aimed at demoralizing the regime and breaking the link between it and the people. A close reading of the American Province Senior Advisers' (PSA) and District Senior Advisers' (DSA) monthly reports from the field substantiate this point.(13) They continually note how these irregular military tactics and political-coercive techniques allowed the insurgents to protract the conflict and keep the government on the defensive. Furthermore, it allowed the insurgents to maintain a type of psychological influence over elements of the population. This type of "veto control" kept the population aware of the dangers of going over to the GVN, and the insurgents sought to create in their propaganda a "we will return" frame of reference.

In addition to these cyclical patterns of combat and political activity which allowed the VC/NVA to conduct the war when they chose, the data suggest that their strategy also allowed them to determine where they would conduct activities. The map in figure 3.3 (see p. 91) identifies those provinces where the enemy was most active. However, as we will show in a later section, within these provinces the insurgents usually sought to control only certain districts, while periodically projecting power and influence into other provincial areas. As with the cyclical patterns, this geographical pattern is an integral part of such protracted conflicts.

While the three-stage military process gives the impression that insurgent victory results from military success, the theorists of revolutionary warfare place primary emphasis on the establishment of a competing ideological system and political structure. According to Thompson, while the insurgent organization is divided into two parts, the infrastructure is the essential element.

> In revolutionary war this organization is established in two parts. The most important is the communist party underground structure within the population, created on the cell system both territorially in towns and villages and functionally in student, labor, and other organizations. It is the role of the underground to carry out propaganda, subversion, sabotage, assassination, and other terrorist incidents. (14)

If effect, the major task is not to outfight but to outadminister the regime. Therefore, ideological thrust, organizational form, and programmatic content are essential, for the insurgents must demonstrate to the populace that there are alternative structures that will satisfy their aspirations. Only through such a process will the insurgents be able to socialize and mobilize the populace into backing their cause. (15) No less of an authority than Bernard Fall noted that "it can be postulated that no revolutionary war can be won without at least a measure of popular support."(16) Thus, it was through the infrastructure that the communist party administered the positive and negative measures to propagandize, indoctrinate, and mobilize the population and separate it from the regime. (17)

In Vietnam, the insurgent movement excelled at this process. Their effectiveness is perhaps most concisely summarized in the following quote from Douglas Pike's important study, <u>Viet Cong</u>:

> When I first approached the subject of the National Liberation Front (VC), I was struck by the enormous amount of time, energy, manpower, and money it spent on communication activities. It seems obsessed with explaining itself to itself, to the other side, and to the world at large. . . . If the essence of the Chinese revolution was strategy and the essence of the Viet Minh was spirit, the essence of the third generation of revolutionary war in South Vietnam was organization. . . . This assumption seems to me to be beyond debate. The Communists have brought to the villages of South Vietnam significant social change. . . . The Communists in Vietnam developed a socio-political technique that carried it to heights beyond anything yet demonstrated by the West working with developing nations. The National Liberation Front was a sputnik in the political sphere of the Cold War.(18)

THE STRATEGY OF 1969-1972: AN OVERVIEW

From the perspective of political-military strategy, the U.S. involvement in Vietnam passed through quite distinct phases. In the aftermath of Tet, the Nixon administration rejected the previous administration's approach to the war and, through the Vietnamization strategy, shifted the focus to what was frequently referred to as the "other war." This was the pacification war, and the goal was to eliminate VCI influence and control in the rural areas and bring them under the governance of the GVN.(19) In many respects, this new U.S. strategy paralleled the counterinsurgency doctrine of 1961-1963, with its emphasis on the economic, political, social, and psychological integration of the rural population into the Republic of Vietnam.

This dramatic reversal in strategy was marked by two important changes in U.S. civilian and military leadership in South Vietnam. First, Creighton Abrams was appointed Commander, U.S. Military Assistance Command, Vietnam. Unlike his predecessor, Abrams gave priority to pacification and civic action. In 1969, he was instrumental in initiating the new "Strategic Objective Plan," which was based on the concept of area security. The objective was to provide continuing security for the rural population through a fusing of combat operations and pacification. On the civilian side, Robert Komer, who was appointed in 1967 to direct the Civil Operations and Revolutionary Development Support (CORDS) was able to expand the scope and pace of pacification. Originally given official priority at the Honolulu Conference in 1966, "on the ground" these programs were accelerated only in the period following Tet. Although he officially left Vietnam in 1968, Komer remained a forceful advocate of these programs, as did his successor at CORDS, William Colby.

Vietnamization was designed to transform the GVN into a government capable of "holding its own" against the insurgents. Guy Pauker captures the spirit of the 1969-1972 strategy in the following terms:

> Vietnamization is . . . much more than transferring of equipment to the South Vietnamese and training them to use and maintain it. It involves the consolidation of the emerging politico-military system in South Vietnam. . . . to face the challenge of Vietnamization the GVN must pursue a correct rural strategy and gradually increase its popular acceptance by demonstrating that . . . it is able and willing to offer tangible, immediate benefits to the masses. It must also follow a policy of military "sufficiency." The GVN should aim at maintaining at all times a favorable military balance of forces while accepting the fact that communist violence will continue and that it cannot secure total control of territory in the short run.(20)

In sum, the conduct of the war would be turned over to a revitalized and properly prepared South Vietnamese government and army, and the U.S. role would be rapidly phased out.

Conceptually, the strategy of 1969-1972 consisted of the following programs: (1) to provide security and protection for the rural populace (area security); (2) to severely weaken the VC political organization in the rural areas; and (3) to create a sense of political community between the GVN and rural population through political, social, and economic reform. With respect to area security, the goal was "to combat the entire enemy threat. Area security aims to provide security to individuals and groups at all levels, from the peasant's household to an entire geographic or political subdivision, against both internal and external threats." To accomplish these objectives, ARVN and the other elements of the Republic of Vietnam Armed Forces (RVNAF) would require significant improvement and expansion. The area security program designated specific responsibilities to the different RVNAF elements.(21) Each was to focus on one of the different elements of the VC/NVA force composition. For instance, "the ARVN had the primary mission of locating and neutralizing enemy main force units, base areas, liaison, communications, and logistical systems in clearing border zones. These regular forces also prevent enemy main force incursions into . . . secure areas.(22)   The Regional Forces (RF) were concerned with "enemy provincial and local units," and additionally were to assist "in neutralizing the VCI, interdicting enemy LOCs, and protecting local resources."(23)   The Popular Forces (PF) were responsible for local enemy guerrillas.   The PF was also to participate in local VCI neutralization.   Finally, the National Police were responsible principally for VCI neutralization but were also to assist in village and hamlet defense.

According to official recommendations, in order to successfully implement the area security step of the Vietnamization strategy, the RVNAF would require an increase to between 1.13 and 1.18 million troops.(24)   Qualitatively, it would require extensive improvements in the specific areas of leadership, training, equipment, and commitment.

In sum, area security was the first step in deploying the improved capabilities that resulted from the new strategy. The critical question was whether RVNAF could maintain area security when U.S. troops and air support were no longer available.(25)   Conceptually, it is important to understand that area security meant the physical occupation of a particular area by GVN/U.S. forces.   Security should not be confused with the process of control.   This distinction between security and control was explained in an important 1970 report of the Vietnam Special Studies Group (VSSG), a committee within Kissinger's National Security Council.(26)   The report defined "security" as friendly force occupation of a particular area; while "control" was the physical, political, and psychological mobilization of the population in this area to actively support the government.   According to the report:

> The immediate objective of the war for both sides is to be able to exercise control over people and resources and to deny them to the other side. . . . The establishment of durable control involves effective anti-subversive mechanisms, a government that is sensitive to popular attitudes, and adequate government performance in economic, political, and social matters as well as military and administrative matters. . . . A considerable degree of GVN security is a prerequisite to GVN control.   High levels of insecurity may follow losses in control or decline in the rate of control progress.(27)

In other words, GVN control of the rural areas can occur only after security has been established.   Control enhances security and solidifies it, but security without control can result in a very tenuous situation which can change drastically if the occupying forces are redeployed. Thus, for the GVN to win the "other war," it must establish both security and control in the countryside.

Interestingly enough, given their protracted strategy, the insurgents were not so constrained. A principal comparative advantage the enemy enjoyed was his ability to exercise control over a significantly larger portion of the population than he could secure from GVN/U.S. military incursions. In fact, it was not uncommon to find areas that the GVN/U.S. forces secured but the VC controlled. This was due to the greater emphasis the VC placed on low-level political organization, the clandestine nature of their control apparatus, and possibly to their receiving significant popular support. According to one expert, the "Viet Cong hold the psychological offensive in the countryside because they have an organization which permits their power to appear ubiquitous."(28)

For Vietnamization-Pacification to succeed, it was necessary for the GVN to significantly weaken the insurgent political control apparatus. Only thereafter could the GVN proceed from security to control. Two programs initiated prior to 1969 were assigned responsibility for destroying the VC political apparatus - Chieu Hoi (Open Arms) and Phung Hoang (Phoenix). The former sought to persuade the enemy to surrender through various rewards and protection against punishment; the latter aimed at neutralization through a direct attack on targeted members of the VC infrastructure (VCI).

The area security and counterinfrastructure programs were the basis for the most important part of the refurbished and revitalized pacification process. Pacification had a long and checkered history of failure in South Vietnam.(29) The strategy of 1969-1972 sought to reverse this and establish a rural development program that had the support of the GVN. The major elements of the program included:

1. revival of a functioning rural administration program (including hamlet self-government);
2. rural economic revival to provide incentives to farmers (including land reform); and
3. providing essential rural services including medical, educational, and refugee care.(30)

Through these different aspects of pacification the GVN would establish legitimacy with the rural population. According to Pauker, "In order to face the challenge of Vietnamization, the GVN must pursue a correct rural strategy and gradually increase its popular acceptancy by demonstrating that, unlike the Communists, it is able and willing to offer tangible, immediate benefits to the masses."(31)

To summarize, the strategy of Vietnamization combined with improved pacification was expected to transform GVN-rural population relations through the establishment of a sense of political community, while the RVNAF was to be prepared to fight a protracted military conflict. This was by no means going to be an easy task, as Brian Jenkins pointed out in a 1971 report on Vietnamization:

> South Vietnam faces a tenacious enemy that is determined to go on fighting. North Vietnam has not abandoned its objective of total victory. The Vietnamese have a tradition of long wars, and the North Vietnamese government has thus far shown itself more capable than the South Vietnamese government of imposing on its people the regimentation and austerity necessary to fight one. . . . Within its borders, South Vietnam also faces the persistent threat of the Viet Cong. . . . They are feared, and in some areas . . . they are still popular. . . . South Vietnam must be able to sustain its defenses in a war that, with occasional interruptions of peace, could continue indefinitely.(32)

HES - MEASURING VIETNAMIZATION AND PACIFICATION

Among those factors differentiating the new strategy from the previous strategies employed by the United States in the Vietnam conflict was the type of evaluating instrument devised to monitor the various programmatic aspects of it. The Hamlet Evaluation System (HES) was a fully automated procedure for quantitative evaluation of Vietnamization-Pacification at the hamlet level, identifying problem areas, and providing an ongoing hamlet data base.(33) The stimulus for its development was provided by the Secretary of Defense who instructed the Assistant Secretary of Defense for Program Analysis and Evaluations to devise an effective monitoring system. In Vietnam, this responsibility was assigned to the Research and Development Division (RAD) of CORDS. The result was the Pacification Evaluation System (PACES), "a fully automated procedure for measuring, reporting, and evaluating the status of pacification throughout the Republic of Vietnam."(34) PACES was divided into six subsystems, the most important being the Hamlet Evaluation System.(35) According to RAD documents, HES was the "data bank for the Pacification Evaluation System" and provided "the official U.S. statistics on hamlet and population control."(36)

The monthly HES reports were used extensively by the Military Assistance Command, Vietnam (MACV), as well as by various executive agencies in Washington. Within CORDS, there was general acceptance of HES as an effective management tool. According to one critical examination of HES, "Komer was quite emphatic about the importance of HES as a powerful tool for setting priorities, allocating resources and placing emphasis to implement programs."(37) However, the HES reports were used in a much broader context by the Johnson and Nixon administrations in their conduct of the war. For instance, the Users Guide to the Hamlet Evaluation System notes that HES "provided a data source for analysis in support of important activities such as the Paris Peace Conference."(38) Indirectly, Kissinger was also influenced by the HES data through the Vietnam Special Studies Group (VSSG) which he established in 1969. The VSSG was specifically charged, according to Kissinger, "to solve the perennial problem of obtaining an accurate assessment of the situation in the countryside."(39) The major data base used by the VSSG was the Hamlet Evaluation System.(40) One of the major studies produced by the VSSG (Kissinger cites it at length in his memoirs) was the previously cited "Situation in the Countryside." The impact of HES-based reports on such critical decisions as troop withdrawals and peace negotiations is not easily determined. Nevertheless, we do know HES data were a primary source of information for the VSSG which worked directly for Kissinger.(41)

HES was administered each month to some 2,000 villages and 12,000 hamlets throughout the Republic of Vietnam. Responsibility for administering the monthly evaluation was assigned to 220 specially selected U.S. civilian and military personnel. These District Senior Advisers (DSA) were the CORDS representatives at the cutting edge of the war - the district.(42) The DSA headed an advisory team whose primary purpose was to work with local GVN officials in implementing pacification. Administering the HES questionnaire was an additional responsibility of the DSA. According to the User's Guide to the Hamlet Evaluation System, "The DSA is tasked with the responsibility of reporting monthly on all villages and hamlets in his district . . . the DSA is required to answer . . . 21 security/political related questions for each hamlet every month."(43) To answer these questions, which ranged from friendly-enemy political and military activity to the various aspects of economic development, the DSA was to obtain information from "various sources; including GVN civilian and military personnel, U.S. field personnel, and advisory group personal observations."(44)

Initially, the DSA assigned the specific rating or score for each of the 21 variables, but this was altered because adviser scoring on the indicators did not conform to a single criteria. The original scoring process was replaced with the Hamlet Evaluation System 1970 (HES-70). Under this system, the DSA supplied only factual information and made no subjective judgments. This was converted into a score at MACV-CORDS-RAD. A specific variable could be scored A, B, C, D, E, N. The variables were divided into three catagories concerned with hamlet security, political issues, and socioeconomic development.(45) Once each of the 21 variables was given the appropriate score, an overall evaluation of each hamlet was calculated (A, B, C, D, E, N, X, V). Initially, the overall rating was based on an averaging of the 21 variables. However, when HES-71 replaced HES-70, the weighting process gave greater emphasis to political war tactics.(46)

The overall score derived from the 21 variables signified the degree of GVN success or failure in pacifying a particular hamlet. What follows are the descriptions-definitions of the overall summary scores of the 21 variables.

Category A. Friendly local security and law enforcement forces conduct adequate security operations in the hamlet both day and night - Armed enemy military forces are very highly unlikely to have entered the hamlet during the month - At most sporadic covert VCI activity - The enemy does not collect taxes - Many hamlet households have members participating in GVN-sponsored self-development projects - GVN hamlet chief is elected and present day and night.

Category B. Friendly local security and law enforcement forces conduct adequate security operations by day and marginal by night - Sporadic covert VCI activity, no overt activity - Enemy collects taxes sporadically - Some hamlet households have members participating in enemy activities - Largest enemy guerrilla unit regularly present in or near the village is a squad, largest main force is a platoon - GVN hamlet chief is elected and present day and night.

Category C. Friendly local security and law enforcement forces conduct marginal security operations - Regular covert VCI activity, sporadic overt activity - Enemy collects taxes - Up to half hamlet households can have members taking part in enemy activities - Largest enemy guerrilla unit regularly present in or near the hamlet is a squad to a platoon, largest main force is a platoon or larger - Enemy base areas are often located in or near the village - GVN hamlet chief is appointed and in the hamlet only during day.

Category D. Friendly local security and law enforcement forces conduct only marginal activities - Regular covert VCI activity and overt activity day and night - Regular enemy tax collection - Many hamlet households have members taking part in enemy activities - Largest enemy guerrilla force is a platoon, largest main force is a company - Large enemy base area is often located in or near a village.

Category E. When friendly security forces are present they do not conduct security operations - Armed enemy military forces are regularly present - VCI is the primary authority in the hamlet - Regular enemy tax collection - all or nearly all hamlet households have members participating in enemy activities - Enemy guerrilla units are a platoon or larger, main forces are a company or larger - Major enemy base areas are often located in or near the village.

Category N. Not evaluated.

Category X. Abandoned.

Category V. The enemy are reported to be in physical control of the hamlet.(47)

These monthly results were used to identify trends in the Vietnamization-Pacification process. In fact, it became almost the sole tool for measuring its various programmatic aspects. The summary scores for all the hamlets were grouped into the following categories for analysis and decision making: secure (A, B, C), contested (D, E), not visited (N), abandoned (X), enemy controlled (V).

    Did HES identify and measure those factors that permitted an accurate evaluation of this new strategy, or was what HES could measure most easily the objective by which performance was measured? From the point of view of survey research methodology, HES must satisfy the dual requirements of "reliability" and "validity." Reliability is concerned with "the consistency in results of a test . . . the tendency of a test or measure to produce the same results."(48) The issue of the reliability of the data acquired by the DSA will be examined later. Here we are concerned with the issue of validity - "the capacity of a measuring instrument to predict what it was designed to predict."(49) In the case of this system, serious validity questions can be raised. The first pertains to the grouping of A, B, C hamlets as "relatively secure." Given the categorical definitions listed above, the inclusion of C hamlets with those rated A-B seems very dubious. How can a hamlet that is experiencing regular enemy covert activity, has from a squad to platoon-size enemy force present in the area, and also has a portion of the hamlet population taking part in enemy activities be considered secure? It would seem that such a hamlet was experiencing the type of protracted war tactics that the insurgents employed during the last years of the U.S. involvement to maintain active influence and "veto control."(50) According to the report by Bole and Kobata, which was based on extensive interviews with over 60 percent of the DSAs from the 1971-1972 period, "it is the authors' experience that neither U.S. nor GVN officials could, with high assurance, move freely in C hamlets, and yet to the reviewer of HES output at high levels, all of the groupings in the A-B-C-grouping tended to have the aura of the better A and B ratings." (51)   This same conclusion is frequently found in the monthly reports of the DSAs and the Province Senior Advisers (PSA) which were filed with MACV-CORDS.(52) Furthermore, given the description of the D-E categories, was it appropriate to list these hamlets as contested? Weren't they really under varying degrees of VC control.   In light of these comments, it is our opinion that a more accurate classification would rank A-B hamlets as GVN secured, C hamlets as contested, and D-E-V hamlets as experiencing increasing degrees of VC control.   In the HES data analysis part of this study, this classification design will be employed.

A second validity problem results from the "averaging" process.   Methodologically this is debatable, and the results could be misleading.   For example, a "hamlet with indicators rated as one A, two Bs, nine Cs, five Ds, and one E would be given an overall rating of 2.83 . . . a C category hamlet."(53) Such averaging can be deceptive, masking certain developments that present a very different picture of the situation. And yet, as Komer notes, there was a definite tendency to look only at the overall averages as you go up the line to the Secretary of Defense.   The top policymakers also focused on countrywide and corps summaries.(54)   As was noted earlier, the insurgency was not country or corpswide; in fact, in many instances, it was neither province nor districtwide.

Finally, the HES rating was, in many cases, subject to drastic and rapid change.   Therefore, to look at the score as indicative of an irreversible trend was erroneous.   A village could be pacified one day and VC the next day.   What this suggests, as the following excerpt from the Office of the Assistant Secretary of Defense (System Analysis) SEA Reports notes, is a quite different situation from that presented through a reliance solely on HES data.

> The HES system represents a snapshot of security and development at one point in time.   The monthly statistics merely provides a series of these snapshots and creates an impression of steady progress and widespread GVN influence among the people of South Vietnam.   But security and development are dynamic, not static events; and much of the movement and interaction in pacification is not reflected by the summary HES reports.(55)

VC influence and control, as we noted previously, was achieved through a different type of presence.   Quoting again from the SEA Reports, the nature of this difference is explained as follows:

> A large percentage of the South Vietnamese . . .
> live in areas that are subject to VC domination or
> influence for at least one month out of the year.
> These people simply cannot afford to openly support
> the GVN knowing that an active VC infrastructure
> still operates in their village and that enemy troops
> will return one day soon. . . . The bulk of the
> South Vietnamese people live in a . . . contested
> status at least once a year. (56)

While this explains how a hamlet rated A or B could be overcome rapidly by the Viet Cong, (57) the more important insight
to be drawn is from the questions this and the other criticisms
raise about the validity of the HES instrument. The signi
ficance of this in terms of understanding the rapid demise of
the Republic of Vietnam will become more apparent in the data
analysis sections.

REASSESSING VIETNAMIZATION AND PACIFICATION

How successful was the strategy of 1969-1972? According to
official circles, it was very successful. For example, Guy
Pauker of Rand described the results of Vietnamization as "a
feat of political alchemy." (58) It would not be an exaggeration
to argue that Pauker's conclusion was shared by many U.S.
officials connected with Vietnamization. Certainly this was the
prevailing view of those in the Office of the Assistant Secretary of Defense, for Systems Analysis-Southeast Asia Office
who were charged with analyzing the war for the Secretary of
Defense. (59) Their periodic SEA Analysis Reports, which had
a "direct impact on the Washington decision process," (60) were
very positive in their overall assessment of Vietnamization.
According to Thomas Thayer, its director during the 1966-1972
period:

> Pacification has been successful. There was wide-
> spread evidence and agreement that the government
> of Vietnam exercised a predominant influence over
> the vast majority of South Vietnamese people. . . .
> The South Vietnamese forces appeared to be doing a
> good job. They had repulsed the 1972 offensives
> without the help of U.S. ground forces, but with
> the aid of heavy American air and logistics sup-
> port. (61)

Komer went even further in his appraisal, concluding that the
strategy "spurred a GVN-sponsored rural revolution. Politically, socially, and economically the traditional face of the

countryside was transformed."(62)   With regard to rural security, Komer notes that "the figures for the end of 1971 rate
about 97 percent of South Vietnam's 17.9 million population as
'relatively secure,' and 3 percent as 'contested,' and only
about 7,000 people still under VC control."(63)   In sum,
Komer saw the overall result as "GVN domination of the countryside . . . at the expense of the Viet Cong."(64)   Finally,
Kissinger implies that Vietnamization succeeded by arguing that
Hanoi finally capitulated at Paris in 1972 because the war in
the countryside had been lost.   According to Kissinger, "Vietnamization, for all the anguish caused by protests, had bought
time at home with the steady reduction of American forces.
. . . And it had generated pressures on Hanoi . . . it evoked
the prospect that eventually a strengthened South Vietnamese
government would be able to stand on its own."(65)   In Kissinger's view, Hanoi reached this conclusion after its Easter
offensive of 1972 collapsed:

> I was convinced that, whatever the outcome of the
> offensive, it would end the war. . . . One way or
> another, there would now be serious negotia-
> tions: their substance would depend upon which side
> prevailed. . . . If South Vietnam collapsed, the
> war would have ended in a debacle. If Saigon, with
> our help, held back the entire North Vietnamese
> army, Hanoi would have no choice but to come to
> terms."(66)

Although the GVN success could not be "interpreted as an
augury of total victory," for Hanoi it was "a major setback"
and, in Kissinger's view, forced it to "give up its political
demands" and negotiate a settlement.(67)
     It is the position of this author that a reexamination
of the data from the war will result in a much different
interpretation of the strategy of 1969-1972.   The reassessment will proceed along the following lines: (1) an examination of the accuracy and relevance of the security-pacification
data; (2) an appraisal of the RVNAF; (3) an evaluation of
the counter-VCI programs; and (4) an overview of rural
development-political community progress.

          GVN Security and Control: A Quantitative Examination

This section examines the summary HES monthly scores for
selected provinces for the period of January 1970 to December
1972.   This time frame was selected because it was in the
spring of 1970 that Vietnamization began to seriously take
hold.   Although the strategy was initiated after the Tet
offensive, the period prior to the spring of 1970 was char-

acterized by significant post-Tet enemy military activity. December 1972 was the final full month of involvement for the United States; the peace accords were signed in January 1973.

The data analyzed are taken from a computer file that aggregates the raw monthly HES data at the province level.(68) We will examine trends in the percentage of hamlets in each of the selected provinces receiving overall security scores of A, B, C, D, E, N, X, V for the period under study. One of the unfortunate limitations of the data set is that specific districts, villages, and hamlets cannot be studied over time. The summary scores examined are from the HES-71 scoring system discussed above (see figure 3.2 for the HES-71 model aggregation outline). Hamlets were chosen as the unit of analysis rather than population figures because the latter had serious reliability problems. According to a special assessment of HES in 1972:

> The population focus of the HES generates frequent anomalies in HES ratings. For example, HES scores for an area will show improvement in cases where thousands of area residents are forced by tactical activity from their relatively insecure "C" villages into camps located in "AB" rated zones. In other words, although population has been uprooted, and territory lost, the HES will nevertheless show at least a temporary pacification advance in terms of "AB" population.(69)

While hamlet figures do not give the population size in the different rating categories, there is an abandoned hamlet category which has important implications. Finally, the hamlets reported are only in the rural areas and do not include urban areas.(70)

The rating system used in this analysis is the one specified in the previous section: secure (A, B), contested (C), enemy controlled (D, E, V), abandoned (X), and not evaluated (N). The purpose of this analysis is to determine the degree of GVN security, from a quantitative perspective, in the countryside at the time of the final withdrawal of U.S. troops.

Was the Vietnamization-Pacification strategy as successful as Nixon administration officials contended, or was control for the countryside still highly contested? To answer these questions, we will look at provinces within the four corps regions to determine how many were still either being contested or in enemy hands. We shall define a contested province as one in which at least roughly half the hamlets in the province are ranked below the two secure categories in the period, immediately prior to the peace accords. To support the argument that Vietnamization-Pacification was successful, the enemy had to be defeated in those areas that had been traditional enemy

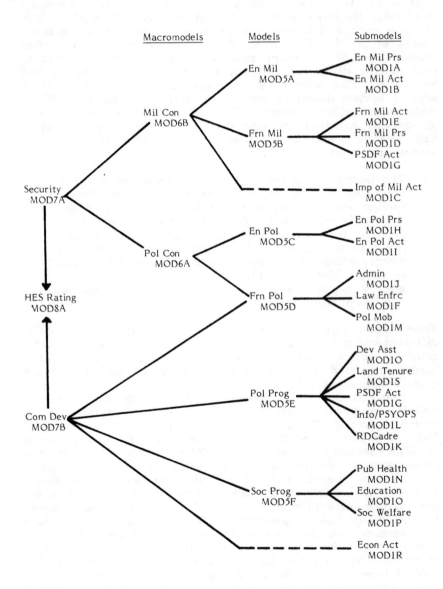

Figure 3.1.   HES70 Model Aggregations

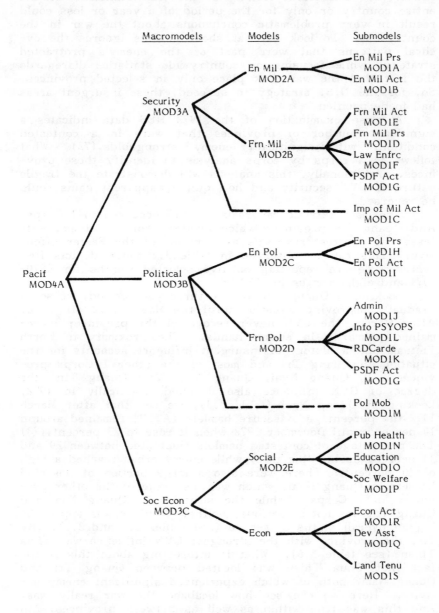

Figure 3.2.   HES71 Model Aggregations

strongholds. Many of these areas were the same provinces where the French experienced their greatest difficulties in the South.(71)   Therefore, looking at the HES statistics for the entire country or only for the period of a year or less could result in very problematic conclusions about the war in the countryside.   To look only at short periods ignores the cyclical patterns that were part of the enemy's protracted strategy, while focusing on countrywide statistics disregards the fact that the war took place only in selected provinces. So, for the U.S. strategy to succeed, these insurgent areas had to be pacified.

A close examination of the 1972 HES data indicates a significant number of provinces that were in a contested condition, with significant enemy strongholds.(72)   What follows is a corps by corps analysis to identify these provinces.   Additionally, this analysis will demonstrate the fragile nature of GVN security and how quickly apparent gains could be reversed.

The most extreme reversals of 1972 occurred in I Corps. And Quang Tri province, which borders North Vietnam, suffered the greatest reversals as a result of the Easter offensive.   This can be observed in table 3.2 which depicts HES scores.   We are reporting on five selected months for 1970-1971 and eight months in 1972.

Looking at Quang Tri for the three year period, we see a gradually improving situation until the March 1972 offensive. After March, the GVN never recovered the province; it remained primarily in enemy hands.   The proximity to North Vietnam and a history of insurgent influence accounts for the situation in Quang Tri and most of the other I Corps provinces.   In Quang Ngai, Quang Nam, and Quang Tin, the degree of GVN influence also declined drastically in 1972. Looking at Quang Ngai (table 3.3), we see that after March 1972 the percentage of secure hamlets (A, B) remained around 10 percent until December 1972 when it rose to 23 percent.(73) The percentage of contested hamlets fluctuated between 20 and 33 percent during this time, while enemy areas reached a high of 40 percent.   There were also a large portion of deserted hamlets in Quang Ngai, which was also true of the other provinces in I Corps.   While the situation in Quang Nam and Quang Tin was not as serious, neither province was approaching an overall status of secure (see tables 3.4 and 3.5).   By far, the province with the strongest GVN influence was Thua Thien (see table 3.6).   What is interesting about this is the fact that Thua Thien was located between Quang Tri and Quang Nam, both of which experienced significant enemy activity.   Here we can see how localized the war really was. And this was true within as well as between provinces.   In sum, at the time of the Paris Accords, an important part of I Corps was either contested or under enemy control.

Table 3.2.   Percentage of Hamlets* in Contested Condition, Quang Tri Province

	A	B	C	HES Category D	E	N	X	V
1970								
January	3.8	50.5	38	2.9	0	0	4	0
March	5	65.7	24	.6	0	0	4	0
May	4.6	60	28.9	1	0	0	4	0
July	5	69.5	19	1	0	0	4	0
September	4.8	61.6	15	.3	0	0	17.8	0
1971								
January	11.5	62.9	7	5	0	0	17.7	0
March	9	55.9	16.8	.5	0	0	17.5	0
July	9	50	23	0	0	0	17.7	0
September	11	63.6	7	0	0	0	17.5	0
1972								
January	10	65.9	6	0	0	0	18.7	0
March	0	58	9	39.6	0	0	19.6	36
April	0	0	4	0	0	0	19.6	80
May	0	0	0	0	0	0	19	80
July	0	0	0	0	12.7	0	15.7	68
September	0	0	0	0	29	0	15.7	55
November	0	0	0	12	19.6	0	15.7	52
December	0	0	0	.2	0	0	53	46.7

*The number of hamlets fluctuated between 571 in July 1970 and 489 in February 1972.

Table 3.3.   Percentage of Contested Hamlets,*
Quang Ngai Province

	A	B	C	D	E	N	X	V
1970								
January	0	15	32	24.8	2	.2	17	8
March	0	12	31	11	1	.5	36	7
May	0	12	32.8	10	1	.3	36	7
July	0	22.9	27.8	55.7	.6	0	34.8	8
September	.6	30	23	5.6	.4	.1	34.8	5
1971								
January	.1	31.5	23	4	.1	0	35.9	4.5
March	.1	33	18.5	8.7	0	0	37	2
May	.1	32	21.8	6.7	0	.1	36	2
July	2	27.8	25.6	6.6	0	0	35.6	2
September	0	37	20.9	2.8	.3	.4	37	.8
1972								
January	1	39.8	18	3.6	.7	.4	35.5	0
March	.6	37.9	17	7	.7	.7	35	0
April	0	5.7	31	20	.9	.3	34.7	7
May	0	9	33.6	12.5	1	.3	34.6	8.7
July	.1	11.7	27.7	15.5	.6	0	37	6.8
September	0	5	21.7	16	2.6	4.6	32.5	17
November	0	5.8	22	17.6	8	0	37.7	8.5
December	.3	23	20	10.6	2	0	39	3.9

---

*The number of hamlets fluctuated between 435 in January 1970
and 637 in December 1972.

Table 3.4.   Percentage of Contested Hamlets,*
Quang Tin Province

	A	B	C	D	E	N	X	V
1970								
January	.9	44	25	7	1	0	0	21
March	1.5	44	23.9	18	1.8	0	0	20.5
May	1	33	20	5	2	.9	21	15.7
July	1	30.8	17.9	6	1.6	1.6	28.9	11
September	3	35.6	10.7	5.9	1.6	1	28.6	12
1971								
January	3	35	14	3	2.9	0	40.5	.6
March	3	32	18	4	1	0	39	1
May	4	34.8	16.8	2.9	.8	.4	39	.6
July	6	34	17	1.6	0	0	38	1.8
September	11	33.9	13	1	0	0	40	0
1972								
January	16.9	29.5	11	1.8	.2	.2	39.8	0
March	5	34	19.9	.4	.2	0	39.8	0
April	0	21.8	27.6	3.9	.6	0	39.8	6
May	.2	26.9	20	4.5	.4	0	39.6	7.9
July	0	23.9	23	5.8	1.8	1	38.8	4.9
September	0	22.5	14	5.8	26	0	29.6	18
November	1.6	22.9	18	11	3.6	0	31	12
December	18.7	32	5	1.8	.6	0	36	4.8

---

*The number of hamlets fluctuated between 326 in January 1970
and 500 in December 1972.

Table 3.5.   Percentage of Contested Hamlets,*
Quang Nam Province

	A	B	C	D	E	N	X	V
1970								
January	1	34	36	19.5	1	.3	1.8	5
March	3	39	34	13	.3	1	4.8	3.9
May	1	18	29	9.6	0	0	38.8	2.5
July	4	24	13.8	7.6	0	.1	47.7	1.8
September	4	26	1.5	4	.3	.3	48.6	.1
1971								
January	3.8	24	21	3.8	0	0	47	0
March	4	18.6	23.7	5.8	.5	0	46.9	0
May	4	20	23.9	4.8	.3	0	46.8	0
July	4	17.7	25.7	5.5	0	0	46.6	0
September	7	21.9	17.8	6	0	0	46.8	0
1972								
January	7.5	21.5	18.8	5	.1	.1	46.5	0
March	4	16.8	25	7	.1	.1	45.9	0
April	.6	15.9	26	9	.5	.6	46	.5
May	.5	13.9	25.5	11.5	.8	.1	45.9	1.5
July	3	11.7	27.7	9.5	1	0	46	.3
September	.5	6	25.8	15.6	1.8	.1	43.9	5.9
November	.5	8	24	14.9	4	0	43.9	3.9
December	3.7	29.5	15.9	39	.1	0	43.9	3

---

*The number of hamlets fluctuated between 317 in January 1970 and 588 in December 1972.

Table 3.6.   Percentage of Contested Hamlets,*
Thua Thien Province

	A	B	C	D	E	N	X	V
1970								
January	5.7	41	42.5	3.3	0	.2	7.1	0
March	9.7	35.8	28.5	2.5	0	4.9	18.0	.3
May	10.6	40.9	34.2	1.1	0	0	12.9	0
July	12.5	44.9	29.8	.5	0	0	7.6	0
September	13.5	54.4	23.5	.4	0	.4	6.8	0
1971								
January	15.4	64.3	12.3	.8	0	0	7.4	0
March	16.6	61.2	14.1	.8	.2	0	6.8	0
May	15.7	66.1	10.2	.4	0	0	7.4	0
July	14.7	69.8	8.7	0	0	0	6.6	0
September	10	67	16	.4	0	0	6	0
1972								
January	17.7	62.3	13.4	.2	0	.4	5.8	0
March	10.4	55.2	27.5	1.0	0	0	5.8	0
April	0	15.4	64.8	9	4.4	.2	5.6	0
May	0	21.4	63	5	0	.2	8.6	1.4
July	3	4	39	5.8	0	.2	0	0
September	3.8	47.6	28.6	14	0	0	5.4	0
November	3.8	47	29	14.6	0	0	5.4	0
December	18.8	53.7	8.6	3	0	0	5.6	0

*The number of hamlets fluctuated between 421 in January 1970 and 499 in July 1972.

In II Corps there were four provinces - Kontum, Binh Dinh, Phu Yen, Pleiku - that to varying degrees faced serious enemy threats. Kontum is a good example of how fragile the HES ratings could be. Between January 1970 and March 1972, the percentage of A-B hamlets in Kontum increased from 30.9 percent to 80 percent. In April, the number of A-B hamlets plunged to 1.8 percent, and for the remainder of the year never exceeded 5 percent. The number of contested hamlets in Kontum also remained low after April 1972, never going above 8 percent. There were an enormous number of deserted and enemy controlled areas in Kontum at the time of the U.S. final withdrawal (see table 3.7).

The situation in Binh Dinh, while better than Kontum in terms of secure areas, nevertheless faced some serious problems at the time of the U.S. exit from South Vietnam. In the first place, after March 1972, secure hamlets fluctuated between 9 and 16 percent, far below the percentage necessary to consider the province secure. Second, enemy controlled areas in Binh Dinh ranged from 25 to 30 percent during this period, while contested hamlets fluctuated around 16 percent (see table 3.8). While Binh Dinh was not in as serious a condition as Kontum, unlike Kontum, it was a trouble spot for the entire 1970-1972 period, never coming close to approaching the 80 percent secure rate Kontum achieved prior to the Easter offensive.

Other provinces experiencing problems in II Corps, although not as extreme as the previous examples, were Pleiku and Phu Yen, both of which experienced large percentages of deserted hamlets after March 1972. As one might imagine, the conditions of these refugee relocation areas did not enhance the GVN's attempt to gain the support and loyalty of the rural population. After March 1972, neither province approached the 50 percent secure status; Pleiku reached a high point of 34.8 percent and Phu Yen 20 percent. In both provinces, enemy controlled and contested hamlets constituted a large percentage of the total (see tables 3.9 and 3.10).

Finally, Phu Bon experienced serious setbacks to what was considered an impressive growth in secure hamlets since January 1971. At that time, Phu Bon contained more than 65 percent secure hamlets. However, after the Easter offensive the figure never surpassed 40 percent (see table 3.11).

The least active enemy areas, according to the HES reports, were the provinces in III Corps. Many of these provinces had been centers of enemy activity prior to 1968; but, in the 1970-1972 period, the situation drastically changed. A good case in point is Long An. During the 1960-1965 period, the VC instituted a campaign of violence and military activity aimed at achieving control of the province. By 1965, they were able to "gain control of approximately 90 percent of the population and area of Long An Province."(74)   This was

Table 3.7.   Percentage of Contested Hamlets,*
Kontum Province

	A	B	C	D	E	N	X	V
1970								
January	0	30.9	39	10	0	5	14	0
March	0	36.6	30.8	12	0	.9	19	0
May	0	28	33	19.8	0	0	18.8	0
July	0	69	23	7	0	0	.4	0
September	0	55	38.8	1.9	0	0	3.8	0
1971								
January	0	68	29.5	.7	0	0	1.5	0
March	0	51.9	45.6	.7	0	0	1.5	0
May	0	70.6	24	.7	0	0	4.5	0
July	0	67	24.9	3	0	0	4.5	0
September	0	69.8	24.5	1	0	0	4.5	0
1972								
January	8.6	67.5	18	0	.7	.3	4.5	0
March	0	80	13.9	0	0	0	5.6	0
April	0	1.8	4.9	26	21.5	0	5.6	40
May	0	0	0	4	1.8	0	5.6	88
July	0	.8	3.5	6.5	3	0	70.7	15
September	0	4	8	2	1	.1	70.7	12.9
November	0	4.9	6	3.5	1	.2	70.6	12.9
December	0	4.9	6	1.6	.6	11.7	63	11.5

---

*The number of hamlets fluctuated around 300 for the period.

Table 3.8.   Percentage of Contested Hamlets,*
Binh Dinh Province

	A	B	C	D	E	N	X	V
1970								
January	.1	18.6	47.8	16.9	.9	0	13.7	1.6
March	0	20	43.7	20	.1	3	10.7	2
May	0	19.8	44	19.7	0	0	14.6	1
July	.6	25	43	15	.1	.7	13	1
September	0	28	39.6	17	.4	.1	12	1.9
1971								
January	.4	31	41.9	11.5	.1	.7	13.6	0
March	.2	30.5	38.8	16	.5	0	13	0
May	0	18.6	23	11	.3	1.9	44.7	.9
July	.2	16.6	24.5	10	.4	0	44	3
September	.6	17	21.7	10	1.6	0	44	3.6
1972								
January	0	20	22	10.9	.8	0	44	.9
March	.6	17.7	22.7	11.7	.8	0	44	1.5
April	.6	10.7	17.7	7	1.9	0	44	17
May	0	11.7	16	8	2	0	44	17
July	0	12.5	12.7	8	3.9	.2	44	17.7
September	0	9.6	12.7	8.6	5.7	.3	44	18.6
November	.4	10	13.9	6	5.9	7	41	15
December	.5	16	14	6	5	3	39.7	14

---

*The number of hamlets fluctuated between 714 in January 1970
and 1,043 in December 1972.

Table 3.9.   Percentage of Contested Hamlets,*
Pleiku Province

	A	B	C	D	E	N	X	V
1970								
January	1	18	18.5	10	4.6	36.8	5.6	5
March	.2	15	16.9	9	17	3.7	21	15.8
May	.1	13	18.9	11.5	29	0	21.9	5
July	1	15.6	24.8	10	29.5	.3	14.5	3.6
September	.2	15	24	18	25.9	.7	15	.5
1971								
January	1.6	17.6	23.7	11.8	26.5	.6	17	.8
March	1.5	16.8	20	19	21	.4	20.6	.1
May	.3	17.6	22.5	23	13	.9	21	.6
July	1.5	17	25.8	18	15	.3	21.5	.1
September	.3	17.9	28	8	22.5	.9	21.5	0
1972								
January	1.5	28.5	20.8	4.6	20	1	22.8	0
March	8	26	15.7	4	20.5	1.8	23	0
April	6	23	22	2.5	19.9	1.6	23.8	0
May	6.6	23.7	19	3.7	19.9	1.5	24.9	0
July	6	27.5	16.6	2	19.8	3	24	.1
September	4.8	30	9.	4.5	17	.4	25	7
November	5.3	28.8	11	7.9	17.9	.6	25.6	2.6
December	5.5	28.8	12	6.7	17.6	.9	25	2.5

*The number of hamlets fluctuated between 599 in January 1970 and 663 in December 1972.

Table 3.10.　Percentage of Contested Hamlets,*
Phu Yen Province

	A	B	C	D	E	N	X	V
1970								
January	.4	47.5	37.5	13.7	0	0	.8	0
March	0	35	33	20.8	2	0	.8	t.5
May	0	29	38.7	23	1	0	.8	7
July	0	31	37	23.7	.4	0	.8	5
September	0	39	50.8	21	.8	0	.8	.8
1971								
January	1.6	33.7	49	12.5	.4	0	.8	0
March	0	32	43	16	.4	0	2	0
May	0	34	35	17	0	0	3.6	1.6
July	.2	24.5	22.6	8	.2	0	31	0
September	1	23.8	28	9.9	0	0	40.7	0
1972								
January	1.9	19	21	8	0	.2	41.9	0
March	1.2	30	20	5	0	0	42	0
April	0	21.8	15	14.5	4	0	41.9	.7
May	0	11	16.8	28	1.6	0	41	2
July	.2	12.7	17	23	1	0	42	3
September	0	11	17	19.6	2	1	41.6	7
November	0	14	17.7	22	1	0	41.6	2.8
December	0	17.7	17.7	18.6	.7	0	42	3

*The number of hamlets fluctuated between 240 in January 1970 and 418 in December 1972.

Table 3.11.   Percentage of Contested Hamlets,*
Phu Bon Province

	A	B	C	D	E	N	X	V
1970								
January	9.6	46.8	18	2	0	2.8	20	0
March	5	41	30.5	16.9	.5	0	20.9	0
May	6	36.7	32	2.8	.5	0	21	0
July	11.8	53	11.8	1.6	0	0	21	0
September	0	66	7.9	3.9	.5	0	21	0
1971								
January	8.9	58.9	9.5	.5	0	0	21.9	0
March	9	46.7	19	1	0	0	23.6	0
May	9	49	16	1	0	0	24	0
July	.5	46	25.5	1	0	1.5	25	0
September	0	48	26.5	0	0	0	25	0
1972								
January	0	40.7	31.8	0	0	0	45	0
March	0	23.5	19	3.5	0	0	53.5	0
May	0	26	16	2	1	0	53.5	0
July	0	25.8	18.9	1.6	0	0	53.5	0
September	.9	25.8	17.9	0	1.6	0	53.5	0
October	.3	32	14	0	0	0	53.5	0
November	.3	36	9.8	0	0	0	53.5	0
December	.3	36	8	.3	0	0	54.5	0

*The number of hamlets fluctuated between 177 in January 1970 and 306 in December 1972.

essentially the situation presented by Jeffery Race in his study, War Comes To Long An.(75) By early 1971, this was significantly reversed according to the HES data presented in table 3.12. And, unlike the provinces examined above, it remained this way throughout 1972, with over 70 percent of the hamlets rated A-B. What is interesting about this development is that the VSSG raised questions about the longevity of these developments in 1970; but, in the case of Long An, unlike other provinces that experienced severe security reversals, the situation remained quite stable.(76)

The province with the most serious security problems in III Corps at the time of the U.S. withdrawal was Binh Long. Located in the northern part of the region along the Cambodian border, Binh Long's secure hamlets (A-B) had exceeded 80 percent by March 1972 (table 3.13). In April, the Easter offensive reached the province and 75 percent of the hamlets reverted back into the enemy controlled categories. By December 1972, the situation had not appreciably changed. Phuoc Long, which is located due east of Binh Long, also experienced a significant improvement in security during the period under study. In fact, by July 1971, all of its hamlets were rated secure. In April 1972, the province suffered major enemy activity and the percentage of secure hamlets fell to 10 percent by May. However, unlike Binh Long, the majority of the hamlets in Phuoc Long regressed into the contested category but the security ratings improved after the spring (table 3.14). Still, a small core of hamlets remained under enemy control. Finally, Tay Ninh, the province immediately south and west of Binh Long, received a lot of cross-border enemy military activity, according to Thayer, but its HES security ratings do not in any way reflect this activity as disruptive to security in the area.(77)

There were three additional provinces in III Corps - Hau Nghia, Long Khanh, Binh Duong - with a large number of contested but few enemy controlled hamlets. As shown in tables 3.15-3.17, the number of contested hamlets fluctuated between 13 and 50 percent after March 1972. Given the previous definition of the "C" category, it is reasonable to assert that there was cause for concern in these areas. In terms of a rank ordering, Hau Nghia had the most serious situation with the number of contested hamlets close to or exceeding 50 percent. Long Khanh was second with over 30 percent contested as the United States withdrew its troops after December 1972. Finally, the number of contested areas in Binh Duong after the beginning of the enemy upswing ranged between 13.6 and 33.3 percent. In December 1972, 30.3 percent of the hamlets were contested and close to 13 percent were enemy held. While these provinces were not nearly as serious as those in other corps, nevertheless, with the withdrawal of U.S. military power, hard questions were raised about what

Table 3.12.   Percentage of Contested Hamlets,*
Long An Province

	A	B	C	D	E	N	X	V
1970								
January	.2	28	48	16	2	0	.7	3.8
March	0	41.8	41.3	12.6	1.5	0	.7	1.8
May	0	44	39.6	13.9	1	0	.7	.2
July	0	47.4	43.8	7	.5	0	.7	0
September	.5	57.5	38.5	1.7	.5	.2	.7	0
1971								
January	.7	65.8	30.5	1.5	.2	0	1	0
March	3.8	69	25.6	.2	0	0	1	0
May	3.8	66	27	1.5	0	0	.7	0
July	3.8	71	21	3	0	0	.7	0
September	4	74	18.6	1	0	0	.7	0
1972								
January	4	73.5	18.8	1.5	0	0	.5	0
March	11	67	18.5	2	0	0	.5	0
April	9	65	18.8	6	0	0	.5	0
May	8.6	67	18.8	4.8	0	0	.5	0
July	11.6	62.6	21.5	3.5	0	0	.5	0
September	11	63	19.5	5	0	0	.5	0
November	11.6	62.9	23	1.7	0	0	.5	0
December	11.9	64	20	3	0	0	.5	0

---

*The number of hamlets fluctuated between 387 in January 1970
and 394 in December 1972.

Table 3.13.   Percentage of Contested Hamlets,*
Binh Long Province

	A	B	C	D	E	N	X	V
1970								
January	0	12	50	22.9	0	0	14.7	0
March	0	27	49	4.6	0	0	18.7	0
May	0	18.7	60	2	0	0	18.7	0
July	0	28	46.8	6	0	0	18.7	0
September	0	49	34	1.6	0	0	14.7	0
1971								
January	0	57	27.8	0	0	0	14.7	0
March	0	75.6	9.7	0	0	0	14.6	0
May	0	63.8	14.6	.7	0	2	14.6	0
July	0	80	1.5	0	0	0	18	0
September	0	79	2	0	0	0	18	0
1972								
January	0	80.7	.7	0	0	0	18	0
March	0	81.5	0	0	0	0	18.7	0
April	0	0	6	5	0	0	18	70
May	0	0	6	5	0	0	18	70
July	0	0	6	5	0	0	18	70
September	0	0	6	7.6	.7	0	18	66.9
November	0	0	6	7.6	.7	0	18	66.9
December	0	0	6	7.6	.7	0	18	66.9

*The number of hamlets fluctuated around 125 for the period.

Table 3.14.   Percentage of Contested Hamlets,*
Phuoc Long Province

	A	B	C	D	E	N	X	V
1970								
January	0	19.6	76.6	3.5	0	0	0	0
March	0	68.4	29.8	0	0	1.7	0	0
May	0	64.9	31.5	3.5	0	0	0	0
July	0	80.7	19.2	0	0	0	0	0
September	0	89.4	10.5	0	0	0	0	0
1971								
January	0	96.4	3.5	0	0	0	0	0
March	29.3	58.6	12	0	0	0	0	0
May	31	56.8	12	0	0	0	0	0
July	0	100	0	0	0	0	0	0
September	12	86.2	1.7	0	0	0	0	0
1972								
January	50	50	0	0	0	0	0	0
March	55.1	44.9	0	0	0	0	0	0
April	0	24.1	62	0	0	0	0	13.8
May	0	10.4	52.2	11.9	0	13.4	0	11.9
July	0	47.7	34.3	5.9	0	0	0	11.9
September	22.7	60.6	4.5	0	0	0	0	12.1
November	0	70.1	16.4	0	0	1.4	0	11.9
December	17.9	68.6	0	0	0	1.4	0	11.9

---

*The number of hamlets fluctuated around 60 for the period.

Table 3.15.   Percentage of Contested Hamlets,*
Hau Nghia Province

	A	B	C	D	E	N	X	V
1970								
January	0	9.5	53.6	35.2	.7	0	.7	0
March	0	9.5	58.8	30.8	0	0	.7	0
May	0	13.1	53.2	31.3	1.4	.7	0	0
July	.7	37.9	46.7	13.8	.7	0	0	0
September	.7	39.7	53.6	5.8	0	0	0	0
1971								
January	0	36	57.3	6.6	0	0	0	0
March	0	27.2	52.2	20.5	0	0	0	0
May	0	25	60.2	14.7	0	0	0	0
July	4.4	42.6	47.7	5.1	0	0	0	0
September	6.6	45.5	44.8	2.9	0	0	0	0
1972								
January	1.4	60	36.2	2.2	0	0	0	0
March	8.1	44.4	44.4	2.9	0	0	0	0
April	3.6	35.7	54.7	3.6	0	2.1	0	0
May	2.1	38.6	50.3	5.8	0	0	0	2.9
July	9.4	28.4	45.2	16.7	0	0	0	0
September	7.2	33.5	48.9	10.2	0	0	0	0
November	3.6	36.4	48.9	10.9	0	0	0	0
December	5.1	41.6	51	2.1	0	0	0	0

---

*The number of hamlets fluctuated around 135 for the period.

Table 3.16.   Percentage of Contested Hamlets,*
Long Khanh Province

	A	B	C	D	E	N	X	V
1970								
January	1	11.3	74	11.3	0	0	2	0
March	4.7	37.1	44.7	3.8	0	0	9.5	0
May	3.8	53.3	29.5	3.8	0	0	9.5	0
July	3.8	61.9	22.8	1.9	0	0	9.5	0
September	7.6	36.1	44.7	1.9	0	0	9.5	0
1971								
January	6.7	36.5	42.3	4.8	0	0	9.6	0
March	3.8	38.4	43.2	3.8	0	0	10.5	0
May	3.8	47.1	32.6	5.7	0	0	10.5	0
July	3.8	49.5	34.2	2.8	0	0	9.5	0
September	3.8	60	23.8	2.8	0	0	9.5	0
1972								
January	.9	7.12	15.7	2.7	0	0	9.2	0
March	0	69.4	19.4	.9	0	0	10.1	0
April	0	62.9	23.1	3.7	0	0	10.1	0
May	0	55.4	28.1	4.5	0	1.8	10	0
July	3.6	44.5	35.4	6.3	0	0	10	0
September	3.6	42.7	37.2	6.3	0	0	10	0
November	.8	54.8	26.5	6.3	0	1.7	9.7	0
December	8.8	43.3	32.7	5.3	0	0	9.7	0

*The number of hamlets fluctuated around 110 for the period.

Table 3.17. Percentage of Contested Hamlets,*
Binh Duong Province

	A	B	C	D	E	N	X	V
1970								
January	0	53.3	37.7	7.4	0	0	1.4	0
March	0	68.3	22.3	4.3	0	0	4.3	.7
May	0	78.3	22.3	5.7	0	0	3.5	0
July	0	79.8	14.3	2.1	0	0	3.5	0
September	12.2	71.9	11.5	.7	0	0	2.8	0
1971								
January	.7	74.4	18.4	3.5	0	0	1.4	0
March	1.4	74.1	21.5	2.1	0	0	1.4	0
May	1.4	79.1	15.8	.7	0	0	1.4	0
July	1.4	79.1	16.5	3.5	0	0	1.4	0
September	7.1	64	18.7	1.4	0	0	1.4	0
1972								
January	11.5	72.6	12.2	2.1	0	0	8.6	0
March	10.7	74.8	11.5	1.4	0	0	2.1	0
April	8.6	58.9	16.5	10.7	.7	0	1.4	2.8
May	9.4	64.9	14.5	6.5	0	0	10.7	2.9
July	1.4	72.2	17.5	5.1	0	0	5.1	2.1
September	10.1	65.2	13.7	6.5	0	0	6.5	2.1
November	6.6	47.4	33.3	8.1	0	0	8.1	2.2
December	2.9	51.8	30.3	10.3	0	0	10.3	2.2

*The number of hamlets fluctuated around 135 for the period.

would happen in such areas.   This will be addressed thoroughly in the following section.

In the IV Corps region, while there were no provinces with as serious a security situation as certain ones located in I and II Corps, there were provinces with a significant percentage of hamlets in the contested or enemy controlled categories.   Among the IV Corps provinces with the most serious security problems were Chuong Thien, Kien Hoa, and Vinh Binh.   In the case of Chuong Thien, a continually improving security situation during 1970-1971 suffered a sharp reversal in the spring offensive of 1972 (see table 3.18).   Chuong Thien had always been an area of enemy activity, and it could be argued that GVN success in 1970-1971 was really a reflection of the enemy's decision to restrict this activity.   This would seem to be the case given the reversals after April 1972.   From this point to the final U.S. withdrawal, A-B hamlets fluctuated between 20 and 25 percent, enemy hamlets between 30 and 35 percent, while most months were characterized by a plurality of hamlets falling into the contested category.   In the case of both Kien Hoa and Vinh Binh, during the period after April 1972, over half of the hamlets in each month's HES ratings generally fell into either the enemy or contested category.   And in each case, the number of hamlets in the enemy and contested categories did not drastically differ (tables 3.19 and 3.20).

Finally, there were six provinces in IV Corps that had a significant number of contested and a sprinkling of enemy hamlets after the initiation of the Easter offensive of 1972. These six provinces included An Xuyen, Kien Giang, Bac Lieu, Dinh Tuong, Vinh Long, and Phong Dinh.   While each of these provinces tended to have over 50 percent secure hamlets, the large number of contested and smaller number of enemy hamlets marked an important regression from 1970-1971. Furthermore, this regression, in light of the U.S. withdrawal, was not a good sign for the future in these areas.   For reasons of space, we will look at only one example.   By March 1972, Dinh Tuong had close to 65 percent of all its hamlets ranked A-B, with 23 percent of the remainder classified contested.   With the offensive the A-B hamlets fell to 53 percent, with 34 percent contested and 12 percent enemy controlled in November 1972.   One can find similar situations in the other five provinces in IV Corps.

Based on these data, it is apparent that a number of provinces in South Vietnam continued to be characterized by high levels of enemy activity and control.   This can be seen geographically on the map in figure 3.3.   Many of these areas were traditional enemy strongholds; and, in the case of provinces in I and II Corps, this situation dates back to the first Indochinese War of 1946-1954.   In the delta region, this can be traced to the late 1950s when   the insurgents prepared for the

Table 3.18.   Percentage of Contested Hamlets,*
Chuong Thien Province

	A	B	C	D	E	N	X	V
1970								
January	0	14	61	9	1	0	4.5	9.6
March	0	22.7	52	13	1.7	0	4.5	5.6
May	0	23	51.7	14	1.7	.5	4.5	3.9
July	0	17	57.9	14.7	1	0	4.5	4.5
September	0	39	38	13.6	1	0	4.5	3.9
1971								
January	.5	50	23	21	0	0	4.5	0
March	1	40	38	14	1	0	4.5	0
April	.5	44.8	32	17	.5	0	4.5	0
July	3.9	48	32.9	10	0	0	4.5	0
September	6.8	43	31.8	13.6	0	0	4.5	0
1972								
January	1	47.7	34	12.5	0	0	4.5	0
March	1	47.7	34	12.5	0	0	4.5	0
April	0	21	43	19	5	0	4.5	6.8
May	0	23.8	39	21	2	0	4.5	9
July	.5	22.7	41	21	3.9	0	4.5	5.6
September	0	20	41	27	2	0	4.5	3.9
November	0	22	36.9	28.9	3.4	0	4.5	3.9
December	2	27	32	26	2.8	0	5	3.5

*The number of hamlets fluctuated around 180 for the period.

Table 3.19.   Percentage of Contested Hamlets,*
Kien Hoa Province

	A	B	C	D	E	N	X	V
1970								
January	.9	14	31.6	21.5	5	.1	3	22.5
March	.4	17	30	20	6.5	.6	4	20.8
May	.4	15	29	19.6	8	4.6	4.5	17.9
July	.3	22	31	17	4	0	4.8	19
September	0	27	34	18	2	.1	5	12
1971								
January	0	27	36	19.6	11	0	5.6	0
March	.1	30.9	30	22	10	.6	5.7	.1
May	.1	31	31	22.9	9	0	5	0
July	.3	34.8	35	17	7.5	0	4.9	0
September	3	39.7	32	13	7	0	4	0
1972								
January	9	37.6	26.8	15.7	6.7	0	3.5	0
March	.9	44.9	27.7	15	7	0	3.5	0
April	.6	40.8	26.8	16.6	11	0	3.5	0
May	.9	41.9	28	17.7	7	0	3.5	0
July	.7	47.6	27	15	4	.1	4	0
September	1.8	41.6	25	20.8	5	0	4	.6
November	1.8	48	23.7	16	5	0	4	0
December	3.6	50	22	14	5	0	4	0

---

*The number of hamlets fluctuated between 612 in January 1970
and 649 in February 1972.

Table 3.20. Percentage of Contested Hamlets,*
Vinh Binh Province

	A	B	C	D	E	N	X	V
1970								
January	0	12	44	28	2.6	0	0	12
March	0	25.9	43	17	1.9	0	.4	11
May	0	21	46	19	1.9	.4	.4	10.7
July	0	27	41	19	1	0	.4	10.7
September	0	41	37	11	.4	0	2	6.8
1971								
January	0	43	33	17	1.7	0	2	1.9
March	0	48	28.7	17	2.6	0	2	.7
May	0	43.6	32	18.5	2	0	2	.7
July	0	48	29	18	1	0	2	.7
September	2.6	52.4	31	9.7	1	0	2	.2
1972								
January	2.6	55.6	30	8.5	.4	0	2.6	0
March	1.9	56	28.7	9	.9	0	2.6	0
April	0	52.7	27	16	.4	0	2.6	.2
May	1	54	26.5	14.8	.4	0	2.6	0
July	1	46.9	29	17	1	0	2	1
September	1.7	51	27	15.8	1	0	2	.4
November	1	42.5	28	22.8	2	.2	2	.2
December	1	42.5	21.8	27	4	.2	1.9	.2

---

*The number of hamlets fluctuated around 410 for the period.

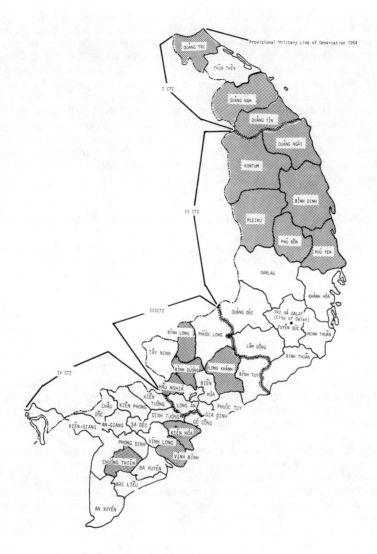

Fig. 3.3.   South Vietnam, December 1972.

*The provinces shaded are those with serious or very serious security problems at the time of the U.S. withdrawal

**There were six provinces in IV Corps discussed in the chapter which were identified as having security problems but not to the degree of those identified on the map.   These included Dinh Tuong, An Xuyen, Kien Giang, Bau Lieu, Vinh Long, and Phong Dinh.

war in the south.(78)   While these enemy areas did not constitute half of the provinces in the south, such distinctions
are meaningless in protracted war.   What is important is that,
from a quantitative perspective, using the HES data, one could
safely conclude that, at the time of the U.S. withdrawal, the
countryside of South Vietnam was far from in the hands of the
GVN.   The enemy was still actively contesting many areas, as
well as controlling others.   At that time, the situation in the
countryside was still to be decided.   The crucial question was
whether the GVN could recover its losses and return to the
security levels of 1970-1971.   To answer this question we must
examine evidence from a much different body of primary materials, for the HES data will not answer this.

GVN Security and Control: A Qualitative Examination

While the quantitative analysis of HES data from 1972 identifies
a number of areas where the GVN faced serious security problems, due to the nature of the data certain crucial issues
cannot be addressed.   For instance, how reliable were these
data?   If the data were frequently inflated, this would obviously alter our previous deductions.   A related deficiency
was that the data could not be used to determine whether a
hamlet was proceeding from the security to the control stage,
or whether the GVN could recover its Easter offensive losses,
especially in light of the U.S. withdrawal.(79)   Finally, how
did those U.S. advisers directly involved with Vietnamization-
Pacification assess its progress and prospects for the future?
      To answer these questions, several sources were utilized,
including the Province Senior Adviser and District Senior
Adviser monthly reports.   As CORDS established itself, civilian and military personnel were selected for these positions.
Their role was to work directly with their GVN counterparts to
implement the programmatic aspects of Vietnamization.   As part
of his responsibility, each adviser submitted a monthly evaluation of his province or district.   These reports provide
insights to the questions raised above.(80)   The second source
consisted of the results of questionnaire interviews administered to the final contingent of province and district advisers
assigned to Vietnam during 1971-1972.(81)   The questionnaire
contained specific questions pertaining to HES reliability,
pacification and development progress, and future prospects at
the time of the U.S. withdrawal.   Special reports of the
Pacification Studies Group (PSG) of CORDS were a third
source of information.   The PSG played the role of trouble
shooter for CORDS by carrying out local spot checks of pacification and development progress.   Finally, the aforementioned
Vietnam Special Study Group constituted a fourth source of
information.

The first question addressed concerns HES reliability. Was the HES data previously analyzed an accurate and consistent presentation of the unit being evaluated, or was it biased? From the perspective of many of the DSAs who had primary responsibility for filling out the HES forms for each hamlet in their districts, these results were inflated. In fact, almost two-thirds of the respondents were of this opinion, concluding that HES did not represent the real situation on the ground.(82) According to an ordering of DSA responses by Bole and Kobata, "HES bias, defined here to mean those influences which were responsible for HES inflation, could be the result of numerous factors: training; command pressures; counterpart pressures; negative and positive incentives; language capability; sources of HES assessment information; attitudes and predisposition towards job, and the Vietnamese."(83) Perhaps the most serious of these factors was the DSA's source of information. Those who had to rely on Vietnamese sources had less confidence in the HES evaluations. "Higher up" pressure from both U.S. and GVN authorities (especially the latter) also had a marked influence on the HES data. According to Bole and Kobata, "the district chiefs viewed the HES as their report cards and the questionnaire results indicate that 65 percent of the DSAs felt that their counterparts were interested in influencing HES ratings higher. Did the higher importance . . . influence DSA HES ratings? The data would support the answer yes."(84)

As responsibility for HES was turned over to the GVN in 1972, the issue of reliability becomes even more crucial as one "Special Assessment of HES Reliability" in October 1972 demonstrates."(85) The following comments concerning certain provinces are drawn from this report:

Quang Tin - Security ratings inflated - the flight of refugees to the province capital from insecure areas has given Quang Tin an inflated security rating at the present time.

Kontum - Security ratings valid - but population almost exclusively in Kontum City. Outlying areas are very insecure.

Pleiku - Security ratings inflated - Le Trung District (75% of Pleiku's population) does not accurately report enemy presence.

Phu Bon - Security ratings inflated - Phu Thien District (60% of Phu Bon's population) ignores enemy presence.

Khanh Hoa – Security ratings inflated – the Vietnamese HES officers refuse to recognize the presence of the enemy.

Ninh Thuan – Security ratings inflated – 100% Vietnamese reporting has led to inflated reporting.

Binh Thuan – Security ratings inflated – Vietnamese reporting officials occasionally refuse to acknowledge enemy presence.

Vinh Binh – Security ratings satisfactory – Vietnamese officials occasionally try to hide major enemy actions.

Bac Lieu – Security ratings inflated – The Province Chief has encouraged all district chiefs to cover up enemy incidents that adversely affect HES scores.(86)

In addition to raising questions about information reliability, many of the advisers interviewed felt that HES was quite ineffective in assessing enemy potential and covert political-military activities. For instance, according to a former district adviser, "as I expressed to my superiors on a number of occasions, the potential of the enemy was vastly underrated [by HES] in my district. Although incidents were at a very low level during the first six months of my tour, the potential of the enemy . . . failed to really influence the HES, regardless of my attached comments."(87) The following account by another DSA is one of the most glaring examples of the VC ability to conceal its activities:

I inherited a village that was rated B and had even been an A at one time. This village was looked upon by two DSAs before me as the model village. All the answers to the HES made it B and I carried it as B for some months before I found out the horrible truth about this village and two others that were like it. For, you see, my best village, which also has the best village chief, village administration, etc., was also the best VC-run village I had. The village Chief was a hard core VC, and all his staff were VC. So if this village was so infested with VC, how was it able to pass as a B on the HES? . . . If a village were VC and knew how to play the game with the RVN, and they knew how . . . the villagers would not say a word about the setup. . . . The VC had this village locked up so

> they really didn't need to cause trouble. Run or
> establish a VC hamlet with a complete infrastructure
> that plays the game . . . and see if the hamlet
> would not come out B; then move this up to the
> village level and see how it would work.(88)

Given these problems of HES information reliability and its
proclivity for underrating enemy potential and covert operations, the advisers developed an informal evaluation process
they labeled "Gut HES." While its origins are unknown, it
constituted the DSAs' personal assessment of the status of
Vietnamization. According to many of the DSAs interviewed, it
depicted a much more accurate assessment of the situation.(89)

The following statements concerning the programmatic
aspects of Vietnamization, drawn primarily from the DSA-PSA
interviews and monthly reports, reflect such "on the ground,"
"first hand" analyses and provide important insights into the
conflict at the time of the U.S. withdrawal. And these insights, concerning a number of the provinces examined quan-
titatively above, present a bleak assessment compared to
official U.S. estimates.

This negative assessment was particularly evident in
comments concerning the ability of the enemy to parry the
Vietnamization-Pacification programs through the effective use
of protracted war tactics. Through these comments, we can
observe how the enemy, even during periods of low activity,
was able to maintain influence and inhibit GVN pacification
progress. This is evident in the following remarks from a
July 23, 1970, PSG report of the pacification and development
programs in Cam An village in Quang Nam province concerning
enemy effectiveness: "a relatively small number of enemy,
operating only infrequently against Cam An village has been
able to cause serious disruption of the security situation and
the pacification programs."(90) A PSG report on developments
in Bac Lieu province draws similar conclusions:

> The tranquil atmosphere of Bac Lieu Province is
> deceptive. A cursory inspection gives the impres-
> sion that all is going well in the province because it
> is, at present, free from enemy main force units or
> even local force units larger than a company. This
> illusory situation must be recognized and considered
> given the fact that . . . the VC effectively control
> and administer large portions of all districts with the
> possible exception of Vinh Loi. The provincial
> government has not been able to accomplish any
> lasting success leading to the elimination of local
> guerrillas or neutralization of the infrastructure.(91)

The enemy's effective use of such tactics to maintain influence
and disrupt the 1969-1972 strategy is frequently noted in the
U.S. advisers' monthly reports from among the provinces previously identified as problem areas.   In fact, by examining the
monthly reports, one can identify the specific time period when
the enemy shifted his strategy to focus almost exclusively on
pacification.   A good example is the following observation of
the senior adviser in Tay Ninh province taken from his March
1970 report: "While the enemy still maintains the ability to
mount significant offensive operations . . . the overall enemy
focus [is now] aimed at the pacification programs."(92)   The
type of actions initiated under this new strategy included such
unconventional military-political tactics as terrorism, kidnapping, indirect fire, small unit engagements, propagandiz-
ing, and taxing.(93)   The following comments from the October
1970 report by the PSA in Binh Thuan parallel the situation in
Tay Ninh.   "The VC have been carefully avoiding any confrontation with friendly forces. . . . Present enemy strategy
within the Province is to keep the Main Force and NVA units
out of contact with friendly forces . . . the VC are using
selective terrorism directed against low level GVN cadre and
the civilian population to retard the pacification program."(94)
     How effective were these tactics in disrupting GVN pro-
grams?   According to the monthly reports, in various selected
areas they took their toll, even though the enemy investment
was held to a minimum.   The following observation of the
senior adviser in Phu Yen in 1970 poignantly notes just how
effective these protracted conflict tactics could be.

> Last year the enemy did not mount any real attack
> on pacification here.   This year he has a real good
> plan and so far he has been generally successful.
> . . . In assessing the current situation in Phu Yen,
> one should see the history of pacification as long
> term and uneven march upward.   But every year or
> so, in a given province, there is a "bear market,"
> to use the Wall Street term.   The line goes down.
> . . . We should remember six months ago when the
> GVN in Phu Yen had the initiative and the enemy
> activity   was   low. . . .   Pacification   progress
> depends - to a large extent - on what the enemy
> decides, for the GVN does not yet have anything
> approaching   full   control   over   the   course   of
> events.(95)

And as the May 1970 report from Phu Yen observes, these
enemy activities were recurring periodically in a number of
province locations.   "During the reporting period, the enemy
continued to place pressure on GVN pacification programs.   He
assassinated a total of 58 . . . and abducted a total of 167.

He also conducted a number of small military engagements and frequently entered areas to propagandize."(96)

This same pattern can be observed in other provinces. The PSA in Kontum remarked in January 1971 how the purpose of enemy actions is to present "just enough sting to remind the population that it is still around."(97) According to the senior adviser in Binh Dinh, such tactics "generate an atmosphere of fear among GVN village and hamlet leaders . . . selective terrorism definitely has a serious adverse impact on hamlet security."(98) In a later report, the same adviser observed that such "economy of force" measures permitted the enemy to employ minimal force while effectively "reminding the populace that they are still in the hills and to support them."(99) The effectiveness of this form of proselytizing in limiting GVN pacification was also noted by the PSA in Pleiku in June 1971. The two most frequent enemy themes were: "do not support the GVN for they can't win"; and "U.S. forces are withdrawing because they have lost the war."(100) These and similar observations concerning the effectiveness of enemy tactics in maintaining influence and keeping a number of provinces in a contested state can be found in the monthly PSA and DSA reports.

The seriousness of this is especially apparent when we look at its effect on the rural population, the main target of the 1969-1972 strategy. Again referring to the province advisory reports, we find comments that strongly suggest that the enemy tactics were able to influence the rural population in various areas not to commit itself to the GVN. For instance, the PSA from Binh Tuy noted in December 1970 how the "people lose interest in their development when their security is threatened. The continued presence of enemy forces able to achieve local superiority has had an effect on the people of Binh Tuy."(101) Similarly, the senior adviser in Tay Ninh expressed serious concern about the "decided psychological effect on the population of the enemy pressure on pacification."(102) Finally, the PSA in Quang Ngai in January 1972 notes the economy and effectiveness of enemy tactics in explaining how, through "carefully selected targets and methods . . . coupled with a vociferous propaganda offensive," he can "keep his presence and power in front of the people."(103) If these low-level actions that were employed only periodically could achieve such an impact on elements of the population, what impression would a major thrust like Tet 1968 or the Easter offensive of 1972 have on rural attitudes toward pacification?(104) These comments, in conjunction with the previous quantitative analysis present a much different situational analysis than that of the Nixon administration at the time of the U.S. withdrawal.

The final question that must be addressed in this section concerns the future prospects for Vietnamization and Pacifica-

cation at the time of the 1972 settlement. To begin with, the
issue of the final U.S. withdrawal from Vietnam was frequently
a cause for serious concern. For instance, the 1970 VSSG
five-province study of the "Situation in the Countryside" noted
the importance of the U.S. role in improving security in these
regions.

> In Thua Thien, Binh Dinh, Long An, and Dinh
> Tuong, it was the vigorous offensive activity of
> U.S. forces more than ARVN forces which gave the
> Allies the upper hand in the main force war in 1968.
> After the enemy's main forces were gravely weakened
> by the Tet and May offensives . . . it was prin-
> cipally U.S. units which applied relentless pressure
> on the enemy throughout the following year. Large
> enemy formations were either dispersed and forced to
> become largely inactive . . . or they were forced to
> retreat to remote jungle bases . . . under these
> conditions . . . GVN control gains became possible.
> . . . Friendly – particularly U.S. – strategy and
> tactics were also closely related to control.(105)

Various PSG studies(106) as well as PSA and DSA monthly
reports note the importance of U.S. involvement in GVN security gains. Witness the following remarks by the PSA in
Binh Tuy in December 1970: "Should the U.S. forces be withdrawn, continued pacification and development will be impossible."(107)   Such a negative projection was not an isolated
case, especially among the last contingent of district and
senior advisers assigned during 1971-1972. In fact, 60 percent of the final group of DSAs interviewed by Bole and
Kobata felt that, at the time of the U.S. withdrawal, their
district was not pacified; and they believed "that it was not
likely that the district involved would ever be secure."(108)
Of the last group of PSAs interviewed, half stated that their
province was not pacified and they did not think at that time
that things would improve with the U.S. withdrawal.(109)
     In the conclusion to the previous section it was stated
that the enemy was still actively contesting many areas and
controlling others, according to the HES data. It was further
remarked that, at the time of the U.S. departure, the situation in the countryside was still to be decided. The evidence
analyzed in this section enhances these conclusions. Given the
fact that HES was somewhat biased upward, and especially so
once the GVN took responsibility for it, it would seem safe to
conclude that the situation may have been somewhat worse than
that revealed by an assessment based solely on HES. The fact
that HES did not effectively take into account enemy potential
or covert actions strengthens this deduction, as does the fact
that many of the U.S. advisers viewed enemy protracted war

tactics as having an important debilitating effect on the programmatic aspects of the 1969-1972 strategy. Finally, this section raises serious questions about the probability of progress in pacification and development in the aftermath of the Easter offensive and in light of the final U.S. withdrawal. Certainly, many of the advisers presented a bleak picture. This, then, raises the serious question of regime survivability. For South Vietnam to survive, it had to recover its loses from the Easter offensive and move forward with Vietnamization-Pacification. To do this, it had to rely on the RVNAF. It is to this issue that we now turn.

The RVNAF and Vietnamization

A crucial element of the strategy of 1969-1972 was the ability of the Republic of Vietnam Armed Forces (RVNAF) to ensure the security of the rural areas and repel VC/NVA probes. With the final stages of the U.S. withdrawal in 1972, this became even more critical. To meet this need, the RVNAF troop strength was significantly enlarged during 1968-1972 and the training, equipment, and supply levels appropriately upgraded. Table 3.21 traces this development and also contrasts it to the declining U.S. troop strength.

Table 3.21. Comparative Troop Strengths, 1964-1972
(in thousands)

	1964	1965	1966	1967	1968	1969	1970	1971	1972
RVNAF Regular Forces	250	303	323	343	427	494	513	514	570
Regional Forces	196	132	150	151	220	261	283	284	301
Popular Forces	168	136	150	149	172	214	251	248	219
TOTAL RVNAF	514	571	623	643	819	969	1,047	1,046	1,090
TOTAL US FORCES	23	184	385	486	536	475	335	158	24

Source: Southeast Asia Statistical Summary, Office of the Secretary of Defense (Comptroller), February 14, 1973, Table 3.

By 1972, the position among many U.S. officials was that the RVNAF had been effectively transformed. However, a closer examination of these developments reveals important warning signals that suggest that, at the time of the withdrawal of U.S. forces, the RVNAF still faced difficult problems. These can be divided into the following categories: (1) serious questions persisted as to whether RVNAF could succeed in the absence of U.S. military support; and (2) while the RVNAF reached a troop strength of nearly 1.1 million, serious flaws remained qualitatively.

With respect to reliance on U.S. military support, throughout the 1969-1972 period, the eventual prospects of RVNAF reaching the point where it could operate without U.S. support remained a question mark for certain U.S. officials. This is reflected in the following comments taken from a March 1970 report by the PSG concerning the redeployment of the U.S. 9th Division from the provinces of Dinh Tuong and Kien Hoa: "During the months following the 9th's departure . . . enemy battalions reappeared. It is estimated by intelligence personnel that at least two main force battalions are again operating in the Dinh Tuong-Kien Hoa area."(110) Similar developments were identified in other provinces. For instance, the senior adviser from Quang Tin noted in January 1972 that, with the departure of the U.S. division, certain districts suffered a deteriorating security situation as the enemy forces became more active.(111) In Vinh Binh during the same period, the PSA observed how the "increasing lack of U.S. air assets . . . limited air mobile operations." This, in turn, allowed the enemy forces freedom of movement to expand the level of conflict.(112)

It should be noted that, even as the U.S. troop levels dwindled in the 1968-1972 period, U.S. airpower was able to restrict enemy activity and achievements. This was particularly apparent during the Easter offensive of 1972 when awesome U.S. air attacks prevented much larger setbacks than actually occurred, even though the setbacks that did occur had an important effect on security in a number of provinces. The degree and importance of this U.S. force is reflected in the increase of the number of sorties flown by U.S. pilots in comparison with the VNAF in South Vietnam in 1972 (see table 3.22). The importance of the U.S. escalation is even more significant when one takes into account the fact that the number of sorties flown by the United States against North Vietnam increased from 24,000 in 1972 to 106,000 in 1972.(113)

The second problem with the RVNAF, which is directly related to the first, concerns the quality of these forces. Examined from a qualitative perspective, a number of disturbing developments emerge. To begin with, RVNAF desertion rate was a serious problem throughout the war. In 1971, for example, after three years of upgrading the RVNAF's training,

Table 3.22.   Combat Sorties Flown in South Vietnam
(in thousands)

	1965	1966	1967	1968	1969	1970	1971	1972
U.S.	81	170	227	282	255	130	40	119
VNAF	24	33	34	25	34	29	34	56

Source: Thomas Thayer, "How to Analyze A War Without Fronts," Journal of Defense Research (Fall 1975), p. 825.

equipment, and supply levels, desertion from the RVNAF was over 140,000.(114) What is even more disturbing, according to a 1971 Defense Department study, was that the "desertion problem . . . is concentrated in the ground combat unit."(115) According to one account of the 1968-1972 period, "12 to 13 percent of the troops deserted. In the two years of heavy combat (1968 and 1972) the rate went up to 16 percent."(116) However, as the report goes on to explain, the situation was even worse once these percentages were broken down.

> The regular forces account for about 60 percent of the desertions, with the Regional and Popular Forces accounting for about 23 percent and 17 percent, respectively. More important, the ground combat units of RVNAF (20 percent of the force) accounted for 50 percent of all desertions and for 80 percent of the desertion from the regular forces. The data indicate that 30 percent of the average ARVN (Army) combat strength deserted every year.(117)

The desertion problem was further compounded by the fact that only "14 percent of all deserters . . . returned."(118) For combat units, the return rate was even lower. For example, in 1971 the average was 9 percent, while in 1972 it dropped to 3 percent.(119) As a result of this, combat units were chronically below authorized personnel levels. And when one includes delays in replacements and other problems, the result in 1970 was that the average combat battalion had 26 percent fewer troops than authorized. In 1972 the average was 28 percent.(120) In sum, the desertion problem was serious and there was no indication at the time of the U.S. withdrawal that things were going to improve. Such developments not only "cast further doubt on the RVNAF's ability to sustain operations" without the United States to fall back on, as one report notes,(121) but additionally, could significantly affect the success of the overall strategy.

A second continuing problem was that of RVNAF leadership.(122)   One of the main reasons for this was that the Vietnamese officer generally owed his position and promotions more to political connections than to battlefield performance.(123)   Of course, this had a serious effect on combat performance since good leadership is critical to good performance.   An additional problem that handicapped the performance of RVNAF was a lack of time in training.   Especially for combat units, training is a continuous function.   According to the analysis of available data from 1968 to 1970, the following trends in combat units can be depicted:

> Advisors reported that about 17 percent of the units trained for less than 20 minutes per week on average, during 1970.   About 50 percent trained for less than 2 hours per week, or an average of less than one day per month.   About 17 percent of the units trained about 4 hours per week or more.   Thus, not much time was devoted to the training of South Vietnamese maneuver battalions during 1969-1970. To compound the problem, about half of the training that was conducted was considered ineffective or marginal. . . . In 1970 . . . the advisors rated about 22 percent of the training as being poor and an additional 40 percent as being only fair.   So some units didn't train at all, and half of the training that was conducted was considered ineffective or marginal.(124)

The RVNAF (and especially ARVN) was also handicapped by an overreliance on heavy weapons and air firepower, conventional tactics, and an inability to counter protracted warfare tactics, as the result of U.S. indoctrination.(125)   Finally, the RVNAF was plagued by corruption.(126)   What these developments portray is an RVNAF that had serious problems all through the period of American involvement, including the 1969-1972 period.   Given this, what would the likely impact be on the prospects for Vietnamization and Pacification?   With the United States no longer capable of delivering the type of blows it did in 1972, would RVNAF be able to stand on its own?   The above discussion strongly suggests that the RVNAF was in trouble.   And this meant pacification was also in trouble. After all, before pacification could have the opportunity to take root, the RVNAF had to be able to ensure security.   This issue will be returned to in the conclusion, but first we must examine the effectiveness of the U.S.-GVN in countering the enemy's protracted warfare tactics.

Neutralizing the VC Infrastructure:
Chieu Hoi and Phung Hoang

Given the protracted nature of the enemy's strategy, in order to establish security as the first step toward pacification, the enemy's political organization (infrastructure or VCI) had to be severely weakened. The principal aim of the Chieu Hoi and Phung Hoang programs was to cut into the VCI strength, and taken together they constituted the psychological operations element of the 1968-1972 strategy.(127)

Chieu Hoi (open arms), although first initiated in 1963, reached its peak during the 1969-1972 period (see table 3.23). Through this program, the GVN offered VC and NVA members an opportunity to defect, gain a political pardon, and even receive vocational training. Two types of cash rewards were employed to lure potential defectors. The first consisted of a reward for a defector who came in with a weapon or led government forces to weapons. The second was through the "Third Party Inducement Program." Under it a person who induced a member of the enemy to surrender received a reward that varied with the defector's rank.

Table 3.23. VC-NVA Defectors, 1963-1972
(in thousands)

1963	1964	1965	1966	1967	1968	1969	1970	1971	1972	Total
11	5	11	20	27	18	47	33	20	11	203

Source: Southeast Asia Statistical Summary, Office of the Assistant Secretary of Defense (Comptroller) March 25, 1971-January 17, 1973, pp 1-17.

Despite the success of Chieu Hoi during 1968-1972, the program effect on the Viet Cong political structure was not far-reaching. To begin with, during the entire course of the program, defectors tended to come from the lower ranks. Of all the defectors, an estimated 20 percent came from the enemy's political organization, and senior cadre accounted for only 5 percent.(128) The overall defector figures are also misleading because of the reward system. By 1969, according to a special report on Chieu Hoi, the program became a money-making enterprise for many South Vietnamese, including GVN officials.(129) In effect, many of those defecting were not members of the VC/NVA, and in some cases individuals defected on more than one occasion.(130) Finally, by 1971, recurring evidence suggested a coordinated enemy strategy of infiltration of the Chieu Hoi Centers, wherein the agent would defect and then join a local paramilitary force.(131)   Thus, while Chieu Hoi removed VC/NVA from their military and po- litical forces, it does not seem to have significantly affected the VCI (or, for that matter, enemy military force levels). The same can be said about the impact of Phung Hoang.

Phung Hoang or Phoenix aimed at neutralizing high rank- ing VCI cadre(132) in order to dismantle the political ap- paratus.   To carry this out, specific Phung Hoang forces were established and attached to special district intelligence centers where all intelligence on VC personnel was collected and collated for targeting purposes.   If we look at the figures on neutralizations (i.e., arrests and/or deaths resulting from Phung Hoang actions), it would seem that the program was successful.   In 1968, 13,000-14,000 VCI were neutralized.(133) In 1970, about 21,000 VCI were reported out of action, while in 1971, the number was 18,000.   However, the problem with these figures occurs when the quality of the VCI taken out of action is examined.   The purpose of the program was to dis- mantle the driving force behind the VC/NVA forces, the lead- ership of the enemy political organization.   This was never achieved.(134)   In 1968, for example, when non-VCI were eliminated from the figures, actual enemy losses drop to as low as 5,200.(135)   Furthermore, of these "less than 1% . . . held positions of top leadership" in the VCI, and this was con- sidered too low to cause the VCI any serious problems.(136) The years 1970-1971 saw no significant changes in the pro- gram's effectiveness.   It was estimated that less than 3 percent of all the VCI neutralized during this period were full or probationary VCI above the district level.(137)   Further examination of the data shows that three out of four elimina- tions during this period were from the lowest levels of the VCI - village or hamlet - and the majority of these were not party members.(138)   All through the 1968-1972 period, assessments of Phung Hoang were not very positive.   For example, an analysis of 1969 neutralizations concluded that these not only had "little impact on the strength of the infrastructure . . . but the estimated VCI strength increased."(139)   A 1971 re- port noted that "Phung Hoang has changed very little . . . no one seems to be able to improve it."(140)

In sum, with respect to the health of the VCI, the above figures on Chieu Hoi and Phung Hoang, when added to the conclusions in the previous three sections, strongly indicate that the infrastructure remained intact and in place despite the tremendous allocation of allied resources and effect to pacify the countryside.

Economic-Social Development and Political Community

Once a hamlet was secured by the GVN and VCI influence was eradicated, the final steps in the pacification process were social and economic development and the establishment of political community. However, while the strategy was conceptualized to begin with the establishment of security and then proceed to these other programs, what generally occurred was an attempt to establish the various programmatic elements of the strategy concurrently. In fact, as was noted previously, the monthly pacification scores analyzed in this study were a combination of 21 security, political, and socioeconomic variables. In the case of the latter, these variables included public health, education, social welfare, development assistance, economic activity, and land tenure. While the various elements of socioeconomic development were important aspects of the pacification process, and were effectively instituted in various provinces of South Vietnam, if an area remained contested, improving socioeconomic conditions through large amounts of aid and land reform did not significantly affect the establishment of security. Furthermore, high marks on these variables could have a distorting effect on the monthly summary score if it diluted the seriousness of the security situation in a hamlet.

If we examine a few of these factors, we can observe how such a situation could develop. With respect to the public health variable, if "GVN-approved medical services are accessible to hamlet residents" and a "GVN-sponsored dispensary is located in this village and is accessible to hamlet residents," then, on this factor, the hamlet would be given an "A" evaluation.(141) If the dispensary was located in an adjacent village, the rating fell to "B." In the case of the education variable, a hamlet received highest marks if "most of the children of hamlet residents attend GVN primary school classes located in this hamlet" and "GVN-accredited secondary schools are located in the village."(142) In the case of development assistance, higher ratings were based on how many hamlet households participated "in GVN-sponsored economic improvement programs and self-development programs,"(143) while for economic activity the number of "households that own a TV set" and a "motorized vehicle" boosted a hamlet's evaluation.(144) The point of our argument is that, if a hamlet or village still had an active enemy element, the introduction of such aid would in all likelihood have had little impact on reducing enemy influence on the population, or increasing its support for the GVN. Furthermore, enemy access to the population may have resulted in this aid falling into its hands. And finally, high marks on these variables would have artificially raised the monthly summary score, resulting in an evaluation of hamlet progress that underreported enemy influence and the contested nature of the situation. In sum, it made little sense to give a great deal of importance to socioeconomic development scores if the enemy was still influential and/or in control. As noted previously, in 1972 there were a number of such areas.

These conclusions concerning socioeconomic development can be equally applied to political community. By political community we are referring to a process whereby the government obtains the support of the population through "an adequate government performance in economic, political and social matters as well as military and administrative matters."(145) Using the terminology employed previously, political community occurs when the GVN has "control" of a hamlet, and this occurs only after "security" has been firmly established. Therefore, in contested areas such as those previously identified, political community had not been achieved, even though the HES variables devised for measuring political community indicate the opposite. A brief examination of these indicators will clarify this contradiction. The pertinent HES variables included administration, information/psychological operations, and political mobilization. As in the case of socioeconomic development, while these factors were important to the completion of pacification, a contested hamlet that received high marks on these political development factors was not necessarily progressing toward GVN control. As noted previously, the GVN may have occupied an area and carried out political changes but the area still remained contested if the enemy maintained influence. Therefore, a high mark on administration, which was based on whether the "hamlet chief is elected and regularly present in the hamlet day and night" could quickly change in a contested area.(146) With respect to information/psychological operations, one is right in questioning the meaning of a high rating based on whether "static GVN visual displays are regularly posted in the hamlet" and "hamlet residents [are] exposed to GVN monies, cultural team performances, etc., periodically" in a contested hamlet.(147) The same would be true of a high political mobilization score which results from the number of households participating in hamlet defense, or civic and other GVN-sponsored local organizations.(148)

It must be admitted that at the time of the U.S. withdrawal, a number of provinces were still in a contested state and political community had not been achieved, regardless of HES ratings to the contrary. With respect to socioeconomic development, while large amounts of aid were introduced into these areas, its contribution to GVN control is problematic given the enemy's strategy.

CONCLUSION

In conclusion, two questions will be addressed: (1) at the time of the U.S. withdrawal, what was the state of prospects for pacification; (2) what impact did this have on the fall of South Vietnam in 1975? Conceptually the programmatic elements of the Vietnamization and Pacification strategy were appropriate for this type of conflict. Given the revolutionary warfare approach of the opposition, the strategy focused on the problem areas and identified the proper countermeasures. It was a fundamentally viable counterinsurgency strategy. The failure of this strategy lies not in the plan but in the area of execution.

During the 1968-1972 period, the GVN/U.S. forces faced a wounded but implacable enemy both north and south. And, as a result of an important shift in strategy in the aftermath of the Tet offensive, he was able to maintain his influence and political-military organization in the countryside through the economy of force tactics of protracted warfare, while awaiting the final withdrawal of U.S. troops. The cyclical patterns were not new; the goal was to maintain influence and veto control until a politically and psychologically demoralized United States exited and then settle the war. The goal of the United States during this period was to carry out a transformation of the GVN's governing and war-fighting ability. Based on the findings presented in this study, it is our conclusion that no such transformation occurred and the allegations that Vietnamization-Pacification "brought significant security and development to the rural population" and that a "Peoples War of National Liberation had been defeated" are rejected.(149)

While the process of pacification was supposed to progress from security (friendly occupation of an area) to control (physical, political, and psychological mobilization of the population in an area to actively support the government), this study has demonstrated that, in a number of provinces prior to the Easter offensive, the GVN had not advanced beyond physical occupation. As the result of the offensive, many of these provinces regressed to the point where the enemy was either controlling or actively contesting large parts of them. This situation was first depicted in the quantitative reassessment of the 1970-1972 HES data. These rapid setbacks in 1972 are evidence of the viability of the communist forces as well as the effectiveness of their protracted warfare strategy in maintaining influence and veto control in the countryside. They certainly reflect the fragility of the HES security ratings and consequently of pacification progress. Thus, from a quantitative perspective, at the time of the U.S. withdrawal, the situation in the countryside was "up for grabs." The decisive question was whether the GVN could recover its losses, return to the security situation of 1970-1971, and then proceed from security to control. The remainder of the study strongly suggests that is was not very likely that these developments could occur.

To begin with, the HES ratings examined present a somewhat brighter picture than apparently existed. According to the U.S. District and Province Senior Advisers, the HES evaluations did not accurately represent the situation due to rating inflation (which worsened under the auspices of the GVN), nor did they properly take into account enemy potential and covert operations. Furthermore, these reports from the field seriously questioned whether the GVN could recover and advance its standing in the countryside in light of the U.S. withdrawal. In their view, the protracted warfare tactics of the opposition had a serious restraining impact on pacification progress, especially in terms of the transition from security to control. These tactics permitted the enemy to maintain influence and veto control in the areas he chose to fight the war in, while awaiting the final American exit.

With respect to the future, a large majority of these officials were not enthusiastic about the GVN's prospects. This pessimism was certainly understandable given the state of the RVNAF at the time of the withdrawal. The first step in pacification was the securing of an area by the military. To carry this out, the RVNAF had to take full responsibility with the U.S. forces no longer available. However, the condition of the RVNAF made these prospects very unlikely. Rocked by desertions, poor leadership, inadequate training, addiction to a reliance on firepower and U.S. support, the RVNAF's ability to act effectively was very questionable.

In sum, at the time of the U.S. withdrawal, the enemy troops and infrastructure were intact and in place in a number of provinces. The Easter offensive dealt a serious blow to pacification in 1972, demonstrating conclusively that the war was far from over in the countryside. The GVN was going to continue to face a committed and implacable enemy who would continue to peck away during the so called "cease-fire" through the use of protracted warfare tactics. What impact did this process have on the events of 1975? Certainly it shows the flaws in the argument that the U.S. strategy of 1969-1972 was successful and only a powerful strike from the north, in conjunction with tactical GVN errors, caused the collapse. A more accurate explanation would attribute the swiftness of the collapse to the failure of pacification to wrest control of the countryside from the VC and consolidate its influence among the population. The GVN was unable to overcome many of the problems that had plagued it since the late 1950s, while the communists managed to maintain themselves during the 1968-1972 period and thereafter to improve their position.(150)   By 1975, these developments had undermined the GVN strategy of Vietnamization. This laid the foundation for the strike from the north which resulted in the rapid toppling of a South Vietnamese regime that was unable to defend itself or call on the United States to bail it out as it did in 1972.

NOTES

(1) Robert Thompson, "Revolutionary War in Southeast Asia," Orbis (Fall 1975), p. 967.

(2) Richard Shultz, "Coercive Force and Military Strategy: Deterrence Logic and the Cost-Benefit Model of Counterinsurgency Warfare," Western Political Quarterly (December 1979), pp. 444-46.

(3) See Bernard Brodie, "The Tet Offensive," in Decisive Battles of the Twentieth Century, edited by Noble Frankland and Christopher Dowling (London: Sedgewick & Jackson, 1976).

(4) David Galula, Counterinsurgency Warfare (New York: Praeger, 1964), p. 74.

(5) I did not have access to the complete MACV collection for it is not available for independent researchers as a result of Executive Order No. 11652. However, through the Southeast Asia Branch of the U.S. Army Center of Military History, a number of specific files cited in this study were made available.

(6) During the Vietnam War, the Defense Department assembled a variety of computerized data files intended to measure the effectiveness of the allied war effort so the military planners and commanders could prosecute the war more effectively. Most of these data came from the hamlet and village levels and were reformatted for easy retrieval and analysis. These data are now available through the Machine-Readable Records Division of the National Archives of the United States. The file used in this study was the Hamlet Evaluation System.

(7) Douglas Pike, Viet Cong (Cambridge, Mass.: MIT Press, 1966); Michael Conley, The Communist Infrastructure in South Vietnam (Washington, DC: Center for Research in Social Systems, 1967); Bard O'Neill, D. J. Alberts, and Stephen Rossetti, Political Violence and Insurgency: A comparative Approach (Boulder, Col.: Phoenix Press, 1974).

(8) Thompson, "Revolutionary War in Southeast Asia," p. 958.

(9) Shultz, "Coercive Force and Military Strategy," pp. 459-64.

16(10)   Thompson, "Revolutionary War in Southeast Asia," p. 963.

(11)   Cited in Peter Paret, French Revolutionary Warfare From Indochina to Algeria (New York: Praeger, 1964), p. 16.

(12)   For a detailed discussion see O'Neill, Alberts, and Rossetti, Political Violence and Insurgency, Ch. 2.

(13)   The Province and District Senior Advisors were part of the CORDS personnel and were directly responsible for implementing pacification and other programmatic aspects of Vietnamization. They were both military and nonmilitary U.S. personnel. Much more will be said about them later. Their monthly reports are used extensively in this study.

(14)   Thompson, "Revolutionary War in Southeast Asia," p. 960.

(15)   Thompson notes that "the party knows only too well that if the people are to be attracted, the cause must be directed to their vital interests and must be broadly enough based to embrace most sections of the community irrespective of the party's final aims, which must be obscured," ibid., p. 959.

(16)   Bernard Fall, Street Without Joy (New York: Shocken, 1964), p. 371.

(17)   For a good discussion of how the VC administered these positive and negative measures see Nathan Leites, The Viet Cong Style of Politics (Santa Monica, Calif.: Rand, 1969); on the negative measures see Richard Shultz, "The Limits of Terrorism in Insurgency War; The Case of the Viet Cong," Polity (Fall 1978), pp. 67-91.

(18)   Pike, Viet Cong, pp. vii-x.

(19)   For a comprehensive study of the history of pacification in Vietnam see Chester Cooper, et al., The American Experience With Pacification in Vietnam (Institute for Defense Analysis, 1972); also see Lawrence Grinter, "South Vietnam: Pacification Denied," Southeast Asian Spectrum (July 1975), pp. 49-78.

(20)   Guy Pauker, An Essay on Vietnamization (Santa Monica, Calif.: Rand, 1971), p. vi.   Emphasis added.

(21)   Much of the primary documentation of these programs is drawn from special reports compiled in the office of the Assistant Secretary of Defense (Systems Analysis) during 1968-1972. We will cite these reports two ways since we worked with them in two different forms: they will be cited as OASD (SA), Southeast Asia SEA Analysis Reports with the appropriate microfiche file number and page number; or the title of the specific study and date it appeared in SEA Analysis Reports will be used.

(22) The Pacification Studies Group (PSG) was part of the U.S. Military Assistance Command, Vietnam-Civil Operations and Revolutionary Development Support (MACV-CORDS). A number of the PSG reports will be cited in this study in the following manner: Pacification Studies Group, The Area Security Concept (Aug. 1970), p. 5.

(23) Ibid.

(24) OASD (SA), SEA Analysis Reports 6.2, pp. 274-80; also see James L. Collins, The Development and Training of the South Vietnamese Army 1960-1972. Vietnam Studies (Washington, DC: Dept. of the Army, 1975).

(25) For a discussion see Brian Jenkins, A People's Army For South Vietnam: A Vietnamese Solution (Santa Monica, Calif.: Rand, 1971).

(26) The Vietnam Special Studies Group (VSSG) report used in this study was primarily concerned with an in-depth examination of progress in Vietnamization in five provinces (Thua Thien, Binh Dinh, Long An, Dinh Tuong, Chuong Thien). It will be cited as VSSG, "The Situation in the Countryside" (January 1970).

(27) Ibid., pp. 84, 86.

(28) F. J. West, Area Security: The Need, the Composition, and the Components (Santa Monica, Calif.: Rand, 1968), pp. 1-2.

(29) Komer notes that "these attempts had many names. Civic Action, Agrovilles, the Strategic Hamlet Program, Hop Tac . . . and Revolutionary Development." However, as he explains, while "grandly designed," all were small-scale efforts compared with what was going into the conventional war. Robert Komer, "Was There Another Way," in Lessons of Vietnam, edited by W. Scott Thompson and Donaldson Frizzell (New York: Crane, Russak, 1977), p. 213.

(30) Robert Komer, "Impact of Pacification on Insurgency in South Vietnam," Asian Survey (Aug. 1970), pp. 6-8.

(31) Pauker, An Essay on Vietnamization, p. vii.

(32) Jenkins, A People's Army, pp. 4-5.

(33) Prior to HES, the collection, processing and evaluation of different strategies of pacification, counterinsurgency, and so on had been attempted using manual systems. The result was incomplete data that lacked uniformity in coverage and reporting practices and therefore was unreliable.

(34) MACV-CORDS Research and Development Division (RAD), Pacification and Evaluation System, TAB E, p. 1.

(35) Ibid.

(36)   Ibid., TAB F, p. 1.

(37)   Albert Bole and Katsuji Kobata, An Evaluation of the Measurements of the Hamlet Evaluation System (Naval War College Center for Advanced Research Projects - No. 118) p. 92.

(38)   User's Guide To The Hamlet Evaluation System was prepared by MACV-CORDS (RAD) and can be obtained with the data computer tapes from the National Archives of the United States. We will cite it as User's Guide HES, p. 6.

(39)   Henry Kissinger, White House Years (Boston: Little, Brown, 1979), p. 434.

(40)   While this chapter also uses the HES data, the VSSG created their own weighing and summarizing system that allowed them to rank hamlets into 1 of 10 categories. For a discussion see "The Situation in the Countryside." The data and code book are available at the National Archives under the title Vietnam Special Studies Group File.

(41)   Kissinger, White House Years, pp. 434-35.

(42)   Administratively, South Vietnam was divided into provinces, districts, villages, and hamlets. A group of hamlets made up a village, a varying number of villages comprised a district, and a number of districts constituted a province. The United States divided South Vietnam into four corps shown on the map in figure 3.1.

(43)   User's Guide HES, p. 2.

(44)   Ibid.

(45)   The variables included Enemy Military Presence, Enemy Military Activity, Impact of Military Activity, Friendly Military Presence, Friendly Military Activity, Law Enforcement, PSDF Activity, Enemy Political Presence, Enemy Political Activity, Administration, RD Cadre, Information/Psychological Operations, Political Mobilization, Public Health, Education, Social Welfare, Development Assistance, Economic Activity, and Land Reform.

(46)   The data tape acquired for this study was the All-Derived Hamlet Evaluation System 1970 (ADHES 70). It contains 144,000 records for the period 6-69 to 1-74. For a discussion of the summarizing differences between HES-70 and HES-71 see the User's Guide HES, Section II.

(47)   User's Guide HES, Annex C, pp. 2-3.

(48)   Clare Selltiz, et al., Research Methods in Social Research (New York: Holt, Rinehart, & Winston, 1959), p. 580.

(49)   Ibid., p. 581.

(50) By "veto control" we mean the ability of the enemy to influence the rural population in friendly (GVN) areas to remain uncommitted to the GVN. Thus, while the GVN may secure an area, "veto control" prevents the establishment of political community.

(51) Bole and Kobata, An Evaluation, pp. 86-87.

(52) Access to these monthly reports was gained through the Current History Branch of the U.S. Army Center of Military History.

(53) Erwin Brigham, "Pacification Measurement," Military Review (May 1970), p. 50.

(54) Bole and Kobata, An Evaluation, p. 98.

(55) OASD (SA), SEA Analysis Reports 313, p. 37-38.

(56) Ibid.

(57) West calls this the "We'll be back (in force)" Syndrome, Area Security, pp. 2-4.

(58) Pauker, "An Essay on Vietnamization," p. iv.

(59) One of the major data bases for OASD/SA-Southeast Asia Office was HES.

(60) This quote is from Komer's "Foreword" to the study by Thomas Thayer, "How to Analyze a War Without Fronts," Journal of Defense Research (Fall 1975), p. viii.

(61) Thayer, Ibid., p. 938.

(62) Komer, "Was There Another Way," p. 222.

(63) Ibid., p. 220.

(64) Ibid.

(65) Kissinger, White House Years, pp. 1038-39.

(66) Ibid., p. 1098.

(67) Ibid., pp. 1307, 1344. The demands Kissinger is referring to concerned Hanoi's giving up of the demand "we dismantle the political structure of our ally and replace it with a coalition government."

(68) The data file used in this study is the All Derived Hamlet Evaluation System 1970 (ADHES). It was derived from the Hamlet Evaluation System 1971 file (HES 71) which covered the period 1/70-1/74. HES 71 was comprised of an individual monthly evaluation of each hamlet. The record was made up of the responses to the previously mentioned 21 variable scores. This file contained 550,000 records. From HES 71 the ADHES file was derived and it contained 144,000 records. Where HES 71 contained monthly data on individual hamlets, ADHES aggregated the HES 71 data at the province level.

(69) MACV-CORDS-RAD, "Special Assessment of HES Reliability," p. 1. (This document is not dated, but the data contained in it puts the date in the latter half of 1972.)

(70) According to the same report, "The HES was designed to monitor rural pacification and is not adequate to measure urban trends in a manner meaningful to management." Ibid., pp. 1-2.

(71) The most intense fighting during the French Indochina War occurred in North Vietnam and the northern area of South Vietnam. The southern part was quieter but there were still Vietminh areas. Thayer presents a very good portrayal of the situation on maps. Thayer, "How to Analyze a War Without Fronts," pp. 777-78.

(72) All the data reported in this section are taken from ADHES. The data is presented in percentage tables. This author cautions anyone interested in working with this data tape to be prepared for numerous technical and formating problems before the data are ready to work with.

(73) As the fighting dies down in an area the security ratings go up, even though the enemy may be entrenched in the area.

(74) VSSG, "Situation in the Countryside," summary (Long An), pp. 1-4.

(75) Jeffrey Race, War Comes To Long An (Berkeley, Calif.: University of California Press, 1972).

(76) According to the VSSG Study, "given VCI strength and leaning of the majority of the people toward the VC/NLF, the longer term political prospects for the GVN in Long An are not bright." VSSG, "Situation in the Countryside," summary (Long An), p. 4. In three of the other provinces studied by the VSSG - Thua Thien, Binh Dinh, Dinh Tuong - similar conclusions were drawn (see pp. 89-91).

(77) Thayer, "How to Analyze a War Without Fronts," p. 913.

(78) Pike, Viet Cong.

(79) It is generally agreed that, without extensive U.S. air support during the Easter offensive of 1972, the GVN losses would have been much more serious.

(80) This study relies primarily on the PSA reports for the period 1/70 - 12/72 and secondarily on DSA reports from the same period.

(81) The study by Bole and Kobata, An Evaluation, obtained through questionnaires the responses from 165 of the last 220 DSAs and 32 of the final 44 PSAs on a number of questions concerning their experiences and understanding of progress in Vietnamization.

(82) Ibid., p. 61.

(83) Ibid., pp. 75-76.

(84) Ibid., pp. 77-78.

(85) MACV-CORDS-RAD, "Special Assessment of HES Reliability."

(86) Ibid.

(87) Bole and Kobata, An Evaluation, p. 70.

(88) Ibid., pp. 50-51.

(89) For a number of statements on this issue by former DSAs, see ibid., pp. 94-96.

(90) Pacification-Studies Group, "Evaluation of Cam An Village" (July 1970), pp. 22-23.

(91) Pacification Studies Group, "Pacification and Development in Bac Lieu Province" (May 1970), pp. 1-2.

(92) MACV-CORDS, Province Report, Tay Ninh Province, March 1970, p. 2.

(93) Ibid., pp. 2-3. Similar developments can be seen in the other provinces as the enemy decided to shift his strategy to this approach.

(94) MACV-CORDS, Province Report, Binh Thuan Province, October 1970, pp. 1-2.

(95) Ibid., Phu Yen Province, March 1970, p. 3.

(96) Ibid., May 1970, pp. 2-3.

(97) Ibid., Kontum Province, January 1971, p. 2.

(98) Ibid., Binh Dinh Province, August 1970, p. 6.

(99) Ibid., December 1970, p. 4.

(100) Ibid., Pleiku Province, June 1971, p. 1.

(101) Ibid., Binh Tuy Province, December 1970, p. 6.

(102) Ibid., Tay Ninh Province, January 1971, pp. 1-2.

(103) Ibid., Quang Ngai Province, January 1972, pp. 1-2.

(104) The following comments by the Pleiku PSA note the effects of large actions on population attitudes: "The memory of the massive destruction . . . the impurity with which the VC/NVA moved about will be difficult to erase from the minds of the people." MACV-CORDS, Province Reports, Pleiku Province, March 1971, p. 1.

(105) VSSG, "Situation in the Countryside," pp. 89-90.

(106) Pacification Studies Group, "Effects of the Redeployment of the U.S. 1st Infantry Division," (March 1970); "Redeployment Effects of the 9th Division from Dinh Tuong and Kien Hoa Province," (March 1970); and "Redeployment of the 3rd Marine Division," (November 1969) are only a few examples.

(107) MACV-CORDS, Province Reports, Binh Tuy Province, December 1970, p. 6.

(108) Bole and Kobata, An Evaluation, p. 172.

(109) Ibid.

(110) Pacification Studies Group, "Redeployment Effects of the 9th Division from Dinh Tuong and Kien Hoa," (March 1970), p. 9.

(111) MACV-CORDS, Province Reports, Quang Tin Province, January 1972, p. 1.

(112) Ibid., Vinh Binh Province, January 1972, p. 2.

(113) Thayer, "How to Analyze a War Without Fronts," p. 825.

(114) OASD (SA), SEA Analysis Reports 162, p. 49.

(115) Ibid.

(116) Thayer, "How to Analyze a War Without Fronts," p. 822.

(117) Ibid.

(118) OASD (SA), SEA Analysis Reports 162, p. 70.

(119) Thayer, "How to Analyze a War Without Fronts," p. 822.

(120) Ibid. p. 821.

(121) OASD (SA), SEA Analysis Reports 162, p. 74.

(122) Ibid., 315, p. 165; 313, pp. 32-34.

(123) Combat losses and the diversion of military leaders into nonmilitary jobs aggravated the situation. GVN also refused to systematically replace poor leaders and this affected the quality of command.

(124) Thayer, "How to Analyze a War Without Fronts," pp. 819-20.

(125) Brian Jenkins, The Unchangeable War (Santa Monica, Calif.: Rand, 1972).

(126) Guenter Lewy, America in Vietnam (New York: Oxford University Press, 1978), pp. 180-81.

(127) For a general discussion of the failure of psychological operations, see the comments by former USIS head in Vietnam, Barry Zorthian, in Lessons of Vietnam, pp. 108-10.

(128) J. A. Koch, The Chieu Hoi Program in South Vietnam, 1961-1973 (Santa Monica, Calif.: Rand, 1973).

(129) OASD (SA), SEA Analysis Reports 613, pp. 53-90.

(130) Ibid., pp. 88-90.

(131) Koch, The Chieu Hoi Program, pp. 49-57.

(132) Specific attention was to be paid to the VCI members of the National Liberation Councils and Committees, People's Revolutionary Party, and the National Alliances for Democracy and Peace.

(133) OASD (SA), SEA Analysis Reports 317, p. 61.

(134) "Phoenix," SEA Analysis Reports, June-July 1971, p. 2.

(135) OASD (SA), SEA Analysis Reports, 317, pp. 61-75.

(136) Ibid.

(137) "Phoenix," SEA Analysis Reports, p. 2.

(138) Ibid.

(139) "Phoenix," SEA Analysis Reports, p. 2.

(140) Ibid., pp. 94-102.

(141) User's Guide to HES, p. C-20.

(142) Ibid., p. C-30.

(143) Ibid., p. C-32.

(144) Ibid., p. C-33.

(145) VSSG, "Situation in the Countryside," pp. 84-86.

(146) User's Guide to HES, p. C-25.

(147) Ibid., p. C-27.

(148) Ibid., p. C-28.

(149) This quote is from Stephen Young a member of AID who worked for CORDS. Cited in Lessons of Vietnam, p. 114.

(150) According to Thayer, "The Communist Forces . . . were getting stronger and stronger. They moved their logistics supports into areas of South Vietnam they now controlled and protected it. . . . They built roads, bridges and pipelines, and they introduced several thousand more troops. By the end of 1974 they were in the strongest position they had since at least 1964." . . . "How to Analyze a War Without Fronts," p. 939.

4 Requirements of Strategy in Vietnam

Lawrence E. Grinter

INTRODUCTION

The controversy over the character of American and South Vietnamese military operations in South Vietnam - especially the ground war - existed throughout the period of direct U.S. military involvement in the Vietnam war between 1965 and 1972. Muted in recent years following the defeat of allied policy, the fall of Saigon, and Hanoi's efforts to communize South Vietnam, the controversy has resurfaced with the publication of important new studies and memoirs. The debate over military strategy in Vietnam is important because it impinges on the larger issues of U.S. political-military objectives in the war, and indeed our whole approach toward revolutionary conflict in the Third World. In brief, what happened in Vietnam was that two competing, controversial American schools of thought about military strategy clashed, as both sought to counter the communist's strategy - which presented a third and different kind of formula.

This chapter analyzes United States political-military strategy and operations in South Vietnam with particular attention to the ground war, the assumptions behind the strategy, the operational implications, and the attendant benefits and costs. The chapter explores two fundamental questions:

1. Did the Westmoreland/Abrams' strategy of attrition - big unit, munitions-intensive, mobile warfare - for all its evident success in wearing down communist main force units (at least as measured by body count) do much collateral damage to South Vietnamese society; or on balance, did it aid Hanoi's cause more than it hurt it?

2. Could a different ground strategy - specifically, a popu-
    lation security, long haul-low cost approach - have both
    handled the changing communist threat and minimized dam-
    age to South Vietnam so as to more seriously jeopardize
    Hanoi's cause?

Exploring the first question requires comparisons of empirical
data and then a series of judgments - from hindsight of a lost
war and an ally conquered by a totalitarian adversary.   Answering the second question places us into a more hypothetical
realm, but not entirely because a population security strategy
did exist side-by-side with the attrition war.   While not
receiving more than one-tenth the resources of attrition,
population security gained prominence after the 1968 Tet offensive, and just possibly could have made a fundamental
difference in the war's outcome had it received more priority
much earlier.
      The chapter covers the period from 1961 to 1973.   During
that time, the Kennedy administration increased the United
States advisory presence in South Vietnam from 875 to 16,300
personnel.   Then, in late 1964, Hanoi began infiltrating
regular North Vietnamese combat units into South Vietnam.
The Johnson administration responded with bombing reprisals
against North Vietnamese targets while also expanding the
mission of U.S. troops in the south to limited combat operations.   Escalation begot escalation.   In the spring of 1968,
Hanoi launched the Tet offensive against South Vietnam's
cities, and paid for it with the destruction of most of the
communist attack forces.   However, the shock of Tet changed
the Johnson administration's war policies, and the new Nixon
administration began the disengagement of U.S. combat troops
under the "Vietnamization" program.   Hanoi's new invasion of
South Vietnam in April 1972 brought retaliation from the Nixon
administration, including mining of the DRV's ports and B-52
attacks on its strategic resources.   Then came the final
extrication of the U.S. combat presence from South Vietnam
and the release of our prisoners from Hanoi as peace accords
were signed in Paris between the United States and North
Vietnam.
      The period from signing of the Paris Accords in January
1973 to April 1975 when Saigon surrendered to Hanoi's tanks
will not be treated.   During that period, the North Vietnamese
prepared their final assault on South Vietnam, fortifying and
hardening the logistic systems, moving tens of thousands of
fresh troops and equipment into or adjacent to South Vietnam.
In early 1975, in total violation of the Paris agreements, North
Vietnam reinvaded South Vietnam.   The United States Congress
prevented any U.S. combat reaction and, in South Vietnam's
moment of extremity, cut off all aid.   The country collapsed
immediately thereafter.

PERSPECTIVE

Before we analyze the attrition and population security strategies, the broad outlines of the Vietnam war will be sketched
as background.

The Two Vietnams

The two countries that fought each other to such a ruinous,
tragic conclusion (North Vietnam and South Vietnam) were
organized and led very differently despite a common experience
with French colonialism and a precolonial heritage as China's
protectorate and then fiercely independent smaller neighbor.
The pre-French history of Vietnam is a 2,000-year epic of
pioneer expansion, conflict, and pacification as the Viet
people, imbued with China's culture but separate from it,
moved south, ultimately throwing off Chinese control. Gradually, the Vietnamese divided into two ruling families or
dynasties: the Trinh in the north and Nguyen in the south.
Each regime became an object of European attention as Indochina was penetrated by the West.(1)
     France's occupation of Vietnam in the eighteenth and
nineteenth centuries was accomplished through missionary,
mercantile, and finally military measures. Vietnam was divided
into three French protectorates - Tonkin, Annam, and Cochinchina - each with distinctive arrangements between local rulers
and French military governors. Cochinchina, with its rich
farmlands, was soon detached and directly incorporated as a
territory of France. French investments and settlers flooded
in. Cultural and political ties focused in Saigon. In the
Vietnamese countryside, as in the cities, local security forces
were armed, bought off, or set at odds with each other.
France deliberately - as a tenet of colonial policy in keeping
with the European pattern - constrained the development of
local political institutions and movements. A fragmented polity
would not rise up in revolt.(2) When Vietnamese nationalist
and communist revolutionary groups emerged in the 1930s,
France reacted with force - only to see the system collapse 10
years later as World War II and Japanese occupation created
the political vacuum in which the revolutionaries, with Ho Chi
Minh and the Viet Minh in the lead, struck for independence.
The eight-year Franco-Viet Minh war, known as the Indochina
War, cost the forces under French command almost 95,000
killed out of some 250,000 total casualties. The Viet Minh,
who had 330,000 men under arms at the end of the war, may
have taken a total of one-third of a million casualties, 40
percent of them killed. Another quarter of a million civilians
probably perished.(3) Defeat at Dien Bien Phu broke France's

will to continue the war. French-Viet Minh negotiations at Geneva resulted in the two sides agreeing - over the strenuous objections of the government of Vietnam in Saigon - to partition Vietnam at the 17th parallel. A Democratic Republic of Vietnam (DRV) was established in Tonkin with Ho Chi Minh as President, while the State of Vietnam was truncated to Annam and Cochinchina, becoming the Republic of Vietnam (RVN) with Ngo Dinh Diem as its first president.(4)

Outside Support

From well before independence in July 1954, and of course afterwards, both the communists under Ho Chi Minh and the nationalists under Ngo Dinh Diem and his successors were critically dependent on outside support. Without it, neither Vietnamese government could have survived or sustained its respective war effort. In the first six years of independence, the Republic of Vietnam received over $2 billion in U.S. aid of all types.(5) Until late 1964, when the DRV began its conventional military invasion of South Vietnam, Hanoi was receiving annually about $100 million of Soviet, Chinese, and East European aid - approximately 20 percent of its budget.(6) By 1966-1967, as the drain on both Vietnams' treasuries grew enormous, U.S. dollar expenditures on Vietnam (U.S. force expenditures in country) were running at over $20 billion each year.(7) Hanoi gave out few statistics, but it was probably absorbing over $1 billion of communist assistance each year between 1965 and 1973 with high points in 1968 and 1972 to support its invasions. Reasonable extrapolation of those figures shows that probably $60 billion was spent on allied operations and assistance in South Vietnam, while possibly $20 billion was spent on Hanoi's war effort by her allies. The marked difference in aid received by Hanoi compared to what Saigon absorbed reflect complex circumstances, but they also tell much about the relative efficiency of a Stalinist regime compared to a military authoritarianship.(8) Finally, let us recall that all the ground fighting and attendant destruction and rehabilitation took place in South Vietnam. No ground fighting, or refugee generation, occurred in North Vietnam.

Sanctuaries

The United States, the Soviet Union, and China - the main external powers in the war - each relied on completely safe sanctuaries for their inputs to the Vietnamese belligerents. No communist interdiction of U.S. supplies to South Vietnam, by air or sea, ever occurred. No allied interdiction of Soviet or Chinese supplies coming to North Vietnam's borders occurred until President Nixon, in response to the April 1972 invasion, mined North Vietnam's ports. The DRV's use of Laotian and Cambodian border areas adjacent to South Vietnam as sanctuaries was critical to its prosecution of the war. Given the formal or professed neutrality of Laos and Cambodia under international accord, this was a clear violation of international law. But so was the secret allied bombing of communist targets in Laos and Cambodia.

Asymmetries

The Air War. The United States, sometimes assisted by South Vietnam, conducted air operations over North Vietnam, Laos, Cambodia, and South Vietnam from 1965 through 1973. The scope of these air operations was substantial, and, while most of it was tactical in nature, strategic bombing occurred in the later phases of U.S. participation (Linebacker I and II in 1972). By contrast, neither North Vietnam nor the Soviet Union nor China conducted any air combat operations over South Vietnam, Laos, or Cambodia. The communists relied instead on elaborate camouflage measures, a myriad of logistics routes, and highly sophisticated air defense systems that took substantial tolls of allied aircraft and pilots.

The Naval War. The United States had near total control of the sea adjacent to North Vietnam, South Vietnam, and Cambodia. Neither North Vietnam, nor the USSR, nor China chose to challenge the U.S. naval presence in any meaningful way. (The tiny Tonkin Gulf skirmish in August 1964 between North Vietnamese patrol boats and two American capital ships - causing a political uproar in the United States - was the sole exception.)

The Ground War. Approximately 2 million North Vietnamese troops (NVA) were given assignments in South Vietnam, Laos, and Cambodia. Approximately 1.5 million of these infiltrated South Vietnam where they joined southern Viet Cong forces. Close to 670,000 communist troops were killed in action according to U.S. reports. South Vietnam called up nearly 3 million men (ARVN) between 1965 and 1973; ARVN combat deaths numbered approximately 220,000 of which 95 percent were killed inside South Vietnam. Regular South Vietnamese troops twice fought outside their country - during strikes into the Cambodian and Laotian border sanctuaries adjacent to South Vietnam from which North Vietnamese regulars were launching attacks. Both operations - the unsuccessful strike against COSVN headquarters (Hanoi's field command) in Cambodia, and the ARVN First Division's attempt to cut a critical North Vietnamese invasion route in Laos - proved very costly.

Finally, while 1.5 million North Vietnamese troops infiltrated and fought in South Vietnam, not one regular ARVN soldier saw combat in North Vietnam.

Casualties

The war was a disaster for the Vietnamese - North and South. Estimates vary but most figures tend to place the total number of Vietnamese deaths at between 1.3 and 1.5 million people, out of a combined population base of about 40 million.(9) Applying a ratio of 2.5 wounded for every one killed, gives a total Vietnamese wounded figure of 3.3 million (assuming the smaller figure of killed). Total casualties then, by conservative count, were 4.6 million killed and wounded out of a population of 40 million, or about 12 percent of the Vietnamese people. A holocaust by any standard. U.S. combat deaths in Vietnam totaled 53,000; one recalls that the figure was 420,000 deaths in World War II. Yet it became fashionable among war critics in the West to say that the United States was somehow fighting the war for the South Vietnamese.

How many of the 1.3 million Vietnamese killed between 1965 and 1974 were civilians? Senator Edward Kennedy's Senate subcommittee on refugees stated that 430,000 of all Vietnamese war-related deaths were civilians - nearly all of them South Vietnamese. Other commentators with less access to or interest in actual Vietnam data, placed the figure much higher. Careful comparison of all sources - official and private - yields a probable estimate of about 248,000 South Vietnamese civilian war-related deaths and about 115,000 North Vietnamese civilian deaths from 1965 to 1974,(10) very close to the estimates for the earlier Indochina war. This equated to about 28 percent of total war deaths - a tragedy, but nevertheless a ratio of civilian to military deaths lower than in either World War II or Korea.

Television and Other Media

The war in Vietnam was the first major war in history to be televised. Beginning in 1965, when large-scale combat operations commenced, international media and photo journalists flocked into South Vietnam. At the height of the war, there were close to 500 accredited reporters in country. The most powerful participants in this media influx were the American television networks. They concentrated almost exclusively on filming allied activities, choosing to emphasize U.S. combat operations rather than, for example, South Vietnamese political or military activities. Almost nothing of Hanoi's operations in South Vietnam - their attacks on allied localities and defense forces, or their enormous casualties - was ever filmed by the media or shown to Western audiences. The exception was the 1968 Tet offensive. During the entire war, including the protracted negotiations that finally produced the Paris Peace Accords, Hanoi never admitted to having military forces inside South Vietnam.

THE ATTRITION STRATEGY

The attrition strategy was known by various names. "Search and Destroy" was the most frequent media appellation; "Big Unit War" was often used by professional military personnel. Technically, the strategy devised by General William Westmoreland (and continued with some changes by Westmoreland's successors, General Creighton Abrams and General Frederick Weyand) was multibattalion reconnaissance-in-force operations. The basic concept used principles that the United States had routinely employed in other, more conventional, wars. Relying on superior American firepower and mobility, the battle would be taken to the adversary; U.S. units would seize the initiative and inflict heavy casualties on enemy units. Seeking out and attacking (thus "Search and Destroy") communist main forces in the mountains and jungles would provide a "screen" behind which GVN territorial forces and political/economic cadres would operate in the populated areas. As General Westmoreland, the Commander of the U.S. Military Assistance Command in Vietnam (MACV), described it:

> In the first place, the ARVN had greater compatibility with the people than did American troops. Furthermore, since the enemy's large units would be met most often in his base areas or other remote regions, the greater mobility of American units would provide them with an advantage. Superior American firepower would be most advantageously employed against the big units, and using it in remote regions would mean fewer civilian casualties and less damage to built-up areas.(11)

So United States units would intercept and engage North Vietnamese units <u>away</u> from South Vietnamese population centers. United States and Vietnamese authorities agreed on that. Indeed, the first major engagement between U.S. forces and the NVA occurred in the Ia Drang Valley in the Central Highlands in October and November 1965, when Westmoreland committed the First Cavalry Division (Airmobile) against elements of three NVA regiments committed by General Giap, Hanoi's Defense Minister, as a test of U.S. strategy and tactics. In the fighting, the North Vietnamese lost 1,300 killed compared to 300 Americans dead.(12)   But plans for a continued distinction between the United States and ARVN roles, and a cap on U.S. forces in country, soon broke down.   New communist military pressure and renewed political turbulence in Saigon brought the ARVN defense effort to a near halt.   To try and save the situation, President Johnson sent in new U.S. reinforcements who were soon operating astride populated areas. "I recognized the necessity," Westmoreland later wrote,

> to guard against unintended adverse effects stemming from the presence of U.S. combat forces, but I regarded it essential to U.S. - Vietnamese success that U.S. units be available to reinforce and stiffen South Vietnamese forces in the critical areas of high population density.   Consequently, I planned to build up U.S. forces in an arc around Saigon and in the populous coastal areas and not to restrict U.S. troops to the Central Highlands.(13)

No more fundamental decision was ever made about U.S. prosecution of the war in Vietnam.

Throughout 1965 and 1966, major battles erupted up and down the country at the DMZ, in the A Shau Valley, at Dak To and Tuy Hoa, and in the Third Corps region surrounding Saigon.   Westmoreland's "Operation Attleboro" in October and November 1966 was huge, involving over 22,000 allied troops. MACV reported over 1,100 communist troops killed in action.(14)   By late 1966, U.S. troop strength had grown to 385,000.   But Hanoi was able to match these increases with buildups of its own forces operating in South Vietnam, especially in maneuver battalions - a critical index for measuring ground combat power.(15)   Early in 1967, MACV again sought the initiative, engaging and destroying as much of the communist regular forces in country as possible.   The "Cedar Falls" and "Junction City" operations in the first months of 1967 were examples.   Kill ratios of 10 to 1 were reported by U.S. authorities,(16) although the enemy soon returned to occupy the areas fought over.(17)   United States intervention, which reached 450,000 men by mid-1967, had succeeded in saving the RVN.   But it had failed to break enemy morale. Moreover, U.S. military resource requirements - in both operating scope and manpower needs-seemed to many to have become open-ended.   Most military commanders believed that more men and perseverance could win.   Dissenters in the official community, gradually joined by Secretary McNamara who subsequently resigned, disagreed, believing the war was becoming a bottomless pit.   Some argued for a change of emphasis toward population and territorial security.

In the narrow military sense, when search and destroy operations resulted in contact, they were usually successful. The body count of claimed enemy dead was very high. But seldom did allied operations prevent communist units, once refitted, from returning to action in South Vietnam. The country was simply too large and too difficult to defend. Frontiers extended 900 miles. The eastern and southern borders were bounded by the sea. Estimates are that it would have taken the United States alone a force of 1 million men in country(18) - in addition to Vietnamese defense forces which ultimately numbered over a million men - to have occupied all areas once fought over.(19)

When U.S./ARVN units could get the adversary to stand and fight, major communist casualties often resulted - witness the communist dead reported in the Central Highlands and DMZ battles of 1967 and 1968. At Khe Sanh in the spring of 1968 the Strategic Air Command pummeled surrounding NVA troop implacements with B-52 strikes, resulting in United States official estimates of close to 8,000 NVA killed - many of them buried in the tons of earth blasted by the great Arc Light strikes. At An Loc in 1972, when a North Vietnamese division operating from the Parrots Beak in Cambodia struck into Binh Long province, the ARVN reaction plus U.S. firepower shattered the invading forces. But these were exceptions. In practice, the attrition strategy was essentially a loose framework for operating which allowed subordinate commanders a wide latitude in how to attack enemy units and supporting areas, and whether or not to support population security/pacification efforts. It was a practice which "encouraged subordinate commanders to act according to military convention, even though there were no front lines in South Vietnam from which to launch operations and measure progress as there had been in World War II and Korea."(20) Attrition, therefore often failed because the adversary could not be found, or enemy units would scatter to base areas and reassemble later. Moreover, the enemy made a practice of avoiding large, heavily armed U.S. units, and attacking weaker ARVN units. Poor security, good communist intelligence, compromise of U.S. plans, and terrain complexity compounded allied problems.

General Westmoreland was well aware of the criticism of placing so much emphasis on enemy main force units, that it would leave the guerrillas a free hand in the villages, thus ignoring the revolution at its local roots. His response is important. "What [my critics] failed to recognize" he wrote after the war:

> was that the situation in South Vietnam by the time American combat troops entered the country was different from the situation . . . in Malaya in the 1950s. Where there had been little outside support

> for the insurgency in Malaya, the big units in South
> Vietnam were no longer depending on irregulars for
> sustenance but on North Vietnam. From a military
> standpoint, it was the irregulars that were drawing
> support from the regulars. . . .
>
> I elected to fight a so-called big-unit war not
> because of any Napoleonic impulse to maneuver units
> and hark to the sound of cannon but because of the
> basic fact that the enemy had committed big units
> and I ignored them at my peril.(21)

The General makes a strong case. But this writer knows of
no reliable evidence to back up the claim that in the mid-1960s
regional and local communist personnel - military and political -
were as dependent on NVA regular units as MACV asserts. In
fact, it was a more balanced, multitiered approach: "a sophisticated political-military system with the end objective of
establishing control over both territory and people. Political
and military efforts are balanced to this end."(22) In their
combat operations, the communist high command made a point,
year after year, of concentrating NVA/VC ground assaults at
the local level, in units smaller than battalion - a strategy
aimed at demoralizing the GVN and breaking the links between
the government and the people in the villages.(23)

How, then, can we assess attrition? It has been the
subject of much commentary from many sources. Few of those
involved in the conflict - including military officers implementing the strategy - were particularly enthusiastic about
it. The range of criticisms runs from political restraints - not
being allowed to clean out NVA sanctuaries - to excessive use
of firepower, to overreliance on "body count," to assertions
that attrition was not even a strategy but rather, as in World
War I, an absence of strategy. The U.S. Generals who commanded in Vietnam were surprisingly critical of attrition.
Over half (58 percent) of those answering a detailed survey
by Professor Kinnard of the University of Vermont stated that
the search and destroy concept either was not sound in concept or became unsound in implementation. Specific comments
included "largely ineffective due to enemy intelligence activities," and "should have been employed against specific
objectives in North Vietnam and not against a will o' the wisp
enemy in some unstrategic jungle."(24) Execution of attrition
came in for particular criticism: 86 percent of the respondents
felt it was only "adequate" or "left something to be desired";
42 percent believed large-scale operations like Cedar Falls had
"been overdone from the beginning."(25) Commenting on close
air support and artillery support, 28 and 30 percent felt they
were "too much considering the nature of the war" - a telling
comment on the negative effects of the munitions-intensive

U.S. approach.   One respondent called H and I (harassment
and interdiction) fire "madness."(26)

The body count, as a measure of allied combat progress,
also came in for heavy criticism: 55 percent of the responding
generals felt it was "a misleading device"; 61 percent called it
"often inflated."   Individual comments included: "The im-
mensity of the false reporting is a blot on the honor of the
Army"; "grossly exaggerated"; "a fake - totally worthless";
"gruesome - a ticket-punching item"; "often blatant lies."(27)

What about the effect of the conventional fighting, and
the attrition strategy, on South Vietnam?   Extensive casualties
were borne by the South Vietnamese population during the
war.   U.S./GVN operations to remove people from areas of
fighting were carried out on a large scale.   Attendant to this
was an implicit policy of refugee generation through compul-
sory relocations, combat operations, and crop destruction,
although many U.S. commanders went to great lengths to
shield noncombatants from the fighting.   (On the communist
side, by contrast, vengeance killings and systematic atrocities
such as the murder of 2,700 to 5,000 civilians at Hue during
the 1968 Tet offensive were evidently a deliberate tenet of
policy.)   By the end of 1967, close to a million South Vietnamese were in refugee status.(28)   Between 1964 and 1969, as
many as 3.5 million South Vietnamese, over 20 percent of the
population, had been refugees at one time or another, not
including close to a million more temporarily displaced by the
1968 Tet and post-Tet offensives.(29)

Civilian   casualties   were   high.   War-related hospital
admissions in South Vietnam between 1965 and 1974 counted
over 475,000 people, representing perhaps 80 percent of those
actually wounded which would give a total of about 571,000
war-related wounded.   Somewhere near another 248,000 civilians died as a result of military-related wounds.(30)   Guenter
Lewy estimated the total of South Vietnamese civilian war
casualties from 1965 to 1974 · to be approximately 1.2 million
(342,000 lightly wounded, 570,000 hospitalized, 39,000 assassinated by VC/NVA forces, 248,000 killed).   This was an
enormous number of people, especially when compared to South
Vietnamese military deaths over the same period of about
220,000.(31)

One can only conclude from the above information that the
allies' munitions-intensive ground strategy hurt the political
linkage between the population and the Saigon government and
its U.S. ally.   Senior commanders were sensitive to the problem.   Rules of engagement regularly reviewed by troop units
were published.   Precautions about destruction of property
and loss of noncombatant life were taken.   Significant expense
and risk was undertaken to spare civilians.   "And yet," writes
Lewy, "these sensible ideas ran head on against the mind-set
of the   conventionally trained   officer who,   seeing the war   in

the perspective of his own expertise, concentrated on 'zapping the Cong' with the weapons he had been trained to use."(32) Desire to minimize casualties among U.S. troops, availability of vast supplies of ammunition, lavish use of firepower as a substitute for manpower, the often real inability to distinguish noncombatants from combatants, local commanders' well known penchant for calling in artillery and air support at the sign of enemy resistance, the very questionable practice of H&I fire, and the communists' habit of hiding their forces within populated areas combined to cause needless loss of life to the people caught in the middle, the very people whose support the government needed.(33) Perhaps the most dramatic single indicator of the destruction occurring in South Vietnam, aside from the estimated 250,000 civilian deaths between 1965 and 1974, was the enormous stacking up of refugees in the coastal cities. By 1972, estimates showed that over 40 percent of South Vietnam's population - 2 out of every 5 people - were concentrated in the cities.

It is ironic that attrition, for all its use of firepower and technology inside the country we were helping to defend, was never employed against the country we were fighting. Washington vetoed any invasion of North Vietnam, and allowed NVA sanctuaries adjacent to the Republic to remain safe from ground attack throughout the entire war with two minor exceptions - the May 1970 Cambodian and February 1971 Laotian strikes. Unlike the American Civil War, when Lee took the war out of Virginia and into the North's heartland, comparable punishment of North Vietnam was never authorized. The fear of "a wider war," which so galvanized opposition to U.S. participation in the Vietnam conflict, lay like a pall over the Johnson administration's deliberations.

Secondly, while it proved dangerous for North Vietnamese units to be committed against United States units in combat, it was Hanoi's choice when to commit, for how long, and when to disengage. Seldom could the Americans dictate the initiation or pace of the engagement unless they could surprise and trap the enemy, which they did do periodically. The DRV drafted about 125,000 17-year olds into its military system every year from 1965 to 1975. Over 100,000 regulars were infiltrated into the RVN each year between 1966 and 1969. When they were added to communist recruiting in the south, Hanoi was able to maintain a steady state in armed forces operating against the Republic. In fact, government studies in February 1969 put the total NVA/VC manpower pool at 2.3 million which, even at Tet 1968 loss rates, would have taken 13 years to exhaust.(34)

So attrition never got Hanoi down to the bottom of its barrel, despite the sacrifice of a whole generation of communist youth. In short, Hanoi controlled the strategic expenditure of its resources and the tempo of violence in the south, while American rules of engagement and style of fighting ensured

that the ground fighting, and much of the resultant devastation, occurred in South Vietnam. From this perspective,
attrition was a defensive and costly strategy, one where
tactical victories by the allies ("We never lost a battle with the
North Vietnamese") could not be translated into a strategic
breakthrough.

In summary, I conclude that the strategy of attrition did
not ultimately succeed in South Vietnam for the following
reasons:

1. It was constrained by political guidance which precluded
    U.S./ARVN units from taking the ground war out of South
    Vietnam and into North Vietnam and its sanctuaries.
2. The North Vietnamese army was not destroyed. American
    strategy and tactics could not force the adversary to fight
    on its term.
3. Lavish use of firepower and instances of insufficient
    discrimination in applying that firepower in South Vietnam
    - despite a system of rules of engagements and clear
    sensitivity to the problem among top commanders - caused
    enough damage to South Vietnam to, at times, nullify the
    political linkage between the government, the people, and
    the war effort.
4. The "body count" as an indicator of progress was both
    unrealistic and inflated. Moreover, it became an incentive
    among poorly trained or insensitive commanders to place
    more wanton violence under the mantle of legitimate opera-
    tions.

Here, then, was a strategy which could not hurt the
enemy enough, but which hurt our ally too much.

POPULATION SECURITY

Although the Vietnam war gave way to large-scale conventional
violence during 1966-1969, and again in 1972 and 1975, modest
population security strategies operated throughout the conflict.
The heyday for population security was from 1967 through 1971
under the Nguyen Van Thieu regime, although the Diem government had tried a significant program in the early 1960s.
The later effort - the Revolutionary Development and Accelerated Pacification campaigns - won its spurs after the communist 1968 Tet offensive when the GVN capitalized on the
communists' extraordinary losses during their attacks on the
cities and moved to fill the vacuum in the countryside.

Diem's Strategic Hamlets

Prior to 1961, there were a series of short-lived, ineffective population security programs under the Ngo Dinh Diem government. Weak from the start as it attempted to rebuild South Vietnam from the destruction of the Indochina war, the Diem government could not devote enough effort to village security; urban anarchy, the activities of the gangster sects, and the rebellion of the French-trained army continually drew attention from the countryside. Unlike Ho Chi Minh, who had built a revolutionary organization and army from the ground up, Diem was thrust into a political vacuum with few tools to work with. He began, in the Pentagon Papers' words, "as the most singularly disadvantaged head of state of his era."(35) Consequently, the short-lived pacification and development efforts of those years - Reconstruction and Civic Action (1954-1955), Land Development Centers (1957-1959), Agglomeration Camps (1959-1960), and the Agrovilles (1960-1961) - proved to be little more than trial and error efforts that were poorly administered, insensitive to peasant needs, and often relied on coercion.(36)

The one important population security effort that Diem tried was the Strategic Hamlet program from early 1961 to the fall of 1963. Advice and resource support came principally from the United States.(37) The philosophy behind U.S. aid was anchored in assumptions about sociopolitical reform, winning hearts and minds, and raising economic standards of living while separating the guerrillas from the people.(38) Administered in Vietnam by Diem's brother, Ngo Dinh Nhu (Nhu also ran the Interior Ministry and had control of the police, intelligence, and paramilitary forces), the government set a public goal of stockading close to 14,000 of the Republic's 16,000 hamlets in slightly over one year's time.(39) Desiring to impress the United States with energy and statistical progress, Saigon set to the task and a number of villages as well as hamlets, including established ones with strong community and cultural roots, underwent physical regroupment and stockading. In spite of American (and British) caution and temporary suspensions of funds to the program, the Vietnamese government went ahead with several large-scale and bitter resettlements in afflicted areas near Saigon.(40) Expanding the hamlet effort countrywide, Nhu drove it at a hectic pace. Province chiefs were given quotas, then ordered to establish numbers of fortified hamlets by given dates.

> And this [they] did, often failing to provide the people with adequate alternative means of earning money and leaving them in locations so far from their work and markets that the transportation costs were prohibitive. The inhabitants of the hamlet were not

. . . protected against terror within or guarded
against terror from outside.(41)

By late 1962, GVN statistics put the number of planned strategic hamlets at 5,000, enclosing over 7 million people. By the
close of 1963, there were to be 12,000 hamlets protecting 13
million citizens. Yet, most of it was a statistical illusion, and
the program disintegrated with the overthrow and execution of
Diem and Nhu by the generals and the near collapse of the
war effort in the period of the coups.

The Thieu-Ky Era

From the end of the Diem regime in November 1962 until well
into 1966, each attempt to rekindle a population security
strategy failed. In Saigon, coups and attempted coups followed one another in alarming succession. Institutions of
government deteriorated. Elements of the police and intelligence forces scattered. Political witch-hunts racked the
ministries. No government or leader could claim legitimacy or
rule other than by military decree. The villages were largely
on their own as the ARVN became a temporary occupation
force. No political community existed in South Vietnam.(42)
The fundamental elements of a population security approach
were missing.
    As President Johnson was making the decision to inter-
vene with U.S. combat troops in mid-1965, culminating in over
180,000 U.S. troops in Vietnam late that year, modest Vietnamese pacification and local security efforts appeared and
disappeared. New Life Hamlets, Hop Tac (Victory), Chien
Thang (Will to Victory), and Rural Construction were the
names given to these various efforts.(43)
    Sensitivity to the requirements of providing security
to the people, and the interrelationships between communist
main force units out in the hills and activities of the communist political infrastructure inside the villages, was rare
among U.S. officials and advisers. Army Chief of Staff General Earl Wheeler's oft-quoted statement that "the essence of
the problem in Vietnam is military,"(44) reflected the predominant thinking throughout the U.S. military chain of command, despite clear acknowledgment by both MACV and Secretary of Defense McNamara of the woefully inadequate political
performance of the Saigon government.(45) Those who did
understand the political prerequisites of lasting security
progress in Vietnam either did not have the power to change
U.S. priorities or lost out in the debates, and U.S. military
and economic resources and advisers became substitutes for a
South Vietnamese political effort that would not take hold.(46)
When, following the Tonkin Gulf incident, North Vietnam began

its phased invasion of the south in late 1964 and Saigon went through renewed political turbulence, the war effort nearly collapsed. Those arguing for direct U.S. action - reprisal bombing of North Vietnam and insertion of combat troops into South Vietnam - won President Johnson's approval. The American military intervention of 1965 - three U.S. division equivalents ordered into offensive operations against communist units in the highlands and near Saigon - blocked the North Vietnamese from splitting the RVN in half. However, the ground fighting, coupled with allied aerial bombardment, created waves of refugees threatening to overwhelm the Republic's social services as well as the government's political legitimacy.

As much to cope with the attendant human dislocation as to resurrect village security efforts, Washington and Saigon held two summit conferences in 1966. While the conventional violence escalated, officials lobbying for a new population security approach at the local level sought to focus pacification attention on: provision of continuous local security in the villages; restoration of effective, responsible local government; and improved living conditions. In early 1966, the Revolutionary Development program (Vietnamese name: Rural Development) emerged under the leadership of an energetic ARVN Brigadier General, Nguyen Duc Thang, and an intense ex-Viet Minh cadre training chief, Colonel Nguyen Be.(47) National priority areas were established. By early 1967, about 40,000 GVN pacification and development cadres were assigned or in training. MACV, AID, and CIA supported the program.(48)

However, new waves of refugees fleeing the conventional fighting and renewed instability in the ARVN soon ground the Revolutionary Development effort to a near halt. Then, in the spring of 1967, with Secretary of Defense McNamara pushing the effort and with the appointment to Saigon of Deputy Ambassador Robert Komer as head of a MACV staff directorate called CORDS (Civil Operations and Revolutionary Development Support), U.S. assistance to Vietnamese population security efforts took on a new priority. The Vietnamese began to follow suit. What emerged was the "new model" of pacification as U.S. support - military and civilian - was integrated under MACV and the Vietnamese gave the effort attention at the Prime Ministerial level.

The trends of the Revolutionary Development period and the New Model approach - reenergizing population security, more effective planning and execution, greater complementarity between U.S. and GVN goals - were put to their greatest test by the 1968 communist Tet offensive. Tet sent a great shock through the Saigon government, and it precipitated the start of the American disengagement. But the Tet spasm also decimated communist combat forces in the south - 45,000 dead in the first month. With over a million refugees generated by the fighting,(49) the core question was which side would fill the

vacuum in the countryside. President Thieu took direct command of the situation, and the government reconcentrated
resources on cleaning up the cities and protecting the villages.
The Peoples Self Defense Force was formed, ultimately distributing about half a million arms. The Rural and Popular
Forces were expanded to about 550,000 men. A series of
"Accelerated Pacification Campaigns" began.(50) Despite
inefficiency, corruption, and the inability of the GVN to
eradicate the communist political infrastructure in the localities, a strategic threshold had been crossed. By mid-1969,
in spite of many problems, population security had become the
core of the Thieu government's strategy. It emphasized sustained local security by means of an expanded local militia,
reenergizing village decision making and responsibility, and
land reform.(51) These efforts left much to be desired; but
they succeeded well enough that, when combined with the
expansion of the RVNAF to over 1.1 million men and other
developments adverse to Hanoi's war aims - President Thieu's
and Nixon's uncompromising stance against a coalition government in Saigon, the "Vietnamization" program, and allied
military incursions into Cambodia and Laos - Hanoi evidently
concluded that to save the situation it would have to invade
South Vietnam again, with the shock timed for the U.S. election campaign.(52)

With the full prior knowledge and assistance of the Soviet
Union, North Vietnam mounted its invasion against South Vietnam. Beginning with a devastating barrage of artillery and
armor, a half-dozen armored and infantry divisions struck
across from the DMZ, Laos, and Cambodia. It cost Hanoi some
20,000 dead and 40,000 wounded in the first eight weeks of
the campaign.(53) President Nixon responded by ordering the
mining of North Vietnam's ports and a technologically advanced
aerial interdiction of its logistic arteries and hydroelectric
complexes. While North Vietnam paid dearly for the invasion,
in the south the ARVN was taking serious casualties in the
ground war. NVA forces occupied significant portions of Tay
Ninh, Phuoc Long, and Binh Long provinces. All of Quang
Tri province was lost. On the central coast, Binh Dinh province was seriously jeopardized. Major areas of Quang Tin,
Quang Nam, and Thua Thieu provinces lost government security protection. Although beaten away from South Vietnam's
major population centers, the communist invasion nevertheless
skewed the whole war back to a killing contest of attrition.
Once again, population security was orphaned to the big unit
war.

While the period 1967 to 1972 saw an end to the long
neglect of population security, it must be emphasized that,
even then, it was still a modest effort compared to the resources going into big unit operations and aerial interdiction
in the south. At their height in 1968-1971, pacification and

population security efforts - in terms of Vietnamese and U.S. forces providing security to people on a day-to-day basis - probably did not account for more than one-sixth of the resources the allies were spending on the war. Over the period 1961 to 1973, population security, with its attendant political and economic efforts, probably garnered no more than one-tenth of the war's overall expenditures. In summary, as an alternative to attrition, population security never got a fair test as a strategy, despite the startling cost-effectiveness which it would at times demonstrate.(54)

CONCLUSION

The political costs of the attrition strategy and the political constraints upon it proved to be very high. While attrition did major damage to the main force units Hanoi chose to commit in South Vietnam, attrition did not wear down communist forces to unacceptable levels. Moreover, the scope and intensity of allied firepower, when exploited by Hanoi's policy of disrupting South Vietnamese populated areas, resulted in very serious damage to the Republic. The political costs to the government in Saigon of the uprooting and harm to hundreds of thousands of people were extremely high. Too many RVN citizens bearing the brunt of the war simply concluded that neither Saigon and its U.S. ally nor Hanoi cared sufficiently about their welfare.

A fundamental point was that Hanoi was largely able to control the level of violence inside South Vietnam (and, therefore, the degree of attrition of its own forces), by committing or withdrawing them from combat at times and places of its choosing. Thus, on balance, North Vietnam essentially dictated the strategic tempo of the ground war, while the allies dominated the tactical outcomes. Few more telling lessons about the value of sanctuaries and the paralyzing effect of political constraints can be demonstrated than in this war where Hanoi hid its forces just across South Vietnam's borders, and Washington and Saigon refused, until very late in the war, to attack those sanctuaries.

The alternative to attrition - the population security strategy - never got a fair test. In terms of resources, it was orphaned to the big unit war. But equally critical was the absence of the necessary political requirements. No sufficiently viable political community was developed in South Vietnam despite years of effort, changes of government, and resources expended. The Diem government was elitist, Catholic, traditional, and personalized. It was a family regime - a patriarchy - incapable of organizing South Vietnamese society in a manner that would get enough people to identify with and

fight for the central government. The officers who overthrew
Diem and formed their own governments in his wake - Minh,
Khanh, Ky, and Thieu - shifted the focus of power to cliques
within the armed forces. Despite Thieu's commendable efforts
in the midst of some of the heaviest fighting of the war to
decentralize power and push resources out to the villages, his
priorities were constantly contested by other generals.
Thieu's plans were further sidetracked when Hanoi slammed its
great wall of military pressure against the Republic in April
1972. Population security was pushed aside once again.

     Could the war have had a different outcome? Could it
have ended with a free noncommunist South Vietnam? I am
convinced the answer is yes. But such an outcome would have
required a different mix of political and military ingredients,
and a GVN strategy which early-on clearly emphasized population security and community building. In essence, a different historical basis behind the two Vietnams' emergence as
independent states would have been necessary. First and
foremost, Vietnamese authorities in Saigon - like the communists who came to power in Hanoi - would have had to represent a system of political authority which linked the central
government and the villages into a mutually supportive and
sustainable national community. Ho Chi Minh did this in totalitarian fashion, liquidating his opposition, amputating or
co-opting their organizations, ultimately reorganizing and
penetrating all of North Vietnamese society. When Ho turned
his full attention to subverting South Vietnam in 1959, he had
been actively organizing and preparing the ground for revolution for 30 years. However repulsive his accomplishment was
in what it did to the millions of human beings who supported
him or resisted him, as an exercise in political effectiveness
and the conquest of power it was a masterpiece of political and
social engineering. This in essence, but with obviously
different values and treatment of human beings, is what the
Saigon governments needed to do. They needed to develop
South Vietnam politically, building power and imbedding it
within the population so as to involve the people in their own
defense and welfare. It is not an easy task under the best of
circumstances. Nor can it be done quickly. It took Diem five
years simply to stabilize his control of the main levers of
power in South Vietnam's cities. That was the year, 1959,
when Hanoi put in motion its plan to overturn the Republic.

     It is very difficult to compress the process of political
development. To secure a population's support prior to the
emergence of a political community requires coercion. Often it
fails. Sometimes the tasks can be carried out simultaneously,
but that requires superlative leadership. A population security strategy in South Vietnam was necessary from 1954 to
1965. In the midst of the high intensity conventional warfare
of the late 1960s, we saw this very thing being attempted by

Thieu with the rearming and expansion of the Rural and Popular Forces, creation of the Peoples' Self Defense Force, and
the moves toward local village initiative and land reform. The
people demanded it. The problem was that these tasks should
have been underway before the strain of the big unit war
began.

If the Saigon government had institutionalized its political
power and penetrated the villages before Hanoi raised the
stakes, then we very likely would have seen a much different
outcome to the war. First of all, support for communist
activities in the villages would have been much harder to come
by. Secondly, government defense efforts would have resulted
from demands of the localities rather than being impressed on
them from Saigon. Third, as the emergency escalated, if
Saigon had asked the United States to intervene, U.S. forces
most likely would have been used only as strike forces away
from the populated areas instead, as actually happened, in the
role of substitutes for Vietnamese forces. So the critical years
were 1954 to 1965. If South Vietnam had had an effective,
powerful government in those years, Hanoi's hammer would not
have found nearly so vulnerable a body politic.

Taking the long view, it is clear that the pre-American
and pre-Independence roots of the matter had an inexorable
bearing on the outcome. France, like the United States, obviously did not want to see Vietnam fall to communism. But
by virtue of the traditional French imperial policies of divide
and rule, conjoined later to the instinctive U.S. policies of
high technology and firepower, both Western allies contributed
to the country's tragedy in spite of their own heroic efforts as
well as those of the many Vietnamese who fought with them
against communist totalitarianism.

Ultimately, of course, in spite of the massive external
inputs, it came down to a contest between the Vietnamese as it
has so many times before during their centuries-long history
of conflict, pacification, and uprisings against both their own
rulers and foreign invaders. And, as is always the case in
revolutions, the heart of the problem lay in politics, rather
than force. How could you, as one close observer asked,
solve the challenge of: "reforming and redistributing power in
a political system under severe internal strain"?(55)

The South Vietnamese, for all their extraordinary effort
to stave off Hanoi, were unable to solve that basic political
problem. Robert Shaplen's insight on the situation years ago
unfortunately became the correct conclusion to the story: "And
so it goes - a kind of compulsive mutual-vivisection society, in
which everyone wants to cut everyone else up to determine the
cause of the national disease, which may be incurable."(56)

Nothing that I have written is meant to disparage the
cause for which the United States, South Vietnam, and the
other allies in the war (South Korea, Thailand, Australia, and

the Philippines) fought. The cause and the motives were honorable: to prevent the conquest of South Vietnam by North Vietnam. That we failed, and in the process contributed to our failure by the ways in which we intervened and fought, requires no further elaboration. But, as Guenter Lewy writes, "the fact that South Vietnam, abandoned by its ally, finally succumbed to a powerful and ruthless antagonist does not prove that this policy could not have had a less tragic ending."(57) The sad fate of the people of Indochina since 1975 - the millions who have had to endure what communist regimes in Hanoi, Vientiane, and Phnom Penh have done to them, or in desperation taken their chances on the open seas and in the refugee camps - gives vivid testimony to what people will do for freedom, imperfect though it is, in flight from what they can no longer endure.

NOTES

(1) A classic treatment is Joseph Buttinger, The Smaller Dragon: A Political History of Vietnam (New York: Praeger, 1958).

(2) See Donald Lancaster, The Emancipation of French Indochina (New York: Oxford University Press, 1961); and Dennis J. Duncanson, Government and Revolution in Vietnam (New York: Oxford University Press, 1968).

(3) Bernard B. Fall, The Two Viet-Nams; A Political and Military Analysis, Rev. Ed. (New York: Praeger, 1964), p. 129; Duncanson, Government and Revolution in Vietnam pp. 1-3; and United States-Vietnam Relations, 1945-1967, Part IV, A.5E, U.S. Government Printing Office, Washington, D.C., 1971 (hereafter cited as Pentagon Papers).

(4) Details are in the Pentagon Papers, Parts II and III.

(5) The Pentagon Papers, Part IV, A.4, p. 1.1.

(6) Duncanson, Government and Revolution in Vietnam, pp. 405-06.

(7) Ibid.

(8) The national capacities of different kinds of governments, and their ability to mobilize and absorb resources are analyzed in A. F. K. Organski and Jack Kugler, "Davids and Goliaths: Predicting the Outcomes of International Wars," Comparative Political Studies, (July 1978), pp. 141-81.

(9) Guenter Lewy, America in Vietnam (New York: Oxford University Press, 1978), pp. 442-53.

(10) Lewy, p. 453.

(11) General William C. Westmoreland, A Soldier Reports (Garden City, New York: Doubleday, 1976), p. 146.

(12) Lewy, America in Vietnam, p. 57.

(13) General William C. Westmoreland, USA, and Admiral Ulysses Grant Sharp, USN, Report on the War in Vietnam, as of 30 June 1968 (Washington: USGPO, 1969), p. 99. Also see pp. 114, 132.

(14) Ibid., p. 129.

(15) Ibid., pp. 84, 97-98; Lewy, America in Vietnam, p. 84.

(16) Westmoreland and Sharp, Report on the War in Vietnam, pp. 152-53; Lewy, p. 64.

(17) Lieutenant General Bernard W. Rogers, Cedar Falls-Junction City: A Turning Point (Washington, D.C.: Department of the Army, 1974), p. 158 as cited in Richard A. Hunt, "Strategies at War," p. 31.

(18) Douglas Kinnard, The War Managers (Hanover, New Hampshire: University Press of New England, 1977), p. 42.

(19) "Had I had at my disposal," General Westmoreland later wrote, "virtually unlimited manpower, I could have stationed troops permanently in every district or province and thus provided an alternative strategy," Westmoreland, A Soldier Reports, p. 147. Essentially unlimited manpower - South Vietnamese manpower - did exist. The problem was that Saigon could not mobilize it.

(20) Hunt, "Strategies at War," p. 27. Also see pp. 32-43 for difficulties U.S. combat units had in establishing security in Hau Nghia and Long An provinces.

(21) Westmoreland, A Soldier Reports, p. 149.

(22) David W. P. Elliott and W. A. Stewart, "Pacification and the Viet Cong System in Dinh Tuong: 1966-1967," RAND Corporation, Memorandum RM-5788 ISA/ARPA (Santa Monica, California: RAND Corp., January 1969), pp. 100-03. Also see Jeffrey Race, War Comes to Long An (Berkeley: University of California Press, 1973).

(23) See Thomas Thayer, "How to Analyze a War Without Fronts," Journal of Defense Research (Fall 1975), pp. 800-05; and Richard Shultz, "The Vietnamization Strategy of 1968-1972: A Quantitative and Qualitative Reassessment," p. 51.

(24) Kinnard, The War Managers, p. 45.

(25) Ibid.

(26) Ibid., p. 47.

(27) Ibid., pp. 74-75.

(28) Lewy, America in Vietnam, p. 65.

(29) Ibid., p. 108.

(30) Ibid., p. 444.

(31) Ibid., p. 451.

(32) Ibid., p. 96.

(33) Ibid., pp. 95-105.

(34) Ibid., p. 84.

(35) The Pentagon Papers, V A.5.2., p. 15; and Lawrence E. Grinter, "How They Lost: Doctrines, Strategies and Outcomes of the Vietnam War," Asian Survey (December 1975), pp. 1120-23.

(36) Lawrence E. Grinter, "South Vietnam: Pacification Denied," Southeast Asian SPECTRUM, (July 1975), pp. 49-55.

(37) Details on U.S. advisory support to the program are in Chapter 1, James W. Dunn, "Province Advisors in Vietnam, 1962-1965."

(38) The roots of the perceptions which vitalized the Kennedy administration's approach to South Vietnam's difficulties are surveyed in Richard Shultz, "Strategy Lessons From An Unconventional War: The U.S. Experience in Vietnam," in Nonnuclear Conflicts in Nuclear Age, edited by Sam C. Sarkesian (New York: Praeger, 1980), pp. 140-43.

(39) Robert Thompson, Defeating Communist Insurgency (New York: Praeger, 1966), p. 122. (Thompson was head of the British Advisory Mission to Vietnam at this time.) By late 1962, when troubles were evident, Nhu indicated that only 3,200 hamlets, enclosing about 4 million people, had been stockaded. See GVN data in Pentagon Papers, IV. B.2, p. 28.

(40) The harsh "Operation Sunrise" relocation in the Ben Cat district of Binh Duong province in the spring of 1962, while not typical of most resettlements, nevertheless revealed an extraordinary lack of GVN preparation of the farmers. See Pentagon Papers, IV. B.2, pp. 20-30.

(41) Richard L. Clutterbuck, The Long, Long War: Counterinsurgency in Malaya and Vietnam (New York: Praeger, 1966), p. 67. Also see the USAID appraisal of September 1963 in Pentagon Papers, IV. C.1, pp. 12-14.

(42) See Allen E. Goodman, Politics in War: The Bases of Political Community in South Vietnam (Cambridge, Mass.: Harvard University Press, 1973).

(43) Grinter, "South Vietnam: Pacification Denied," pp. 56-59.

(44) Quoted in Roger Hilsman, To Move a Nation: The Politics of Foreign Policy in the Administration of John F. Kennedy (Garden City, N.Y.: Doubleday, 1967), p. 426.

(45) See The Pentagon Papers, IV. C.1, pp. 30-34, 40.

(46) See, for example, the views of Roger Hilsman, Pentagon Papers, IV. C.1, pp. 35-36; the Army's 1966 PROVN ("A Program for the Pacification and Long Term Development of South Vietnam") study, as cited in Lewy, America in Vietnam, pp. 85, 472; and the British position in Robert Thompson, No Exit From Vietnam, rev. ed. (New York: D. McKay, 1970).

(47) Douglas S. Blaufarb, The Counterinsurgency Era: U.S. Doctrine and Performance 1950 to the Present (New York: Free Press, 1977), pp. 225-27.

(48) Grinter, "How They Lost," p. 1120.

(49) Sharp and Westmoreland, Report on the War in Vietnam, p. 170; and Robert Shaplen, The Road From War: Vietnam 1965-1970 (New York: Harper and Row, 1970), p. 191.

(50) Robert W. Komer, "Clear, Hold and Rebuild," Army (May 1970), p. 21; "Pacification: A Look Back and Ahead," Army (June 1970), p. 24; and MACV-CORDS, "Four Year Community Defense and Local Development," MACV, Saigon, January 10, 1973; Blaufarb, The Counterinsurgency Era, pp. 263-68; and Tran Dinh Tho, Pacification, Indochina Monograph, U.S. Army Center of Military History (Washington, D.C.: 1980), pp. 150-55, 167, 169.

(51) Of relevance is John Paul Vann, opening statement, February 18, 1970, before U.S. Congress, Senate Committee on Foreign Relations, Vietnam: Policy and Prospects, 1970, Hearings, p. 90; Allan E. Goodman, "South Vietnam and the New Security," Asian Survey (February 1972), p. 126; and Roy L. Prosterman, "Land Reform as Foreign Aid," Foreign Policy (Spring 1972), p. 135.

(52) Grinter, "How They Lost," pp. 1115-16, 1130.

(53) Robert Shaplen, "Letter from Vietnam," The New Yorker (June 24, 1972), p. 70.

(54) The cost of outfitting an ARVN division, compared to outfitting and maintaining an American division in Vietnam, was in the vicinity of 1 to 20. RF and PF forces, which constituted 55 percent of RVNAF manpower and took over 60 percent of the casualties between 1967 and 1972, cost even less to equip than regular ARVN units. See Thayer, "How to Analyze a War Without Fronts."

(55) Blaufarb, The Counterinsurgency Era, p. 277.

(56) Robert Shaplen, "Letter from Saigon," New Yorker, January 31, 1970, p. 55.

(57) Lewy, <u>America in Vietnam</u>, p. 441.

5 The Sources of U.S. Frustration in Vietnam

Douglas S. Blaufarb

The contributors of this book have traced in some detail the gropings of the United States and its armed forces for a solution to a problem they were not prepared or trained to deal with: the surmounting of a communist insurgency in a remote and unfamiliar terrain, in a political and social context that could not have been more exotic or difficult for Americans to understand. As we all know, the effort ended in failure. The critical point and the purpose of this book is to determine and explain why, focusing especially on the strategies of the U.S. military. In the opinion of this commentator, the authors of the various contributions, examined singly and then viewed as a whole, come close to a convincing explanation but do not bridge the last gap leading to a full understanding of the phenomenon of frustration which the United States, then indisputably the most formidable military power in the world, encountered in Vietnam.

Let me first summarize the findings of the contributors. Colonel James W. Dunn launches the book with a careful, low-key, and authoritative exposition of the first departure attempted by the army in Vietnam from previous military advisory practice: the assignment of advisers on a territorial basis to work with the civilian government structure, namely the province chiefs and their staffs. In fact, all province chiefs by 1962, when the program began, were army officers on detail to the Ministry of the Interior, and population security was one of their principal responsibilities. The same was true at the next echelon below province, which was the district, where U.S. advisers began to be assigned in 1964. At province level, the available forces consisted for the most part of paramilitary units called the Civil Guard (later the Regional Forces) and at district level, the poorly trained and equipped village defenders called the Self Defense Forces (later the Popular Forces). The decision to assign U.S. military advisers to these internal government echelons, which was based on a recommendation of General Maxwell Taylor, constituted a recognition of the unusual character of the war and an attempt to carry out an elementary precept of counter-insurgency operations, namely, that "the people are the target."

The program, being new, met with many difficulties, the most important being the hasty and incomplete training of the advisers for their novel tasks. Some improvement was made in this aspect after two years of experience and the American command pulled together a rather makeshift plan to concentrate the effort on one priority area - the region surrounding Saigon. The purpose was to dramatize the key concept of U.S. counterinsurgency at the time, namely, "clear and hold," the clearing to be done by the regular ARVN and the holding by the paramilitary territorial forces, supported if necessary by the regulars. Because of poor planning and preparation, and particularly because it was forced upon a reluctant South Vietnamese command, this plan (called Hop Tac) failed and became a dead letter in 1965 as attention turned to the commitment of U.S. combat forces. Colonel Dunn makes clear that, with this turning point, the U.S. military advisory program lost its primary position and the advisers became little more than liaison officers between U.S. and ARVN regulars. In the opinion of this writer, the advisory effort only regained its importance during the reborn pacification programs of 1968-1971, when the Army made an effort to assign top officers as advisers. Be that as it may, Dunn's paper clearly points to weakness in the quality of the American effort, attributable to inexperience and ignorance of the complex Vietnamese background, in short to inadequate training; and secondarily to a lack of commitment by the Vietnamese which, in his account, was particularly evident in the failure of Hop Tac. This order of importance is reversed in subsequent chapters but is perhaps natural in a study of a particular and limited U.S. program.

In the next chapter, Dr. Richard Hunt's explication of the U.S. strategy of attrition and the reasons for both its adoption and its failure, we arrive at the heart of the military problem facing the United States, the fact that it was only secondarily a military problem, the war being fundamentally a political contest for the control and willing support of the rural population in which military force played a subordinate role. Dr. Hunt chose to drive this point home by recounting and analyzing two instances in which U.S. Army regular forces (in both cases from the 25th Division) deliberately and consciously departed from normal practice, attempting to deploy unconventionally and to concentrate on supporting the pacification program of village and hamlet control through a combination of small unit patrols by components of the 25th Division coordinated with the deployment of GVN civilian and paramilitary services to protect and assist the population over the long haul.

The first of these experiments took place in Long An province in 1966 and 1967, where a battalion of the 25th was assigned to an experimental pacification support effort co-ordinated by an officer assigned from the U.S. Embassy (Colonel S.V. Wilson). The terms of deployment and engagement by the battalion are interesting since they evidence rather sharp awareness on the part of the division commander, Major General Frederick Weyand, of the problems posed by the strategy and tactics hitherto followed by the U.S. ground forces. Weyand, says Hunt, "planned to integrate South Vietnamese forces - from police to ARVN - into his operation, to exploit all intelligence jointly by establishing intelligence coordinating centers, and to fire artillery only in daylight hours into non-settled areas after obtaining permission from the province chief. Weyand also pledged to deploy forces in company and platoon formations and refrain as much as possible from larger size sweeps in order to minimize the number of civilians displaced by the fighting." In other words, for the purpose of this exercise at least, one U.S. general seemed to grasp that the war was a political contest and the road to winning the willing adherence of the villagers began by killing and maiming and disrupting the lives of as few of them as possible. Unhappily, the experiment was far too brief and isolated to have any permanent effect. The U.S. units stayed only a short time in the areas they had cleared and the ARVN soon moved on. The VC infrastructure decamped or laid low until they left and then returned, as strong as ever - probably stronger in view of the publicity and failed promises of the combined U.S. and Vietnamese effort.

Hunt's second illustration is equally indicative. Several years after the experience in Long An, a new commander of the 25th Division, Major General Ellis Williamson, decreed that his brigades would be committed for a period in support of the Accelerated Pacification Campaign, launched in late 1968. The area of this commitment was Hau Nghia province, on the Cambodian border, where VC influence had been predominant for many years and the GVN's military and civilian arms were spread thinly indeed. Williamson ordered that one American battalion be committed "to each of Hau Nghia's districts and established liaison teams so the battalions could work closely with district police and military officials. . . ." Dr. Hunt does not say how long the experiment continued, but clearly it was intended to be a short-term departure from normal - a fact which in itself revealed the extent of General Williamson's misunderstanding of the problem he faced. The experiment uncovered other deep-seated problems. For example, Hunt says, "The division tended to equate its presence . . . with local security on the assumption that if it occupied an area . . . the other side . . . could not be there.⁴ General Williamson, ignoring entirely the reality of the VC's clandestine apparatus and its ability to retain its hold in the teeth of hostile occupation, proceeded to quarrel with the rating system and some officers in his division allegedly attempted to have their ratings of the areas his troops occupied changed. The experiment also brought the Americans and the Vietnamese military closer together operationally, a disillusioning experience for the Americans who found the ARVN casual about its responsibilities and willing to let the Americans bear the brunt. Equal disillusionment arose in regard to the sluggish performance of local government officials who failed to exploit the presence of the Americans to get their stalled programs going.

Although he underlines the unawareness and unpreparedness of the Americans for the kind of war they were committed to, Hunt finally concludes that the very nature of the war put the final burden of winning or losing on the Vietnamese. The situations in Hau Nghia and Long An "starkly illuminated," in his words, "the central issue of the war for the South Vietnamese side: the performance of the government and its forces. . . . The gravest danger in the long run to the Republic of Vietnam was the unabated spread of unresponsive and corrupt government administration, poor civilian and military leadership, and lack-luster indigenous forces. These factors directly contributed to the inability of successive governments in Saigon to gain the political commitment of the peasantry, or to preempt the appeal or loosen the hold of the Viet Cong on the villagers."

Both the contributors discussed so far, therefore, have much fault to find with the Americans: gross ignorance and misunderstanding, poor coordination, and stubborn persistence in error. But what begins to emerge just as clearly is the ultimate responsibility of the Vietnamese for their own fate. It was, it begins to appear, the kind of conflict a foreign power, no matter how willing and wealthy, could not win for the indigenous government. Such a power could not simply move in its clanking divisions and multitudinous aircraft, rout the forces of darkness in pitched battle, and then hand the country back to its own forces and government and leave. The principal task of securing the countryside and gaining the allegiance of the population by governing responsively and fairly as well as firmly could not, by its nature, be performed by any entity other than the indigenous government - lavishly helped, if necessary by its affluent ally, but unable to shift the ultimate responsibility from its own shoulders.

This being the case, it was a governing fact of the situation throughout the war that the South Vietnamese performance in almost all particulars fell grievously short of what was required, and this was particularly true of its military (including those assigned civilian tasks), paramilitary, and police services. Thus far have our first contributors brought us without raising, we may note in passing, the broader question of why this should have been so. Was the GVN's problem systemic and general; and, if so, what was the disease that caused these unhappy symptoms? Or was it simply a matter of particular personalities who were incapable or corrupt or both? We shall return to these questions later.

We turn to the contribution of Dr. Grinter, which he describes as a discussion of the controversy over attrition versus population security as the main U.S. strategy. In contrast to Hunt, who focuses on two particular departures from the attrition strategy, Grinter takes a broad view of both approaches, coming down in the end strongly in favor of a population security strategy, which he finds succeeded well enough during the period of its fullest development (1968-1971) that "along with other developments . . . the North Vietnamese government concluded that the only way to save the situation was to launch a massive military invasion of South Vietnam." This, of course, was the Easter Offensive of 1972.

As analyzed by Grinter, the population security strategy had three main thrusts: "sustained local security by means of expanding local militia; reenergizing village decision making and initiatives; and reform." This necessarily simplified summary leaves out such integral elements as the Chieu Hoi program to induce defections from within the communist apparatus and the direct attack on that apparatus mounted under the Phoenix (Vietnamese name Phuong Hoang) program. These and other details of what was an exceedingly complex and ramified effort matter less than grasping the main elements, which Grinter accurately summarizes. It was an effort to focus the military and civilian energies of the government directly into the villages and hamlets, attempting to work far more than previously with sources of local initiative and aspiration, and to allow them freer expression in determining the use of resources.

During this period, due in part to the losses sustained during the Tet Offensive of 1968 but also due to the new energies directed into the rural areas, the communist cause declined to its lowest ebb inside South Vietnam. Whether or not this was a principal motive of the Easter Offensive must remain a matter of speculation but it seems plausible. However, the extent to which the effort succeeded remains problematical for reasons that are developed by Dr. Richard Shultz. Nevertheless, there can be little argument that the affairs of South Vietnam were in far better condition during 1968-1971 and as a result of those efforts to improve population security than they ever had been in the long years before.

Dr. Grinter then raises the natural question: could the outcome of the war have been changed if a different strategy had been followed? His answer goes beyond strategy and focuses on the indispensable quality of political community as the essential ingredient. If the South Vietnamese leadership had been able, in the critical years between 1954 and 1965 before the big unit war began, to establish a sense of political community pervading the South Vietnamese polity and binding its fractured parts into a common commitment to national goals, then the outcome would have indeed been different.

But then Dr. Grinter goes on to make the point that, in his view, the preconditions which might have made such an evolution possible did not exist. As he puts it in a curious but quite telling phrase: "success would have required . . . a different historical basis behind the two Vietnams' emergence as independent states." In other words, history dealt South Vietnam an extremely poor hand. The fragmentation of its society, the result of deliberate French policy, together, we may add, with the by-products of a lengthy and costly struggle for independence from France, created deep divisions that were part of the heritage handed to the courageous but limited leadership of Ngo Dinh Diem in 1954. It required five years for Diem to establish himself as president in fact as well as name and it was then, Dr. Grinter points out, that the Communist party took up the armed struggle.

The implications of this analysis are, therefore, deeply discouraging. If history were the culprit, if the state of South Vietnam as it emerged from the Geneva Accords of 1954, together with the sharply contrasting political sophistication and organizational genius of Ho Chi Minh, made the political tasks of Diem and his successors impossible to achieve, if all that is true, then we are forced reluctantly to conclude that it mattered very little - except to those Vietnamese whose lives and limbs and property might have been spared as a result of a more sophisticated U.S. approach - which of the two alternative strategies posed by Dr. Grinter was followed.

Although he does not trace the implications of his analysis to this conclusion, it clearly emerges from his argument that, in either case, the North Vietnamese would have prevailed, for although the strategy which focused on population security was by far the more effective method of dealing with the kind of threat posed by the communists, the political and social disarray of South Vietnam made defeat inevitable given, first, the dogged persistence as well as the uncanny skill of the communists in detecting and exploiting the weak points of their adversary, and, second, the fact that the U.S. military presence was necessarily a time-limited intervention.

As noted, Dr. Grinter does not draw this conclusion explicitly; he merely implies it by his reference to the necessity of "a different historical basis," if South Vietnam

were to survive the communist onslaught. While bowing to the
rigor of the logic of argument, one does not have to accept its
chilling implications as foreordained. If the United States had
followed a population security strategy from the beginning of
the phase of "armed struggle" (i.e., from early 1960, when
the new phase of communist attack became apparent) and had
eventually, by the power of demonstration as well as its
control of resources, persuaded the South Vietnamese first
that the strategy worked and second that the United States
except to the limited extent necessary to keep enemy main
forces at bay, would not deviate from the principal that "the
people are the target," it is logical to assume that certain
consequences would inevitably have ensued.

Among these consequences would have been a considerable
increase in costs exacted from the communists for persisting in
their efforts and a slowing down of their progress. The other
side of the same coin would have been an increase of confidence on the part of the South Vietnamese resulting from their
ability, with American help, to deal effective blows against
their enemies at some times and some places. Such increased
confidence may not have had political consequences, but it is
not to be ruled out that it could have provided the final
argument in favor of the course which the military leadership
of the Republic - notably General Thieu - almost chose on
several occasions and then pulled back from for fear of up-
setting the fragile structure that kept him in power. This was
no less than the creation of a popular political movement
intended to provide a new and firmer political base for the
regime to replace the various officer cabals which dominated
the government from the fall of Diem to the fall of the Republic. (1)

At this point of the discussion we have arrived at the
crux of the problem of explaining the frustration of U.S. and
Vietnamese efforts to suppress the insurgency despite great
superiority of resources. It was not merely the failure of the
United States to follow a "long-haul, low-cost" strategy
focused on the population rather than the enemy armed forces
- although that was certainly an important element. Most
analysts - including our contributors - agree that the ultimate
responsibility for mastering the insurgency belonged to the
South Vietnamese and from beginning to end they woefully
failed to meet it. Corruption has been blamed and inefficiency, low performance standards, inadequate leadership, and
the rest of the litany of complaint. But all of these stemmed
from one cause and that was the politicization of the military,
its leadership's involvement in the various cliques that Thieu
manipulated in order to retain his hold on power.

Not always, perhaps, but more often than not, history
tends to support the generalization that a politicized army is
an incompetent one. This is certainly true of the type of

regime presided over by Thieu in which he was forced to protect himself by pleasing the powerful subordinates who gave him their support and could also withdraw it if they were not satisfied. Satisfaction, in this context, means honor and privilege, ease of life, an opportunity to build a family fortune by discreet corruption - all without serious demands being placed upon the members of the clique for performance of duty, for courage, leadership, initiative, and all the other qualities that make for military success.

When such a system exists at the top of a political structure, it follows inevitably that it will permeate the entire system. Each major subordinate of the chosen leader builds his own support network of officers loyal to him, using the same inducements. The disease of poor performance and low dedication becomes systemic, embedded at all levels of the structure. The individual officer who resists and attempts to perform his duties according to the precepts taught at the military schools, finds himself exceedingly unpopular. He becomes a threat to the system, is often isolated and shunted off to dead-end jobs, and is ignored by the promotion boards.

This, then, is the fundamental explanation of the disabling inadequacies of the Vietnamese structure, both military and civilian, and for the failure of the United States, despite strenuous efforts, to improve significantly the quality of military leadership and performance by bringing pressure to bear in favor of individual officers who demonstrated talent and dedication. The disease, as we have said, was systemic and could not be cured by focusing on individual cases.

It follows from this argument that the critical matter of performance standards required far-reaching political changes to remove the military from politics, changes which might have taken place had President Thieu had greater confidence in his ability to remain in power without depending on the manipulation of military cabals. Such an increase in confidence might, in turn, have been forthcoming if an effective population security strategy had been followed from the beginning.

The point needs to be made at this juncture that a population security strategy both depends on and helps to create the sense of community which most of our contributors agree was a vital missing ingredient in the South Vietnamese polity. That condition was reinforced by the method by which the countryside was governed, a method which tended to perpetuate the most fundamental division in Vietnamese society, that between the urban, educated classes that provided the cadre from whom province and district chiefs and their staffs were drawn and the largely illiterate peasants in their conical hats and black pajamas laboring in the fields. This was as true during the years when the military manned the governing positions as it was before that change was made. Even after Thieu's reforms of 1969 and 1970, which gave village chiefs greatly increased authority over local matters and security as well as election of village councils by popular vote, the devolution of power stopped at the district office. There and at province level, decisions of vital importance to villagers were made by men they regarded as foreigners. Many of them were from the north, speaking a barely intelligible language. More important, they had little sympathy or understanding for the problems of the ordinary rural dweller, and often made common cause with the local landowners and Chinese traders who controlled the economy in the countryside.

Here, too, an increase of confidence on the part of the regime could have brought Thieu to make the long-promised step of turning over some degree of authority in the district and province governments to elected councils. Such a step, combined with the development of a nationwide political movement to contest free elections, could have, if pressed with energy and a commitment to democratic processes, gone a considerable distance toward replacing the rickety and ineffective system of corrupted military authoritarianism with a gradually growing sense of political community. It would not only have taken the military out of politics and freed the President's hands to reward and punish the military leadership on the basis of performance, but also would have helped to narrow the yawning gap between governors and governed in the countryside.

Looking at such developments from a different perspective, a long-haul, low-cost strategy would also have reduced the intensity of the opposition to the war in the United States, especially if it had been accompanied by a growth of democratic process. U.S. casualties would have been lower and evidence of success would have armed the administration with effective arguments against opponents of the war.

Such favorable developments in both the United States and Vietnam would not, of course, have necessarily followed upon the adoption of a population security strategy. Nevertheless, we are justified in assuming that many new possibilities would have been opened up and that the picture would have been far from as totally bleak as implied by Dr. Grinter's analysis.

In our pursuit of the sources of our frustration in Vietnam, we have now seen that blame is shared rather equally between the United States and the Vietnamese and that, specifically on the U.S. side, the fault lay with ignorance of the very special context and environment in which the war was fought together with the failure to adopt a strategy appropriate to the nature of the war. On the Vietnamese side, the primary failure was one of inadequate performance of military and police functions together with unwillingness to take the final steps necessary to build an effective political community embracing the entire body politic.

We turn now to Dr. Richard Shultz's study of the pacification and Vietnamization programs at the height of their
claimed effectiveness, the period 1968-72. Relying heavily on
the reports and comments of those Americans at the cutting
edge of the pacification process, the province and district
advisers, Dr. Shultz examines closely the underlying reality
behind the claims made then and later by such official spokes-
men as Henry Kissinger and Sir Robert Thompson to the effect
that the communist insurgency had been defeated in the countryside. He finds much to disagree with in those findings.
To begin with, the Easter Offensive of 1972 brought a major
setback in the half-dozen provinces directly affected by the
invasion. Even more important, Dr. Shultz finds that the
communist infrastructure remained largely intact throughout
the country, despite the attack on it that formed a major part
of the pacification effort. He analyzes the two major anti-
infrastructure programs, Chieu Hoi and Phuong Hoang, and
finds them seriously flawed and largely ineffective. He
similarly delves into the Hamlet Evaluation System (HES) which
produced the readings of security and control that underlay
the optimistic official views and finds that HES had a built-in
upward bias which invalidated much of the statistics it produced.

Dr. Shultz's scrutiny of the effectiveness of the Vietnamese armed forces yields similar results. He finds that the
departure of the U.S. armed forces in the early 1970s left the
RVNAF with inadequate strength to handle its responsibilities
and, even more damaging, he cites evidence to the effect that
the quality of the RVNAF and its performance under fire were
severely constrained by desertions, by poor leadership, and
by lack of training. His conclusion, therefore, is that the
alleged success of pacification and Vietnamization was illusory
and that the collapse of South Vietnam in 1975 under the
pounding of the DRV was foreordained. Specifically, he
blames the failure of pacification and Vietnamization to build a
political community within South Vietnam as the ultimate cause
of the collapse.

With the details of this analysis there can be little fault
to find since Dr. Shultz's documentation is extensive and in
some cases incorporates material not previously available. One
can object that his emphasis slights important aspects of
pacification such as the improvement of the paramilitary forces,
and the devolution of power to village chiefs and their elected
councils. It also ignores the very considerable improvement in
economic conditions in the countryside, particularly in the
Mekong Delta. It focuses rather too exclusively on the provinces that were impacted by the DRV's 1972 offensive and
others where guerrilla warfare continued, ignoring the majority
of provinces where the communists were reduced to a skeleton
organization and had to follow a low-profile policy, maintaining

only enough activity to remind the population of their continued existence. Nevertheless, the total picture in 1972 by
no means supports the official claims that were made at the
time, and Dr. Shultz is correct in saying that pacification and
Vietnamization in 1972 were a long way from achieving the
control of the population along with its willing support that
were their long-range objective.

Where one can enter a demurer is in his further conclusion that the collapse of 1975 stemmed directly from this
failure. From first to last, the final communist offensive was a
conventional ground operation which relied on massed regular
forces, tanks, and artillery, all of which were rapidly and
skillfully maneuvered to exploit, surprise, and shock. Confronted with this carefully prepared offensive, the South
Vietnamese army, already stretched thin and running short of
supplies, panicked, abandoning position after position without
resistance, clogging the roads in headlong flight and, in fact,
disintegrating in ignominious disarray.

It is difficult to see in this tragic denouement of the
Vietnamese drama the role that Dr. Shultz believes was played
by the absence of political community except in the somewhat
different sense noted above in our discussion of the deficiencies of the RVNAF. Certainly, these deficiencies - poor
leadership and morale, lack of training, general failure of
professionalism - were in large part responsible for the debacle
of 1975, although some responsibility also belongs to the U.S.
Congress which had refused to authorize the additional supplies requested by the administration and thereby dealt a
serious blow to Vietnamese morale. The deficiencies of the
RVNAF, in turn, stemmed from the involvement of the military
in politics and the placement of the survival of the Thieu
regime at the head of its priorities, before military proficiency
and the values that go with it. The creation of political
community may have evaded the programs whose purpose was
to achieve it, but it is difficult to draw a casual connection
between that fact and the collapse of the RVNAF in 1975.

To sum up this writer's view of the sources of U.S.
frustration in Vietnam, the responsibility is equally distributed
between Americans and Vietnamese. The American failure
stemmed from ignorance of the arena in which the conflict was
fought and from the reluctance to set aside precedent and
traditional mental sets reinforced by bureaucratic inertia to
adopt a military strategy of population control featuring
dispersion of units and deemphasis of heavy weaponry combined with a commitment to keep units in place as long as
necessary to eliminate the enemy's covert apparatus. Partly,
this failure stemmed from an unwillingness to unify the American effort at an early stage and place it under civilian
control.

On the Vietnamese side, the most glaring weakness was the total inadequacy of the performance standards of military and civilian services caused largely by the politicization of the military. By not risking a new political approach for fear of losing power, Thieu in the end not only lost power but his country as well. A second, quite significant Vietnamese failure was the unwillingness to break up military control of provincial government by instituting the election of provincial councils, a measure which would have helped bridge the gap between governors and population in the countryside and thus advance the creation of the sense of political community which was ostensibly the goal of the GVN's efforts.

What then are the lessons we should distill from this distressing history of opportunities missed and of inadequate grasp of the realities of the situation into which our intervention thrust us? They are easy to enumerate but quite difficult to carry out because they call for abandoning, temporarily at least, many traditional thought processes, procedures, and policies embedded in our civilian and military bureaucracies.

The first rule one would want to see followed is not actually a lesson of Vietnam except in the broadest sense. It is that no two insurgency situations are alike. The lessons of Vietnam cannot be blindly applied in Africa or Central America or wherever we may in the future find our interests sufficiently challenged to force us to contemplate intervention. On the contrary, any such intervention should be based on the most careful study of the political, social, and geographical terrain of the specific country involved, a study focused on several key points. This approach, in fact, is merely taken from the book of rules followed by the communists, who usually carry out a "study of the balance of social forces" prior to a major policy shift.

The key points to be covered by this type of study involve such basic matters as the strengths and weaknesses of the polity we seek to aid, the kind of leadership available, and its ability to make a successful national appeal to the entire population. The quality of the armed forces, of course, is a matter of major concern and particularly their political role, if any, and the effect of that role on their performance. It is vitally important that such an analysis by entirely detached and coldly impartial. Far too often, matters of this sort are dealt with wishfully, with the preferred conclusions of the analysis influencing the judgments it contains.

Of critical importance in this process is another lesson of Vietnam, namely, the inherent limits on the ability of one nation, no matter how powerful, to influence the intimate internal processes of another. To put it simply, the United States cannot base its decision on whether or not to intervene in an insurgency situation upon the assumption that it can substitute its will and ability for that of the leaders of the country to be aided. We can advise and assist - if necessary, with massive quantities of manpower and materiel - but we cannot take the political decisions or exercise the direct leadership of the native population that will be required. Indeed, our help may be welcome but our advice spurned, as so often happened in Vietnam. We should be prepared in advance to deal firmly with such tactics and not, as has often happened in so-called client states, find ourselves helplessly forced to swallow the defiance of the leaders we are attempting to assist because of our public commitment to them and their cause.

But if we are prepared to give advice on which a country's or a government's future may depend, we must be quite confident that the advice is good and especially that it is based on solid knowledge of the peculiarities of the country concerned. Here again, we have a lesson of Vietnam - one particularly difficult to carry out. Our knowledge of that country was pitifully inadequate during the critical early years. Language and culture, geography, politics, and history were all terra incognita. If we find ourselves again in such a situation we may also - for history seems to enjoy these ironies - find ourselves forced by events to decide quickly, before the necessary grasp of the context can be acquired. We can hope, however, that since the mid-1950s the vast development of area specialization in our universities and within the government has made it less likely that we will be forced by events to decide quickly in a virtual knowledge vacuum as was the case in Vietnam.

One clear conclusion that Vietnam forces us to accept is that "reform" of a society, even so apparently obvious and desirable an improvement as raising performance standards in the armed forces and the police, really goes to the heart of the most sensitive of internal questions: the distribution of power and rewards in the society being aided. When we ask an authoritarian and military-based regime (and most underdeveloped nations evolve toward this pattern) to improve its military leadership, punish corruption and poor performance, and reward proficiency, we are asking it to do something which in its view is extremely dangerous since its stability depends on the loyalty of the senior generals, many of whom could be adversely affected by such reforms. There are no doubt various ways around this obstacle. All require careful and delicate negotiation, steady pressure, and detailed knowledge of the context. The lesson of Vietnam that emerges from these considerations is that reforms of any kind are sensitive and delicate in the extreme, and their desirability is by no means universally apparent, especially to the regime which we are proposing to reform while, at the same time, we publicly support and defend it.

Another - and perhaps the most obvious - lesson of Vietnam concerns strategy, specifically the proper mix of conventional versus unconventional approaches to the military problem. If the insurgency we are faced with is of the pattern perfected by Mao and Giap, then our experience urges strongly in favor of heavy emphasis on an unconventional approach which we have also called a long-haul, low-cost strategy, making the people the target. This means abandoning concentration of force and firepower in favor of distributing small packets of troops widely and keeping them in place indefinitely until the threat has disappeared.

Heavy armament and tactical air support are superfluous to this kind of war and interfere with the objective of making the people the target. Much of the combat takes place at night when planes and tanks are at a disadvantage anyway. The scattered friendly units (whether regular or paramilitary, Americans or indigenous with American advisers) patrol and ambush and collect intelligence to refine the targeting of their operations. Larger units, but no larger than one or two battalions, are held in reserve to support the combat patrols in the event they encounter larger enemy forces than they can handle.

Many refinements can be added to this strategy but, essentially, it is an extremely simple form of warfare, in fact, it is primitive: a few men with assault weapons and faces blacked out doing the same simple but dangerous tasks night after night in hundreds of different locations. It is extremely tedious work and often weeks can go by with no contact. It has virtually no appeal for professional soldiers whose entire careers have been pointed toward a climactic tank battle with a sophisticated enemy supported by aircraft, heavy artillery, and the most sophisticated weapons in our armory.

This leads us to the internal problems that counterinsurgency warfare poses for the United States. It is a type of combat that goes against the grain of our military training and doctrine and which, even today, after the painful Vietnam experience, has little acceptance in the military. If another involvement of the United States in unconventional combat were to threaten, the tendency of our military leadership would be to deal with it in the same way - such are the forces of bureaucratic inertia. The answer is the obvious one of taking steps ahead of time, the earlier the better, to prepare at least some units and specialists to train and advise and, if necessary, to fight in an unconventional, long-haul, low-cost mode. Tomorrow would not be too soon.

The same problems afflict the civilian side of the equation. Effective counterinsurgency involves numerous civilian agencies as well as the military - an aspect we have not considered in this chapter - and involves them in ways that depart from their normal practices and patterns. The only certain way to achieve a program that is both unified and effective, i.e., counters the tendency to revert to standard goals and procedures, is to create a new ad hoc organization to combine the inputs of the various organizations involved, including the military. In order to assure that the military's natural tendency to revert to large-unit, mobile warfare does not prevail, the leadership of this unit should be civilian. Such a suggestion is certain to raise an outcry among the nation's soldiery and its friends in Congress and the press since many accept it as axiomatic that civilians have no business managing the military when live ammunition is being fired at human targets. This overlooks the fact that the commander-in-chief of the U.S. armed forces is a civilian. It also ignores the single most effective military intervention carried out by the United States in Southeast Asia. It occurred in Laos and was conducted from start to finish under civilian direction.

The proposed ad hoc organization must, of course, be adequately staffed and must have command authority over participating elements, another prescription which is simple to propose and exceedingly difficult to carry out, given the normal bureaucratic sensitivities it will offend and abrade. In Vietnam, it took many years for a unified and potent pacification organization to emerge; and, up to the end the military remained independent of civilian control in the field. Even with President Kennedy's call to perfect itself in "a new find of warfare" still ringing in its ears, the U.S. military refused to alter its ways and no authority emerged to force the required changes. The lessons implied by such realities are not encouraging but the point must continue to be made in the hope that someone in authority will finally hear it.

If any single formula can sum up the lessons of Vietnam, it is to be found in the central importance of a deeper knowledge of all aspects than we possessed at the time of our critical decisions - knowledge of the enemy, knowledge of the area, and knowledge of ourselves and how our system works or fails to work when faced with unexpected challenges. Until we can summon that kind of knowledge to the service of our policy goals, the outlook is for a continuing series of inadvertencies, some of which may succeed but most of which will either sputter out or, more likely, end in bitter failure.

NOTE

(1) For further detail on this little-know development, see, e.g., John C. Donnell, "Expanding Political Participation - The Long Haul from Villagism to Nationalism," Asian Survey (August 1970), pp., 700-01.

6 American Culture and American Arms: The Case of Vietnam

Donald Vought

It has been a full two decades since military, academic, and government functionaries began exposing each other to various aspects of the "What" concerning the U.S. role in Vietnam. The "What" took the usual forms of what has happened, is happening, or should happen. A few short years later, journalists joined in the reportorial exercise expanding the audience to include the general public. By 1968 – a year which serves as a convenient watershed for nearly any aspect of our Vietnam involvement – the flood of "What" literature was being supplemented by a growing number of "How" exposés, commentaries, and studies. When viewed either separately or cumulatively, the mass of Vietnam literature, with a few gratifying exceptions, leaves the reader with a mixture of incredulity, rage, and sorrow, as well as a gnawing question: "WHY"? The mix varies based on one's personal views of the Vietnam experience, but the why is nearly universal and generally unanswered.

The preceding chapters have addressed the how and what to selected aspects of U.S. military activity in Vietnam. This chapter will attempt to explain some of the whys of this traumatic but revealing time in our national history; it will not rehash political decisions or military operations. Others have done that and, given the recent resurrection of our Vietnam involvement as a subject worthy of study, I suspect that we will see additional advocacy studies and a few balanced examinations of various aspects of the war for some years to come.

Vietnam becomes less enigmatic when viewed in terms of U.S. style. If you can gain understanding of how a culture approaches certain questions (i.e., how a society thinks), you can determine with a surprisingly high degree of accuracy what it will do in given situations, and this is especially true of war. Americans have done poorly in both the study of and the use of study findings concerning national style. As a society, we subject ourselves to periodic orgies of criticism or glorification, but these are generally emotional manifestations of cultural characteristics and not analyses. The influences of American culture are implicit in the characteristics which we will examine in the Vietnam context and which we can observe working in the 1980s. In short, Vietnam was a nearly inevitable result of American style of the time as was the irrational reaction to our failure in Vietnam.

Concentrating on the military applications of our cultural values, we will provide a framework for the "Why" of Vietnam and the "Why's" of subsequent developments using the following format. First we must define the fundamental cultural values. Then we will look at how these values affected our military institutions on the eve of the Vietnam war. Next we will attempt to attribute our actions in Vietnam to these cultural values. This will be followed by a brief summary of the lessons learned from Vietnam and a projection of how our values will influence our military forces in the 1980s.

AMERICAN VALUES

"Values . . . are images formulating positive or negative action commitments, a set of hierarchically ordered prescriptions and proscriptions."(1) As with any culture, there are literally scores of characteristics various observers have attributed to American society and labeled as values. Most are simply behaviors or behavior patterns, wherein a cultural value is manifested in a particular context. In order to defoliate the semantic jungle of cultural descriptions, we will accept Geoffrey Gorer's basic value - rejection of authority(2) - and trace its effects on American style. We will show how the three more commonly identified values which have grown from rejection of authority - competition, a tendency to put everything into a moral context of good or bad, and insistence on human equality - affect U.S. life and its military institutions.

In the United States, "father never knew best."(3) Our immigrant forebears fled the perceived constraints of their old world homelands. Having reached the "promised land" of liberty, they seemed to be unified in only one thing - to avoid constraint through denial of authority to restrain. In the family, efforts to "Americanize" the young led to the demise of "pater potestas" both as a role model (why act like an immigrant?) and as an authority figure. Opportunity for personal "betterment" in the land of promise evolved quickly into competition to "do better" than the father. In fact, the young male was expected to "do better" than his father since he had more opportunities by definition.

With multiple cultural traditions all of which were modified
in an attempt to be more "American," we never developed
uniform child rearing norms. Thus, no generation has reached
adulthood with a high degree of shared experiences. A significant exception which has become increasingly common in the
twentieth century is a flaunting of authority through manipulation of the parent. Lacking norms, the parent has been
sensitized to what everyone else is doing as a measure of
"right" in matters of child socialization. What little authority
the family might muster is then subjected to subversion by
offspring through comparisons with what other people appear
to be doing. Since the first decade of this century, the parent, regardless of the generation we choose to examine, has
been encumbered by widespread acceptance of the social myth
regarding the "pure" or "perfect" child who is corrupted or
fails as a result of environmental influences. Popular interpretation soon established the homily that the childs' failure
was the parents' fault. The anxious parents, in addition to
being no match for manipulative offspring, readily see the
child's success as a testimony to their own worth.

Rejection of authority, in either personal or institutional
form, elevates competition to the role of principal social control
mechanism. With no individual or group to legitimately reward
or punish, the "mandate of heaven" devolves upon whoever
grasps it, i.e., wins or succeeds. With no authoritative means
of defining success, "it" like beauty is in the eye of the be-
holder. Since success is relative, it is transitory and vulnerable to reinterpretation or, most frightening of all, to being
overshadowed by one who is more successful. The stress-
generating aspects of life-long struggle for the chimera of
celebrity (why succeed if no one knows and praises you for
your achievement) are obvious. They have been discernible
since the early nineteenth century, growing in intensity until,
by the 1970s, stress constituted a major health problem and
was a keystone of pop psychology.

Competition or, rather, our culturally induced functional
psychosis concerning competition, as the only legitimate social
discriminator, contributes to our characteristic fondness for
mechanical devices. Auren Uris describes our human relations
environment in the economic context when he states that, "the
average company is a cesspool of resentment, frustration,
anguish, and hate."(4) With human relations approaching the
Hobbesian "all against all," machines provide a noncompetitive
outlet. More predictable and infinitely more loyal than our
fellow man, machines have served America well and our faith in
technology has grown into a national cult.

The second value to evolve from our rejection of authority
is more emotional than competative but nonetheless pervasive.
Equality, which began as a philosophical corollary to rejection
of the ascribed social structures of the old world, has grown

to constitute a moral imperative. We have shifted our interpretation from equality of opportunity, as envisioned by the founding fathers, to absolute equality in all aspects of life. The transition from philosophical position to functional norm has not been without costs. With no recognized class distinctions (i.e., no legitimate multigenerational classes or categories), we have failed to nurture any sense of noblesse oblige. This quality's absence extends through business, government, and the professions and has made significant inroads into our military ethos. Perhaps more important, equality and competition have contributed mightily to creating the "atomized society." Since we must compete socially, economically, and politically (yet, being equal we cannot fail), our energies are perforce focused on ourselves. We ignore the past since it constitutes a form of authority or constraint. The future will take care of itself and is a problem for those who must live it. This leaves us only the present and ourselves in which and for which to live. "Now" is the time to pursue the will-o-the-wisp of fame, fortune, and status suspecting all the while that the illusive goals are so transitory as to be hardly worth the effort. The result is an endemic narcissism broadly defined as the cult of privatism, an escape from historical and social continuities.(5)

Concurrently with the hardening of competition and equality into cultural imperatives, we find a growing tendency to moralize, particularly with reference to other cultures. The views of our articulate Puritan forebears, recently described as "a metaphysical passion which drew its fuel from a hostility to civilization . . . drawing human will directly from God rather than from man-made institutions,"(6) laid a firm foundation for subsequent moral arrogance. We spent the ensuing 200 years proclaiming rationalism and pragmatism as our creed, but developing a national ideology in the form of a civic religion. Increasingly, government actions were defined as "right" or "wrong" rather than "effective" or "ineffective."

Eschewing temporal authority in any form, the early American increasingly referred to God - the ultimate authority but a source with which man dealt directly - as the arbiter of national fate. The transition to a belief that this was "God's Country" populated by "God's Children" destined to execute "God's Will" was swift and remarkably widespread. The concept of American life as an integral element of God's plan with a heavenly mission to save, or at least demonstrate to the benighted a virtuous life-style, peaked around the end of the nineteenth century. The parents of our Vietnam-period decision makers and grandparents of the instruments who executed the decisions were conditioned to accept the following as eternal truths.(7)

1. God's hand directs all things.
2. Everything turns out for the best.
3. The wisdom of the masses is a reflection of God's will.

Nationalistic corollaries arose implying that the American way was the best and only virtuous way to live, and that other people would be Americans if they had the courage or were released from the restraining bonds of man-made, evil-intentioned institutions. Our historical experience did nothing to temper the growth of an everweening moralism. Foreign observers with political interests to serve at home had established an idealized polity in the "fabled republic" of the 1830s.(8) Americans quite naturally began to believe in their own social virtue. We had won every war we fought, even if some victories were achieved by default. The continent's wealth and size were such that social tensions could be siphoned off without most citizens being aware of them. By the time we entered World War I, there was considerable empirical evidence to support the myth of an American monopoly on social moral virtue. The myth has never been dispelled. We secularized and, at least semantically, rationalized social forms prior to midcentury, but the myth survived into and beyond the Vietnam experience to enhance our ethnocentricity.

The effects of our value triad on political and military matters are logical and self-evident. Consider the problem of resolving government and military functions, virtually all of which are predicated on authority, with the cultural rejection of authority.

Our founding fathers conceived of a system of government that limited the opportunities for abuse of authority. Unfortunately (a functional and not a moral evaluation), their intentions evolved into a popular view of government as an adversary. "They" (politicians who aspired to authority) had to be prevented from achieving it by "we" (society). The politicians who occupied positions of authority established elaborate rituals to prove their commonness and show that they were really "one of the boys." Respect and awe had to be avoided at all cost, and this was generally accomplished through humor and ridicule, which were liberally employed to "bring down the great."(9) Even in questions of morality, we seemingly never lost sight of the fact that the old testament prophets were never governors but monitors of government. The federal structure and separation of powers guarantee that no individual or body will possess extensive authority for more than a brief period. This diffusion of authority requires overwhelming consensus on basic questions for the state and economy to function.(10) Lacking such consensus, the system becomes paralyzed. The pursuit of self-interest in the context of a government structure designed to discourage unified action, contributes to a lack of civic willingness to sacrifice for the common good and a political philosophy which justifies normative rules.(11)

The military was the most suspect of professions at our national inception and, with the exception of brief periods of crusade (e.g., Civil War, World Wars I and II), has retained its unpopular status. Our immigrant forebears frequently arrived with antimilitary attitudes which, when mixed with unbridled individualism and rejection of authority, resulted in a deep-seated antimilitary bias. This bias took several forms which have characterized our history. One is the vague perception that decent folk do not become soldiers. If there is no choice, i.e., you are so poorly motivated and untalented that you have no other way to support yourself, then soldiering is understandable if not acceptable. Not always as obvious as the "No dogs or soldiers allowed" signs of the pre-World War II period, the attitude has prevailed. Even today (1981), with an awakening concern for national defense, there is no stampede to participate as members of the armed services.

Another long-standing view which has only recently been called into question is a preference for militia or short-term volunteer service over a regular establishment. Supportive of this military populism is a faith in the ultimate victory of the righteous with little need for training or motivational activities. From the "embattled farmers" (an embarrassingly small proportion of the population by any reckoning) to Hollywood and television depictions of American warriors who are as unmilitary as possible but inevitably win over the beautifully uniformed authority figures of our "evil" enemies, the impression of victory through virtue is maintained. Our legendary ignorance of history nurtures the myth of military success without military form. The efforts of opponents who were already badly bloodied and allies who absorbed much of the enemy's effort in World Wars I and II were ignored in the popular testimonies to American nonmilitary fighting prowess. An interplanetary traveler might well comment on the strangeness of Americans. They accept and in fact applaud individual bellicosity yet have tended until recently to reject organized fighting or even the need to have organized (military) forces to fight in the common interest.

While not a major factor until the aftermath of World War II brought acceptance of a need to maintain significant armed forces in the Cold War, the civilization of the defense establishment was (is) a logical manifestation of American values. Traditional military values were becoming increasingly anachronistic. The size and cost of armed forces precluded the society's simply ignoring them as it had in the past. The solution was to bring some of society's best into the Defense Department and allow them to infuse the dormant, inefficient, organizational monster with good old American managerial know-how, in effect, to make the military into the image of our other large organizations. In the decades of the 1950s and 1960s, American business acumen still had the mystical aura of rational efficiency which had proven itself on a global scale. We failed to note that creeping trivialization, the concern with impression and form rather than substance and the counting house weltanschauung might have adverse effects on military effectiveness.

Theoretically, we attempted to meld two incompatible ethical bodies. The motivating value for business is individual interest resulting in economic gain. Business is the single exception to our cultural compulsion to moralize. The statement, "it was a business decision," absolves the decision makers from any restraint beyond showing profit. The military, in theory at least, subordinates individual aggrandizement to group or community interest, pays in symbolic rewards, and calls for a strict ethical code. Perhaps most significantly, the profession of arms is most effective when it does not have to "produce," i.e., by its perceived abilities it dissuades competitors, hence does not have to "prove itself" daily.

Equality and the strict hierarchical structure of a military organization are superficially antithetical. While many business organizations demand far more behavioral conformity and subservience to superiors than the U.S. military ever did, the lack of power to compel is a major difference. It is acceptable to have de facto inequality where one can "quit." De jure inequality in the context of governmental compulsion flies in the face of American principles.

Morally, the existence of a military force is an outrage to a people committed to the concept of man's perfectability - if all men would only follow our example. More mundanely, the military is visible; its traditions nearly preclude any "fighting back" against domestic critics; and its low status makes it an irresistible target for social commentators. In short, the most the military could hope for throughout most of our history was obscurity. Interestingly, that's what it achieved most of the time until the post-World War II period.

THE PROFESSION OF ARMS ON THE EVE OF VIETNAM

Glory had been bestowed upon those who fought the big battles in World War II. The upper echelons of our armed forces were filled with products of the great crusade. "Victory Through Air Power," "Victory at Sea," "A Crusade in Europe," and the entire corpus of popular and professional commentary, laced with homeopathic doses of virtuous inspiration, tied victory to technological and productive superiority. Korea provided the major experience for most senior NCOs and field officers. Here the numbers were somewhat reduced, but

addiction to firepower and a tendency to rely on attrition as
the prime determinants of victory characterized their operational style. During the late 1950s - the period of professional
maturation for the field officers and some generals of the Vietnam era - Mutual Assured Destruction made ground forces
mere auxiliaries to strategic weaponry. The upshot was a
defensive, even retaliatory, spirit conditioned to make maximum
use of the destructive weaponry that a technologically advanced society could offer.

Professionalism, like so many terms in a society addicted
to hyperbole, means what the user wants it to mean. Bernard
Barber's attributes seem to encompass most definitions of professionalism both civil and military.(12) We will briefly
identify military compliance with Barber's elements in the era
of the early 1960s.

1. Primary orientation to community interest rather than to
    individual self interest.
2. A high degree of generalized and systematic knowledge
3. A high degree of self-control of behavior through codes of
    ethics
4. A system of rewards that is primarily a set of symbols of
    work achievement

1. Community rather than self-interest. Given the values
of American society, this attribute is truly idealistic. We have
no profession that fully meets this criterion, and we had none
in the 1960s. The U.S. military profession was as good as
any and better than most with regard to the ideal of community interest. Unfortunately, the ideal and the practice
rarely coincided as career interests increasingly relegated the
national or institutional interests to motivational slogans. The
Vietnam-bound military man or woman suffered ambivalence on
the question of interest from two sources: (1) the society
would or could not agree on the community interests; and
(2) the altruism and service orientation which motivated many
to enter or at least accept combat area assignments soured
because leaders pursued career-enhancing goals with increasing relish and did so openly. Between 1962 and 1970, the
military institution, with the help of the parent society's
carping, corrupted its own young.

2. Generalized and systematic knowledge. The cultural
distaste for intellectual pursuit had been refined in the
military subculture to an article of faith. Our military
practitioner, "was happiest when he could find a mechanical
solution to problems."(13) While preoccupation with weapons
and equipment is culturally understandable, it led to some
critical gaps in knowledge and concern. Not knowing is unfortunate, but not knowing that you don't know is dangerous,
and we were to pay dearly for it. Examples of inexcusable

ignorance abound. One of the most apparent and widespread, both in the military and among civilian officialdom, was the nearly total lack of knowledge concerning (1) other people's cultures, (2) low-intensity (revolutionary, insurgency, or whatever term was stylish at the time) conflict, and (3) the profession of arms itself beyond the level of current information relative to one's own duties.

3. A high degree of self-control through codes of ethics. The American has always resented having to tolerate the barbarity of war. Refusing to legitimize the military by granting it a professional (i.e., subcultural) status, judgment is rendered under the same moral code the community used for internal social control. By those standards, military activity is categorically immoral. In the 1960s, there was no code of ethics. Now, some seven years after Vietnam, there still is no code per se. Without such a code, society moralized about military activity creating perpetual stress for the soldier. Without a code, an individual's behavior will mirror the parent society unless there is a period of socialization by the military to inculcate institutional norms. On the eve of the Vietnam war, our armed forces by and large followed a vague unwritten set of norms. The rapid buildup of forces filling from the bottom, however, precluded any socialization. Vietnam involved, to a large extent, a group of Americans in uniform who were not professionals. The remarkable uniformity, within the regular forces, of condemnation of those who acted "unethically" in war crimes and the corruption scandals at the end of the decade attested to this truism. Typically, society was far more forgiving than the military community of these moral lapses.

4. A system of rewards based on symbols of achievement. By any interpretation, the U.S. military displayed this attribute, perhaps to an unhealthy degree. Since symbols of rank were the only visible reward, the highly competitive American could develop dysfunctional (from the organizational point of view) means of pursuing his symbolic rewards. In the post-Korean War military, success increasingly came to be judged on image just as it did in the business world. Look like a winner and you are a winner. Army personnel management offices frankly interpreted their missions as getting as many officers qualified for promotion as possible.(14) Emphasis on appearances and a growing acceptance of the legitimacy of a career manipulation with promotion as the goal laid the foundation for many Vietnam era dysfunctions. A few of the trends arising from the effects of competition on symbolic rewards, which began well before Vietnam but continued to become blots on our military heritage, are listed below:

•   Having the act (school, position, etc.) on the personnel record became more important than the act itself. This led to accelerated personnel turnover as officers scrambled to record 40 years of experience in 20-year careers. Problems of confusion and superficial experience strained personnel resources even before the Vietnam war.

- A growing perception that one had to be perfect in all ways to be promoted led to more concern with seeing that nothing wrong happened "on my watch," or at least nothing reportable, than with organizational function. Additionally, the "Mary Poppins Syndrome," i.e., nearly perfect in every way, fed our characteristic fondness for overstatement resulting in efficiency evaluations that were inaccurate hymns to our magnificence. It is a very small step from "making it look good" to mendacity a characteristic with terrible consequences for any military organization.

- There is a widespread view among commissioned personnel that what is good for me (my career) is ipso facto good for the service. This makes it easier to resolve the conflict between ideal institutional values and contrary actions. One can deceive oneself into thinking that his career progression is in the national interest - a situation analogous to Charles Wilson's famous reference to General Motor's corporate well-being as unquestionably being in the national interest.

- Egocentric leadership philosophy was and is an entirely predictable result of the foregoing. A canon of the era - and regretably of subsequent eras - was that "a unit does well only what the commander checks." No mention is made of the desirability of having a unit that functions without the commander's constant direction, for to do so would have diminished the image of the irreplaceable leader. What matter that the irreplaceable leader was frequently replaced by another irreplaceable leader. In consonance with the managerial style of their civilian masters, i.e., everyone below me is a fool, scoundrel, or malingerer, the "me" oriented leaders contributed to the military version of the atomized society. Armies of virtuosos are short lived and not very successful, but then few of our military and fewer of the political leaders of the day apparently read Caesar's Commentaries or the works of Xenophon.

As the United States began to tentatively insert its armed forces into Vietnam (circa 1960), the cultural realities outlined above provided the bases for some general observations. The society was exuberantly self-righteous, secure in the knowledge that heaven would bless any crusade we undertook just as it had always done. True, Korea was less than a smashing success and there was still the "bad taste" of China and Eastern Europe but, in the latter cases, we didn't try very

hard. After the 1962 Cuban missile crisis, our sense of om-
nipotence matched the world's view of the United States as the
arbiter of human affairs. Our ethnocentrism was unmatched
since the days of Imperial China. The American way was not
just the best way, it was the only way; and it was our duty
to enlighten those who had not yet seen this cosmic reality.
Some in government and military circles viewed Vietnam as an
opportunity to develop our small war capabilities in a relatively
safe laboratory.
      The enthusiasm of the Kennedy administration, with its
youthful and vigorous image, blinded us to some ominous aspects of our national style. The increasing concern with the
trappings of success, a hunger for praise, and a tendency to
self-glorification, as well as a blind faith in technology combined to produce that most dangerous of species - the winner.
Repeatedly losing sight of the accomplishment in pursuit of
celebrity status, winners make careers of proving themselves
winners.(15) "Winners" establishing policy for other winners
to carry out is a perilous combination to execute a strange
type of conflict in a strange land against a strange enemy.
Perhaps most important, the contemporary winner is poorly
equipped to "think small," thus the Vietnam laboratory was
destined to become an arena before an American shot was
fired.

EFFECTS OF CULTURAL VALUES - AMERICANS IN VIETNAM

Strategy

To a disquieting degree, our strategy(ies) invariably took on
the appearance of exercises in self-delusion. Even before the
United States entered the conflict with armed forces, we can
detect the effects of optimism born of positive thinking in
official statements. From 1954 on, the theme was that democracy was flourishing in South Vietnam and our support efforts
would not be needed much longer. Despite periods of devia-
tion, the same themes persisted until the ambassador's inglorious escape from the embassy roof in 1975. While "positive
thinking" has some appeal for mental health therapists, it has
one crucial shortcoming: it does not change the objective
reality to include other people.
      General Westmoreland identified six strategies pursued by
the United States in Vietnam between 1954 and 1969.(16) Only
the first (advisers, logistic and economic support) was not
aimed at dissuading North Vietnam. We tried to frighten and
later punish the north into cessation. While not intrinsically
invalid as a strategy, to succeed you must think like the
people you are trying to dissuade or be prepared to destroy

them in lieu of gaining compliance. Discounting Korea, considered by many as an aberration, U.S. war experiences in modern times were against industrialized states that are more sensitive to disruption than agrarian societies. This was especially true in Vietnam since the Viet Cong were unencumbered by the trappings of statehood. The United States perceived the Viet Cong primarily as a threat to the physical security of the peasant. The peasants, obviously, did not universally share this perception. We and the forces of the government of South Vietnam, therefore, expended prodigeous efforts protecting people from a threat they did not sense (i.e., big units of Viet Cong and North Vietnamese) and, in the process, frequently found ourselves constituting the greater physical threat.

Our ethnocentric policymakers used American logic not Vietnamese logic and found themselves fighting one type of war while the enemy fought another: "One fought battles to influence opinions in Vietnam and in the world; the other fought battles to finish the enemy, keeping tabs by body count."(17) As Richard Hunt pointed out in his chapter on strategies, by focusing on the enemy's armed activities, we surrendered strategic control of the war to the enemy. North Vietnam and the Viet Cong had only to adjust their overt armed actions to control their losses. Coupled with the historically proven willingness of the Vietnamese to die for national identity, Hanoi and its southern comrades could have fought for decades at what was to them an acceptable price. We were not prepared morally to destroy North Vietnam. Combined with the real or perceived threat of Chinese or Soviet reaction, this effectively eliminated destruction as a serious policy option.

Cause and effect linkage in the cultural determinants of our various Vietnam strategies are not sufficiently discrete to profit from a listing. Another requirement complicating the use of strategies as vehicles for cultural analysis is the need to first analyze the strategies' efficacy before attempting cultural attribution. For instance, any effort to show cultural motivations affecting the interdiction campaign requires a prohibitively lengthy cost and effectiveness comparison which generally results in a highly subjective conclusion. To avoid the burden of success/failure determination, we will use pacification as the vehicle to identify some key cultural manifestations. First, as the previous chapters have established, pacification was a recognized strategy throughout our Vietnam involvement. Second, Hunt, Dunn, and Shultz have shown that it was a clear failure on a nationwide scale despite local successes. And third, it was the type of effort least amenable to U.S. style. Parenthetically, we might add that it also provided some of the clearest examples of adaptability, ingenuity, and selfless devotion to mission accomplishment on the part of individual American military professionals.

With the insertion of combat units (1965), attention shifted from pacification to a big unit war and stayed there until 1970. Since pacification and its attendant build-up of political power was widely recognized as the key to rural victory, the "why" of a seemingly contradictory course of action is intriguing. (1) Was it our fondness for high technology war? (2) Was it ignorance of the techniques of the insurgents? (3) Was it an unjustified faith in the South Vietnamese government's fighting and administrative abilities? (4) Did our 12-month replacement system condemn our advisers to failure regardless of other factors? The answer would appear to be a combination of all these factors which have roots in the values discussed earlier.

High Technology War - The Winners' Arena

Inserting combat units into South Vietnam produced a phenomenon within the army that stemmed from competition and the unspoken reality that career considerations had begun to outweigh functional purpose. During late 1962 and 1964, the army's "bright young men" were encouraged to enter Special Forces and, to a lesser extent, to serve as advisers in Vietnam because this was where command attention was focused. Once we started the troop build-up, these same "bright young men" and their not so young colleagues were discouraged from these same activities and told that the U.S. units were where the promotions were to be made. (18) The advisory effort - an integral element of pacification - did not cease; but, as Dunn indicated in his chapter on the 1962-1965 period, the media and institutional limelight shifted, leaving the keystone of the combined U.S.-GVN strategy to function in the shadows.

"The advisory system really never worked."(19) The failure is largely attributable to our American style. Our army had been designed for high technology conventional war with mass battles, clearly identifiable enemies, and such relatively simple objectives as force destruction or the seizure of geographical features. Its operational norms called for a temperate climate, a friendly population, and unlimited material resources. Since none of these conditions obtained in Vietnam in the early 1960s, the selection of people to serve was a crucial function. Logically, selection should involve a determination of suitability and painstaking preparation in the form of training/education. Unfortunately, the personnel system was at a disadvantage to carry out such a requirement. Information in personnel records was intended to serve for promotion purposes in that past assignments (few related to advising in an internal struggle), and qualitative evaluations were about all one could glean from them. Thus, the choices were "good," "not so good," or "poor" performances based upon essentially irrelevant experiences. The prevailing philosophy could be summarized as, if you're good, you're good at anything, and a similarly irrational generality for the poor performer. This concept died hard even in light of bitter experiences.

Between 1970 and 1974 I conducted an annual informal survey of from 50 to 60 mid-career officers at the Army Command and General Staff College. The question was: Will the same characteristics and qualifications which make an effective company or battalion commander make an effective adviser to a foreign army? The "yes" responses were as follows: 1970, 85 percent; 1971, 60 percent; 1972, 44 percent; 1973, 18 percent; and 1974, 14 percent.(20) Responses were influenced by the perceptions of the effectiveness of our advisers and the gradually increasing knowledge of intercultural problems. Following discussion of the adviser's role in alien cultures, all of the classes clustered between 25 and 50 percent "yes" responses in a post test. The reasons why effective commanders did not necessarily make effective advisers are revealing. Heading the list were impatience, setting unrealistic goals under the circumstances, compulsion to achieve visible success, and a tendency to focus on institutional-success indicators which were frequently trivial in the advisory context. Thus, in open discussion, the professional military community itself was able to identify subcultural traits which militated against successful large-scale advisory efforts.

Careful training/education could have compensated for the "cookie cutter" personnel classification shortcomings, and eventually it did modulate the intensity of the problem. It took an unconscionably long time, however, before training/education began to have any effect (1964-1965). There were two reasons for this. First, we were inclined to equate combat experience with knowledge of low intensity warfare (irregular, guerrilla, or insurgent warfare, stability operations, or whatever term was stylish at a given point in time). This led to a tendency to train the junior people while their seniors were given briefings on organizational relationships and macroconditions. The result was that the juniors did what the seniors wanted done and the seniors reacted to unknowns and frustrations by doing what they had always been rewarded for doing - fighting a war American style and trying to get the South Vietnamese to follow suit.

Institutional Ignorance of Low Intensity Conflict

The second factor which inhibited our advisory effort, and to a degree the entire U.S. performance, was institutional ignorance of low intensity conflict. The lack of knowledge was massive and, paradoxically, aggressively maintained. To find serving officers unacquainted with Rome's 200 year pacification of Spain, British experiences in India or the Boer War, Russia's pacification of Caucasia, Nationalist China's nearly successful anticommunist efforts of the early 1930s, or France's painful learning from North Africa in the nineteenth century is not surprising. But, to find an equal unfamiliarity with U.S. experience in the American Revolution, Seminole Wars, Mexican War, Cuba, and the Philippines as well as World War II resistance movements is a condemnation of our professional education system. This nearly total blind spot in our professional preparation is directly attributable to our "now" orientation and a cultural arrogance that leads us to disregard the experience of others: they are not Americans, therefore they did not do it right anyway. We had no doctrine because no people would ever oppose the United States - governments are run by evil-intentioned men yes, a people no. The Americans were universally loved. Our Field Manuals took cognizance of "friendly guerrillas," not grass roots opposition. The inhibiting effects these culturally transmitted attitudes have on learning are awesome. I recall having both my fitness to serve in the armed forces and my loyalty questioned by colleagues in 1966 when I attempted to draw parallels between the political power generating techniques of American Patriots of 1775-1781 and the Viet Cong in 1960-1965.

Perhaps the single most dramatic example of institutional ignorance can be seen in our handling of contemporary French military experience (Indochina and Algeria). In the early 1950s, the French experienced all of the problems and tribulations which later plagued the Americans. Following the French withdrawal from Indochina, their army staff prepared a detailed analysis of their experiences and reached some tentative solutions. Instead of becoming a bible for the Americans of the next decade, this work was not even fully translated until 1967. As late as 1972, no more than a fraction of the army's field officers had even heard of the report.(21) The rationale for ignoring this was frequently expressed as "why study losers." The winner attributes his success to his internal characteristics, the loser blames external factors. Thus, the loser's analysis is generally more objective and more valuable as a source of information about what actually transpired.

Algeria also provides an extraordinarily fruitful area of study for the twentieth century low intensity warrior. Admittedly, the circumstances, cultures, and geography differed from Vietnam - as is the case with all internal wars - but concepts, strategies, and tactics provide vicarious experience for those who would profit from studying them. Unfortunately, few Americans did.

The effects of our rejection of the accumulated experience of man's history of internal conflict was felt at all levels. Coupled with the 12-month tour of duty, this shortcoming cost us dearly. The annual cycle of battle, which was remarkably stable, caught us off guard every time. (22)   S.L.A.Marshall, commenting on the 1966-67 period, stated that the enemy was, "still staging the same stale ambushes . . . and we were falling into the same traps as often as ever." (23)   Operationally, we fought not a 10-year war but a one-year war ten times, to paraphrase the noted American adviser, John Paul Vann.

At the policy/strategy level, the ignorance of or at least failure to consider the lessons of past internal conflicts exacerbated ethnocentric tendencies.   Although a review of policy shifts is beyond the scope of this chapter, we can, I believe, show the effects of ethnocentricity in cameo by referring to President Johnson's 1964 South East Asia Development plan proposal.   Johnson made a public bid to buy off the North Vietnamese, a move which had much appeal for Americans and none for North Vietnam.   The vaguest knowledge of Ho Chi Minh and Vietnam's history could have saved the president from a public rebuff.   The impact of American style on pacification is an often repeated litany of insufficiency and excess, high expectations and poor results.

Insufficiency is reflected in the fact that we were so fascinated by "battles" with North Vietnam and Viet Cong main forces that we did not centralize policy and planning for pacification until 1967.   It was not until after 1968 that we began to concentrate on pacification and the slow process of building political power in the countryside, a move which was seven years too late.   Excess, at first blush a contradiction, can be summarized as too much and too many: too much money to be used in too little time; too many Americans pushing to accomplish too many objectives.   We can explain the lack of concentration on pacification through our lack of knowledge of internal conflict and big battle fixation.

A fair case can be made for attributing most of the problems of our style of waging war to our increasingly individualized competitive penchant.   Low intensity conflict requires a range of violence application from police work to combined arms battles.   Most of the effort in terms of time and results falls toward the lower end of the spectrum.   The United States has no national police or paramilitary forces, so we had to rely on odds and ends of local police and military personnel.   The former were unprepared to use violence above the criminal shoot-out level, and the latter were unaccustomed to applying force below the artillery-barrage level.   Given the poor preparation for insurgency warfare, the absence of adequate preparation for intercultural cooperation, and the inapplicability of much of American experience, the insertion of thousands of highly competitive advisers for one year tours produced fairly predictable results.

Unjustified Faith in Vietnamese Government

To be competitive you must be successful, and the success must be recognized - the more visible the better. This philosophy placed the American at a distinct disadvantage vis à vis his Vietnamese counterpart. The counterpart knew that his adviser needed success; he also realized that the adviser's success was tied to his own. This gave him considerable leverage in dealing with the transient American. In effect, a form of informal blackmail existed where each (American and Vietnamese) played the other's system's success game. To succeed in a 12-month period, the impatient American consistently opted to speed things up by putting more Americans into any given function which faltered. Since all functions faltered, by 1965 we had hopelessly overloaded Vietnamese government capabilities from economic management to the battlefield. The overload was well intentioned but nonetheless dysfunctional. Laboring under an operational philosophy which inaccurately assumed that people would "love" the provider of material benefits and cooperate in furthering the giver's interests, the American soldier/official was encouraged to buy the loyalty of the countryside. The perceived need to demonstrate how marvelous each of us was resulted in a lavishness of goods and advice that was self-defeating.

First, the flow of hundreds of millions of dollars into a tiny agricultural country guaranteed corruption of the Vietnamese and, as it turned out, of Americans as well. In a society where respect is based on virtue, the corrupt functionary is by definition unworthy of respect. Second, as Americans poured in to bolster or replace their "less competent" allies, the image of helper was replaced by the image of master. Thousands of Americans (there were over 4,000 advisers by 1965) who saw themselves as agents of change rotated in and out on a 12-month cycle. Before Komer began to hack at the Gordian knot of bureaucratic tunnel vision in 1967, there was no coherent policy or central control agency for pacification efforts. Considering the whole picture, it is no wonder that our energetic efforts to do all things at once and to do them in bravura fashion lacked focus and frustrated those Vietnamese who were trying to build political power in the rural areas.

The Twelve-Month Tour

The 12-month tour has been blamed for everything in Vietnam from policy failure to corruption. While most of the claims will not survive scrutiny, it was a political decision based upon the assumption that a short exposure would make a deadly nonwar more palatable to the American public. Napoleon once commented on unit cohesion by saying that "soldiers had to eat soup together for a long time before they are ready to fight." Unencumbered by business tycoons, systems analysts, and accountants, he was able to express in a homily the complex psychology of group cohesion. Our personnel system totally disregards Napoleon and the subject of combat unit cohesion. As an example, I recall a unit being readied for Vietnam in 1966. It's strength went from about 1,000 to over 4,000 in less than six months, barely in time for movement to the theater of conflict. There was little time for the integrating process symbolized by eating soup together.

Unit cohesion and the 12-month tour have become emotional and controversial topics. One school claims that the army in particular disintegrated under the effects of officer careerism, rapid turnover, and ambiant conditions wherein the struggle lost purpose and public support. Another school claims with equal vigor that the fighting units did develop cohesion and that the charges of disintegration are based on isolated instances and media attention. The truth appears to be somewhere between the poles. Combat units unquestionably conformed to the human behavior imperatives that have functioned in wars for 10,000 years, i.e., "the sentiment of belonging to each other, was the only thing we found in a conflict otherwise notable for its monstrosities."(24) It is equally true that this was more a credit to the young American than it was to the system that contributed nothing to the development of this essential element of armed conflict.

The 12-month tour exacerbated the problems of poor preparation and the thirst for visible success. The highly commander-centered leadership style which evolved in the 1950s reached its logical conclusion in Vietnam between 1967 and 1971. This "Star Trek" style of command, i.e., the captain does everything, tightly controls all actions, and is nearly omniscient, permeated our army in Vietnam. A good deal has been written about the suppression of initiative and "meddling" in the form of commanders two or three echelons removed actually conducting operations of subordinate units (e.g., a brigade commander running a platoon engaged with the enemy). There is little written in explanation of this behavioral syndrome which stems from the need to have success which is directly attributed to the careerist and the concomitant fear of failure in any form. If there is no accepted measurement of success, one must redefine success or create new measurements to meet the need.

Low intensity warfare denies the measurement of success by frontline traces on a map. With the techniques of business being imposed on the defense establishment and no frontlines to show, what is more logical than to measure whatever you can? Numbers became facts whether they related to anything or not. Possession of these facts bestowed power since they

were the only "tangible" signs of job accomplishment and each
level of command wanted to impress the boss with its knowledge. With no institutional memory - the 12-month tour assured that - these bogus "facts" became weapons in the hands
of advocates for various actions or theories. The situation
became ludicrous. Each year a new team arrived, was appalled
at how incompetent its predecessors had been, built up its own
successes in reports, departed in glory, and the cycle repeated itself. When one adds the interpretive twists of each
echelon as it labored to support its views, it is a source of
wonderment that any useful information emerged.

The thirst for data reached humorous proportions. In
September 1962, I received a radio message asking how many
dogs were in the province I was advising. To fully appreciate
the situation, one must remember that the dog is not considered a particularly significant element of the community by
rural Vietnamese. This plus the fact that the province had
over 400,000 population distributed across an area 35 miles by
about 20 miles made the request quite impossible to fulfill.
Like my counterparts in the other provinces, I forwarded a
completely unsubstantiated guess which became "fact" upon
receipt.

By 1968, reporting varying types of data had become an
end in itself. The huge effort devoted to quantification was
rarely matched by analysis and consumed so much of the origi-
nators time as to be counterproductive.(25) The Hamlet Evaluation System (HES) report provides numerous examples of
data requirements that were completely out of control.
Richard Shultz analyzed HES in an earlier chapter showing
that it was both burdensome to prepare/process and of little
value. From the originator's perspective (District Senior
Adviser), the monthly input was literally an impossibility. A
typical district had 308 hamlets. If the DSA visited four a
day (a virtual physical impossibility in itself) every day of a
30 day month, he could evaluate 120. Assuming another 50 or
60 were clearly government or Viet Cong controlled with no
changes, he still had over 100 about which he must guess or
obtain information secondhand. More important, had he tried
to evaluate those, there would have been little time to carry
out other functions of advising the Vietnamese officials which
was the purpose for his being there.

"Unfortunately, whenever any change is introduced into
our service, it is pursued wildly until it is killed by its own
extravagance."(26) This observation, made almost a hundred
years ago, was still applicable to the U.S. Army in Vietnam.
The army, the other services, and the civilian agencies gradually succumbed to the lure of figures to both justify their
existence and demonstrate success. Perhaps useful in a mar-
keting campaign or cost identification effort for industry, the
amassing of data, especially with much of it spurious, is insuf-

ficient in itself to evaluate progress in an internal war. The charts and computer readouts in all too many instances showed us winning. North Vietnam and the Viet Cong, not having access to our systems analysts and computers, did not realize they were losing. In the end, they didn't.

LESSONS OF VIETNAM

On the whole, American society regarded Vietnam as an aberration, a fall from grace with attendant punishment. As a result, we may have learned the wrong lessons. Moralizing on an international scale suffered an initial setback as the Southeast Asian dominos came crashing down. What can one do when the people you have been accusing your government of abusing set about slaughtering each other with renewed gusto upon the departure of the "oppressive forces?" America followed its historical pattern of postwar internalization, petulantly disavowing any interest in people so benighted as to not do what we would have them do. The volte-face of public attention was swiftly and painlessly accomplished by simply ignoring the rest of the world. Between 1975 and 1979 the three major TV networks together devoted less than 60 minutes to the elimination of some 2 million people in Cambodia, or about 15 minutes per year.(27) By 1977, only 1 to 2 percent of an average television week featured international items, and less than 1 percent of our college population was enrolled in internationally oriented courses.(28)

Despite diminished interest, moralizing survives in a more selective mode. "Human Rights" as a national policy incorporates both Vietnam period guilt (a quality of which we never seem to suffer any shortage) and our cultural arrogance. We attempt to dictate to the world how they, the non-Americans, should conduct their internal affairs. By doing this, we toy with a dangerous precedent of basing foreign policy on our domestic values. The Human Rights activities of the late 1970s would appear to be paced by the availability of pictorial coverage and the perpetrators' sensitivity to U.S. pressure rather than the extent or degree of rights violations. One need only note the relative difference in popular outrage between the use of chemicals by the United States in Vietnam and the Soviet use in Afghanistan to appreciate the change of focus between 1970 and 1980.

In his State of the Union message of January 23, 1980, President Carter indicated that "this is a time of challenge to our interests and our values." The challenge to our values of "competition" and "equality" have been great indeed. Between 1975 and 1980, competition on the international plane has lost some of its appeal as others became competitive. Equality has

suffered a similar fate under the growing realization that,
(1) every human may not want to be an American, and
(2) there are not enough resources in the world to allow all
four billion of us to practice America's high consumption life-
style.

Operationally, these shifting appreciations have apparently
had little effect on the intensity of our ethnocentrism. Official
Washington is still surprised when nations act in their perceived best interests. Recently, the intensity and duration of
the Iraq-Iran War (1980-1981) elicited the following analytical
comment from a White House security staffer, "completely
irrational."(29) In the finest traditions of American ethnocentrism, the conduct of the war may have been irrational
when viewed from within the Washington beltway. It obviously
was not irrational from Baghdad and Tehran.

The status of our value triad as it applies to intrasocial
relations must be established briefly because the domestic
environment affects the military more than slight shifts in
international perceptions. During the period of "Agonizing
Reappraisals" (circa 1965-1975), it became increasingly evident
that our values and our actions or institutions did not always
match. While it is too soon to determine the outcome of the
value-institution disconnect historically, values survive all but
the most devastating trauma.

In consonance with the value survival hypothesis, American society emerged from its Vietnam period of reappraisal
more determined than ever to make the values work. Nothing
is socially authoritative. No value is without its interpre-
tations, and no institution is considered worthy of any but
grudging toleration. Insecurity is all pervasive. We have
sold ourselves unrealistic images of beautiful, talented,
materially affluent Americans who never suffer (take a pill, see
your therapist), never grow old (cosmetics, cosmetic surgery),
and never die (we merely "pass on"). One strives to reach
this imaginary El Dorado through increasingly egocentric competition the rules for which are, predictably, undefined. With
no clear social role for anyone, equally vague self-images, and
goals defined as whatever is "in" at the moment, we have
refined the atomized society to new heights of isolation. A
winning image, the public relations utopia, has become the
only thing worthy of prolonged effort. Pursuit of a winning
image is encumbered by long-term loyalty to anyone or anything since loyalty and even personal preference inhibit exploiting all options.

Our "winners," i.e., those with a winning image, and the
numerically more significant would-be winners, glorify competition as the value that made America great only so long as they
keep winning. The "losers," having been convinced that they
too are beautiful, brilliant, and virtually immortal, press to
restructure the competitive environment in their favor. Since

their failure cannot be due to personal shortcomings - an un-American interpretation given our total equality value - it must be systemic bias, i.e., "unfair" competition. Like the winner, our loser carries on his struggle in lonely desperation, attempting to exploit those who appear exploitable for individual gain.

In sum, the American of 1980 has been culturally conditioned to an egocentric universe. Since the use of champions is unlikely to experience a rebirth as a means of settling armed conflicts, there are serious implications for our future military effectiveness.

Post-Vietnam Military: What We Might Have Learned

Relating "What might have been" is always a painful and rarely an illuminating exercise. Identifying what might have been learned from particular experiences can be more fruitful. In the case of Vietnam, the most obvious lesson is a political one but heavily reliant on military judgment. At what point do you stop escalating cost and commitment? When does cost exceed probable gain? In short, when does risk become a gamble? The problem is mind sets that blind us to objective realities. Vietnam is a classic example of the results of selective cognition, a real life manifestation of an old lyric from Disney's Pinocchio: "when you wish upon a star, your dreams come true." In the case of Vietnam, the dreamers were disappointed.

- Lesson - Don't allow your own rhetoric to force "all or nothing" total commitment. Low intensity conflict when kept low, provides for ways to exert influence (offensively or defensively) without national prestige becoming irrevocably committed. Simply stated, you can withdraw should circumstances indicate that the gain will not justify the cost.

Style. We need to learn to "think small." In Vietnam, our grandiose style overwhelmed the Vietnamese as well as our own ability to control our own creation. Grinter, Shultz, and Hunt touched upon the effects of our fixation with large unit operations, how it failed to secure the population and allowed the enemy to organize the population to his own ends. We can only add that the ineffectiveness of large forces thrashing around the countryside had been established in irregular conflicts centuries before.

True, flexibility implies more than simply doing the same thing in a different way. Military flexibility involves tailoring forces and techniques to accommodate changed circumstances. Vietnam could have taught us that formations and personnel

designed and trained for only one type of war will fight that
type of war whether it is appropriate for the circumstances or
not. The military forces of a nation with worldwide responsibilities and interests cannot afford "one mission" services
simply because it is culturally satisfying to explore the
horizons of technology.

Low intensity conflict, particularly when fought within the
confines of a single society (as opposed to a show of force,
strike/raid actions, etc.), is the least expensive form of armed
conflict. However, owing to its rather personal nature, i.e.,
the combatants cannot do violence without some degree of
knowledge of the effects on the victim, the American public
displays no relish for low intensity conflict. A casual review
of the growth of public disenchantment with Vietnam should
reconfirm the obvious. The loss of a few professionals <u>does</u>
<u>not</u> ignite the flames of righteous indignation. On the other
hand, when you take sons and husbands to fight in remote
areas for nebulous national interests and then show no apparent progress over the years, popular tolerance turns to
outrage.

•   Lesson - Keep it small, use professionals not draftees, and
       prepare them to achieve acceptable results with minimum
       cost and little domestic notoriety.

<u>Low Intensity Conflict</u>. We must recognize that war, or rather
the use of armed force, is a political act, one among a nearly
infinite number of actions or inactions the purpose of which is
to influence the behavior of other peoples, not to kill and
destroy. War is not a means of abrogating responsibility on
the part of politicians, nor is it a self-serving game that
soldiers play. Wars are fought for reasons of state interest,
not crusades to rid the world of infidels. War, like so many
products of our modern commerce, comes in a variety of models
and colors with some optional equipment. Our political and
military decision makers, like the shrewd buyer in the marketplace, should select the model that will suffice for the purpose
at the least cost. Low intensity conflict is an economical
option which we must, as a result of Vietnam (if we failed to
perceive it otherwise), recognize as a legitimate form of conflict for at least the next twenty years. The dangers of great
power confrontation, the destructive capacity of modern weaponry, and the high probability of armed conflict erupting from
the cauldron of Third World development make low intensity
conflict an inevitable reality in the 1980-2000 period.

Given this inevitability and the logic of U.S. interests in
the resource-rich southern hemisphere, the U.S. military
should have learned to prepare for low intensity conflict.

- Lesson - Accept low intensity conflict as a reality of the age and prepare service personnel to engage in it. As a minimum, include the study of low intensity conflict in in-service education, not to the exclusion of high intensity conflict, but as an option for the political leaders of the future. Armed forces which cannot be used because the only trick they know is devastation are nearly as valueless as none at all. The last quarter of the twentieth century is going to call for measured national initiatives which combine economic, pyschological, and military ingredients. We cannot afford a military which provides only a sledge-hammer in situations which demand the surgeon's scalpel.

Post-Vietnam Military: What Did We Learn?

Catherine Ann Porter, in her "Ship of Fools," describes how the passengers on an ocean liner taught each other a great deal during a cruise only to discard the newly found knowledge upon disembarking. In a sense, the story is analogous to our handling of lessons learned from Vietnam. Vietnam became an "unevent" just as Orwell's society of 1984 has "unpersons." The speed and thoroughness of our military memory tape erasure matched that of the society. In 1975, a week before the fall of Saigon, it took me four days to locate a map of Vietnam at the Army Command and General Staff College.

It goes without saying that the Vietnam experience was traumatic for the military profession. The United States had never before "lost" a war. Some consolation was derived from the fact that we did not lose any battles and, by the end of the Easter Offensive (1972), had demonstrated the improbability of our military defeat. The winning battles while losing the war analysis was seized upon by many in and out of the armed forces to formulate a milder version of the German Army's "stab in the back" claims of 1919. Most students of the Vietnam war agree that our failure "resulted more from bad policy and bad strategy than from technical or tactical failures."(30) However, that statement reflects more favorably on our technology and the junior leaders and soldiers who fought on the ground than it does on the military institution or its hierarchy. Considering that it took five years (1962-1967) to centralize pacification efforts (CORDS), nearly eight years (1962-1970) to doctrinalize our approach to pacification beyond protection and good works, as well as seven years to begin funneling major resources into pacification, the leadership of that era has little to take pride in. Admittedly, civilian officials made the policy/strategy decisions but, the recommendations of their uniformed professionals to the contrary, were sometimes less than forceful; and resignations in protest were virtually unknown.

A factor which may prove more telling than any other in the long term was a function of our tactical success. Since the vast majority of U.S. ground force officers who served in Vietnam between 1966 and 1973 did so in U.S. units, their experiences were principally in relatively conventional battles. These men, who have since filled the middle and are moving into the higher leadership positions of the army, view their battle experiences as low intensity conflict. What were, in fact, standard operations in jungles or mountains came to be labeled "low intensity conflict" and are now synonymous with that term. Diagrammatically the situations was as follows:

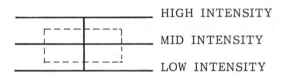

HIGH INTENSITY

MID INTENSITY

LOW INTENSITY

☐ reflects spectrum where U.S. combat troops were employed.

We lost the war in the range of conflict which fell below conventional unit operations, i.e., pacification. Our greatest experience and particularly that of our most successful officers was in the headline-producing battles of U.S. units against VC and NVA regular forces. This provided us with combat experience but little low intensity conflict experience, a phenomenon which has undoubtedly contributed to both the speed and completeness of the memory tape erasure.

The military ethos of 1974 - following the decision to withdraw combat forces - can be likened more to that of 1960 than to 1970. The erasure of the Vietnam memory was encouraged by the public's unseemly haste to forget the whole sordid episode. In addition to the usual postwar rejection of the no-longer-needed reminder of man's imperfections, public distaste extended to the individuals who had dutifully participated in the conflict. The cry of "No more Vietnams," which began even before our withdrawal of ground forces was complete, has been credited with contributing to the inglorious defeat of our erstwhile allies in 1975. By failing to punish North Vietnam for cease-fire violations, we encouraged their mounting aggression and discouraged the southern forces. (31) No one has yet claimed that U.S. support policies caused the fall of South Vietnam, and anyone doing so would be hard pressed to validate the claim. Similarly, one can hardly fail to appreciate the effects of a shift from a level of aid which suffocated the recipient and hindered the development of self-reliance to that of an aloof observer. Obviously, Hanoi perceived the effects clearly and added a touch of irony to the humiliation by finally conquering South Vietnam in a conventional military invasion.

"No more Vietnams" became a national battle cry on a par with the World War II "V for victory." Politically, the slogan was operationalized by reducing executive power and proclaiming to the world that we would not engage in any internal wars outside of selling arms, and then very cautiously. Our great power astigmatism apparently prevented us from seeing that conflict is at least two sided with both protagonists having some options as to how and with what they will fight. The situation is comparable to a child who burns its hand on a stove. While we expect the child to avoid hot stoves for a short time after the unpleasant experience, we eventually educate the child to be able to use a stove without being burned. The United States, however, simply decided to avoid the stoves of low intensity conflict. Since the world has subsequently demonstrated the existence of many such stoves, we perforce operate at a distinct disadvantage. The disadvantage is increased by the fact that these stoves proliferate in the nonindustrial world wherein lie the natural resources so essential to economic reciprocity in an interdependent world.

Within the military, "No more Vietnams" triggered a purge of that which we had laboriously developed in Vietnam. Never quick to incorporate low intensity conflict instruction - it was 1971-1972 before this doctrine was marginally integrated into army in-service education - the subject was virtually stripped from the curriculums of company grade officer and senior NCO courses by 1976. The same fate befell psychological warfare and intercultural communications instruction which were less well integrated at their peak. By 1981, for all practical purposes, the subject area will not be mentioned in the army school system outside of Foreign Area Officer training which involves only some 100 students a year.(32) The completeness of this educational purge may best be demonstrated by a simple comparison. The U.S. Army Command and General Staff College devotes 8 hours to low intensity conflict, Camberley (British Staff College) allocates over 128 hours to such a course. Ironically, Camberley uses the United States in Vietnam as a case study while the U.S. institution merely mentions it in passing. So much for the stove.(33)

Comparisons between 1960 and the post-Vietnam period must be cautiously drawn. U.S. military forces faced a roughly comparable USSR in 1960. By 1975, Soviet technology had moved to a position of operational preeminence in both tactical and strategic terms. With Soviet manpower continuing to reflect a greater number, superpower military balance was no longer tilted in America's favor. The extravagance of our fighting style in Vietnam, where costs per enemy killed rose to 18 times that of World War II, and subsequent neglect had left the services outgunned and outmanned vis à vis the Soviets.

Faced with the reality of no longer being the <u>only</u> military force that can be projected beyond contiguous land areas, the U.S. military began a five year struggle: first, to alert society to the changed realities of world military power; and second, to prepare for that form of conflict that allegedly suits the American best - high intensity, high technology war under nuclear or nonnuclear conditions. Thus, by 1975, in compliance with the public will and in consonance with our cultural values, the U.S. military was fully engaged in doing what it did well with no regard to the usefulness of the activity (i.e., internal wars proliferated while we prepared to fight the European War which we have been preparing for since the early 1950s). There was a rub, however. The revivified cultural values as applied in and to the military denied the human resources which had been available in 1960. Instead of the traditional role of being outcasts but allowed to attempt to form a military subculture for internal cohesion, the armed services were encouraged to behave "decently" like any other business.

The businesslike military of today is indeed a hybrid which has emerged from Vietnam. Vocabularies and philosophies once heard only in board rooms now echo in service schools and organizational headquarters. The production of data in order to show success at the quarterly review continues to absorb effort and generate frustration. Modern management techniques have removed even the symbols of authority from the person of the visible commander and vested them in an impersonal "home office." The "new services" created in the first half of the 1970s came more into alignment with the personnel style of business or, more accurately, of some business. In essence, the services restructured their style to accommodate self-directed, internally disciplined personnel - the archetype of our image of the new post-industrial man, an image which we so assiduously constructed and glorified as the antithesis of the soldier in the late 1960s. Having accomplished the face-lift, the services discovered that those vocal elements of society that had demanded the change did not see fit to participate in their new creation. Instead, the services attracted those least able to function in an unstructured environment. By 1975, the disparity between the new image and the old reality became obvious to all but the political leadership and those uniformed careerists for whom reality is always what the boss wants to hear.

If there is a lesson which Vietnam taught and taught too well, it is the value of a "good" image. Competing for congressional appropriations calls for "selling" programs and policies by skillfull "packaging" of the product. The slice of the budgetary pie is an indication of success for a given service, agency, or program. Thus, the image of austere competence is generally desirable for intragovernmental purposes.

Another image, one with far more serious implications, is the one the services have tried to develop as they struggle to compete for human resources. Speaking at a press conference in October 1979, Robert Pirie (Assistant Secretary of Defense) both summarized the problems of enlistment and demonstrated the new business ethos. In support of pay increases he said, "the objective of our efforts in support of recruiting is to enhance <u>our competitiveness</u> in terms of what we offer the prospective enlistee in order to maintain <u>our share of the high quality enlistment market.</u>(34) (Emphasis mine). Recruiting for an all volunteer force in a society that awards no status to the role of armed service member calls for Madison Avenue's best efforts. First we had to show that the military had learned its lesson and was prepared to modify itself to accommodate the hoped-for recruit, i.e., become less military. Next, we began to develop a "fun" image (travel, enjoy yourself and get paid while doing it). More recently, the image is that of a social service device wherein the recruit is trained/ educated to improve his or her competitive position in the civilian marketplace. The subsequent proliferation of federally funded education support programs has reduced the appeal of the schooling carrot considerably. Additionally, since the "pay off" comes only after separation, it is not difficult to predict the effects on retention and ultimate cost. While the pros and cons of an all volunteer force are beyond the purview of this chapter, the point to be noted here is that the recruitment image is generally <u>not accurate</u>. Fighting, discomfort, and occasional sacrifice are completely omitted. The books depicted on the cover of the Army ROTC application packet for School Year 1981-1982 give mute testimony to the new military's business image. Underneath an officers cap is an academic cap followed by books on organizational leadership, financial management, command, economics, and physics. Noteworthy is the absence of any symbolic reference to war, the army, international relations, or crosscultural communications.

The U.S. military is projecting an image of antiseptic electronic contests a la "Star Wars." With the exception of an occasional vaporization, one is led to believe that the next armed conflict will be over before the station break with little inconvenience on our part. What is potentially more dangerous than recruitment literature which looks like travel brochures or community college admissions pamphlets is that the public and many in the military are beginning to accept the "push button" war image as reality. The "scientification" of warfare has been evolving since Vietnam and has now (1981) reached the logical conclusion that technology and mathematical combat power ratios are war for the United States.(35)

QUO VADIS MILITES AMERICUS

The U.S. military is perhaps more in tune with the parent society today than it has ever been. Faith in technology gives buoyancy in light of seemingly unsolvable recruitment/retention problems. The rebirth of public interest in military games and collectables as well as concern over great power military balance has signaled increased interest. That interest will traditionally lead to higher budgets and more exotic weaponry, but not higher levels of participation, and thus a cycle of contradictions. "Push button" weaponry will replace manpower shortages, but we cannot recruit and retain the caliber of personnel to use and maintain this expensive technology (e.g., by 1982, the army will need some 15,000 computer operators at present force levels - approximately the strength of a division). When considering that low intensity conflict is the most probable form of armed conflict and that much high technology weaponry as well as support systems are unneeded or even counterproductive in such actions, the contradictions are striking.

The attempt to make man more like his machines causes our training to focus on techniques rather than goals, the function of the part rather than that of the whole. The services, faced with poorly educated enlistees, turned to task-specific training at all levels. Task-specific training is valuable so long as the conditions prescribed for execution remain unchanged, e.g., an assembly line. Military operations, however, are characterized by imponderables of enemy, climate, and locale. Thus, when the task requires other than mechanical operation, he who performs it in the unstable environment of armed conflict must understand the principles of the task as well as the cosmos of related tasks in order to respond to changed circumstances. Our current training philosophy does not provide for a view of the forest. All efforts are bent toward conquering one's assigned bush. In 1980, an encouraging note was struck by the resurrection of the Principles of War as ingredients in the army's officer education system. This might signal an institutional shift from the technological high of the late 1970s.

The military as a subculture has been largely eliminated. There is no effort to define an ethic for the military or to socialize members into the profession. At the higher levels, military and civilian managers are interchangeable, so long as there is no armed conflict. Change is perceived as progress, a situation which is stress producing (if not always operationally beneficial) since nothing is implemented before it is changed. This year's "red hot idea" failed four years ago, but personnel movement precludes an institutional memory and no one recalls the previous experience. Even if they did, in today's military one cannot be "negative," it is unprofessional. As it was in Vietnam, the answer to all problems is more money and greater activity.(36)

Should the U.S. government find that our interests would be best served by supporting a faction in an internal war in 1982, we will find ourselves in the same situation that we did in Vietnam in 1962 - ill prepared. We have failed to transmit the hard-earned experiences to subsequent generations within the services. Those with experience are rapidly leaving the services (e.g., NCO or officer entering in 1960 is eligible to retire in 1980). There is little reason to expect action and analyses would be any different from those of twenty years ago since the same cultural values manifest themselves in the same ways as they did then. President Jimmy Carter made a prescriptive statement in 1978 - "we can thrive in a world of change if we remain true to our values." One cannot help but question the utility of such a prescription as it applies to low intensity conflict. Empirically, it would seem that we learned nothing from the Vietnam experience.

During the most turbulent period of domestic unrest which provided the counterpoint to Vietnam, some within the services and the academic community questioned whether or not the contemporary culture could produce a soldier. The performance of individuals in Vietnam and since - their devotion, tenacity, and even selflessness - demonstrates that we as a society can produce defenders in the the finest traditions of the profession. The danger seems to lie in the military institutions (i.e., the service). By being forced into the mold of other organizations, the services cannot control the egocentric even narcissistic effects of the culture. Unless this is changed and soon, there is some doubt as to whether our culture and its military institutions can be relied on to routinely produce steadfast cohorts and the lifelong commitment they require.

NOTES

(1) Donald N. Barrett, ed., Values in America (Notre Dame, Ind: University of Notre Dame Press, 1961), p. 20.

(2) Geoffrey Gorer, The American People (New York: W.W. Norton, 1964).

(3) Ibid., p. 31.

(4) Auren Uris, The Frustrated Titan (New York: Van Nostrand Reinhold, 1972), p. 16.

(5) Christofer Lasch, The Culture of Narcissism (New York: W.W. Norton, 1978), p. 31. Lasch uses the "cult of priva-

tism" in defining modern narcissism, the terms "escape from historical and social continuities" are my attempt to condense Dr. Lasch's lengthy definition.

(6) Daniel Bell, "The End of American Exceptionalism," Parameters 10,2 (June 1980): 7.

(7) These "truths" are extracted from William Holmes McGuffey's readers as interpreted by Lewis Atherton, "Life and Culture on the Middle Border" in The Social Fabric, edited by John H. Cary & Julius Weinberg (Boston: Little Brown, 1975), pp. 39-40.

(8) Edward Pessen, Jacksonian America (Homewood, Ill.: The Dorsey Press, 1969), passim.

(9) Gorer, The American People, p. 41.

(10) Walter Dean Burnham, "Reflections on the American Political Crisis," The Washington Quarterly, Special Supplement (Autumn 1980), p. 5.

(11) Daniel Bell, The Cultural Contradictions of Capitalism (New York: Basic Books, 1976), p. 25.

(12) Bernard Barber, "Some Problems in the Sociology of the Professions," in The Professions in America, edited by Kenneth S. Lynn, et al. (Cambridge, Mass.: Houghton Mifflin, 1965), p. 18.

(13) Henry Steel Commager, The American Mind (New Haven, Conn.: Yale University Press, 1950), p. 8.

(14) While I have never found this "mission" statement in written form, officers serving in two different branches of the Officer Personnel Directorate expressed their agency's goals in these terms in 1959 and 1965.

(15) Michael Macoby, The Gamesman (New York: Simon and Schuster, 1976), p. 48.

(16) William C. Westmoreland, "A Military War of Attrition," in The Lessons of Vietnam, edited by W. Scott Thompson and Donald D. Frizzell (New York: Crane Russak, 1977), pp. 57-58.

(17) Edward Lansdale, "Contradictions in Military Culture", in Thompson and Frizzell, The Lessons of Vietnam, p. 42.

(18) This statement is a paraphrasing of interview comments from both the career managers and the bright young men of the early to mid-1960s. The same "in" vs. "out" activities and the effects on overall personnel balance can be found in the Air Forces Strategic Air Command fixation of the late 1950s.

(19) Douglas Kinnard, The War Managers (Hanover, New Hampshire: The University Press of New England, 1977), p. 91.

(20) The qualities which made an effective commander of the era were not antithetical to those required of the adviser and many people were able to function well in both roles. The dramatic drop in "yes" responses resulted from a growing awareness that the two roles were not necessarily best filled by the same people.

(21) Lessons of the War in Indochina prepared under the direction of General Paul Ely was published in English by Rand Corporation, Santa Monica, CA., in 1967.

(22) Thomas C. Thayer, "Patterns of the French and American Experience in Vietnam," in Thompson and Frizzell, The Lessons of Vietnam, p. 35.

(23) S.L.A. Marshall, "Thoughts on Vietnam," in Thompson and Frizzell, The Lessons of Vietnam, p. 52.

(24) Corinne Brown, Body Shop: Recuperating from Vietnam (New York: Stein and Day, 1973), p. 23. It is informative to compare U.S. unit cohesion that developed in spite of official efforts with the Viet Cong "buddy system" as analyzed by William D. Henderson in Why the Vietcong Fought (Westport, Conn.: Greenwood Press, 1980)

(25) Thomas C. Thayer, "Quantitative Analysis in a War Without Fronts" in Thompson and Frizzell, The Lessons of Vietnam, p. 19.

(26) Captain W. H. Carter, Journal of the Military Service Institute 15 (1894): 752.

(27) William Adams and Michael Joblore, "The Unnewsworthy Holocaust," Policy Review (Winter 1980), p. 59.

(28) Rose L. Hayden, "Global Education for the 21st Century," International Studies Notes (Fall 1977): 19.

(29) Richard Burt, "Mideast Conflict may be a pattern for Future Wars," New York Times Analysis printed in Kansas City Times, October 11, 1980, p. D-1.

(30) Thompson and Frizzell, The Lessons of Vietnam p. iv.

(31) Stephen Hosmer, Konrad Kellen, and Brian Jenkins, The Fall of South Vietnam: Statements by Vietnamese Military and Civilian Leaders (Santa Monica: Rand Report R-2208-OSD (Hist), 1978), p. 43.

(32) The Rapid Deployment Force established in 1980 is not designed to exert long-term influence in internal wars.

(33) For a discussion of U.S. preparedness for low intensity conflict see Donald B. Vought, "Preparing For the Wrong War," Military Review (May 1977), pp. 16-34.

(34) Robert B. Pirie, "The Continuing Military Manpower Crunch," Defense/80 (January 1980), p. 4. This Department of Defense publication was previously titled Command Policy.

(35) Jeffrey Record, "The Fortunes of War," Harper's 260 (April 1980): 19.

(36) For an overview of the effects of short careers and frenetic activity, see Donald Vought, "Farewell to Arms: A Perspective on Retirement," Military Review 60 (February 1980) 2-12.

7

Policy and Strategy for the 1980s: Preparing for Low Intensity Conflicts

Richard H. Shultz, Jr.
Alan Ned Sabrosky

INTRODUCTION

In the international arena of the 1980s, the United States will be confronted with a series of diverse challenges and problems at the strategic level, on the European central front, and in the highly unstable non-Western, nonindustrialized world. However, until very recently, this latter area of threat to American security and economic interests has been ignored, as the attention of U.S. defense analysts focused almost exclusively on the strategic and NATO-Warsaw Pact balances. The irony of this security oversight is that, since the United States has withdrawn from active involvement in the Third World, this security area has experienced a proliferation of crises and conflicts, many of which have been orchestrated by the Soviets or their satellites and surrogates.

A brief examination of international conflict patterns over the last decade will certainly bear this out. These situations, recently dubbed "low intensity conflicts," have been described by Osborn and Taylor as ones "in which exogenous actors have limited objectives even though those of endogenous participants may be less limited. It is conflict in which the military component superficially may obscure more fundamental socio- economic-political issues and goals . . . . It could involve high risks of escalation into regional or even global (control-superpower) wars, but such risks probably will not be high or obvious at the outset."(1) Such conflicts have taken the form of insurgency, guerrilla wars, civil wars, separatism, communal violence, insurrection, and terrorism. That the Soviets and/or their satellites and surrogates are directly or indirectly involved in such conflicts is well documented. For example, Samual Francis has recently pre-

sented an extensive account of their involvement with terrorism, insurrection, guerrilla organizations, and insurgency
movements in many parts of the world.

> Although the Soviets, through the K.G.B., the
> G.R.U., or the International Department of the
> Central Committee of the Communist Party of the
> Soviet Union (C.P.S.U./I.D.), have directly sup-
> ported terrorism in different ways, a far more
> common means of Soviet support has been through
> satellites or surrogates . . . . The advantage of
> using surrogates is that it puts some distance
> between the Kremlin and the disputable policies and
> actions that surrogates must perform. Operations
> that conflict with the publicly stated goals or values
> of the Soviet Union are performed by surrogates.
> . . . Furthermore, operations that would require too
> much commitment of Soviet resources are also under-
> taken by surrogates. . . . That the Soviet aid to
> terrorists is not merely occasional and that it is
> connected to the strategic objectives of Soviet
> political warfare is shown by the nature of Soviet
> and Soviet-surrogate support facilities in the form of
> training, weapons, and propaganda.(2)

In the face of this proliferation of crises and conflicts at the
low intensity level, the U.S. response in the post-Vietnam
period has been nonexistent. As will be discussed below,
disillusionment with U.S. foreign involvement as a result of
Vietnam was a primary reason for this policy of inaction.
And, as Donald Vought has aptly noted, this unwillingness to
involve itself in low intensity conflicts had a significant impact
on the U.S. force structure and operational planning:

> An example of the current manifestation of these
> mindsets and a fundamental indication of the Army's
> rejection of low-intensity war is found in the
> recently promulgated Field Manual (FM)100-5, Oper-
> ations, dated 1 July 1976. In this basic doctrinal
> work . . . only conventional and nuclear conflicts
> are considered. . . . FM100-5 also is indicative of
> the high-technology fixation in that there is no
> mention of the opponent's political will as an object
> of the military action. . . . In sum, I submit that
> the Army, while generally following D.O.D. direc-
> tion, is all but ignoring that form of conflict and
> those portions of the globe where future markets and
> resources compel us to an active role.(3)

Thus, rather than developing a more precise and flexible military instrument that provides forces for response to various low intensity conflicts, the United States has prepared only for conventional high-intensity warfare. This disparity between the type of conflicts the United States most likely will face and the forces available was not significantly resolved by the development of the Rapid Deployment Force (RDF), as we will explain in a later part of this study.

What is the significance of these developments? Perhaps Harold Rood has expressed it most succinctly in his recent book, Kingdoms of the Blind:

> One may not easily weigh the particular value of one small advantage over another similar advantage. But the accumulated effect of many such small advantages may so strongly enhance military capability . . . that victory in war may approach a foregone conclusion. . . . The more the balance tilts toward the Soviet Union, the less likely it is that the West can take advantage of whatever weaknesses or vulnerabilities the Russians may have.(4)

In effect, unless the United States develops the proper forces and equipment that provide it with a range of response options, it will end up conceding access to important Third World resources and strategic locations piecemeal.

In the pages that follow we shall examine in detail: (1) U.S. policy and strategy since 1972; (2) a geopolitical conflict assessment of the 1980s and potential challenges to U.S. interests; (3) , a proposal for restructuring American forces and capabilities for low intensity conflicts, providing the United States with the ability to effectively project its power into the Third World.

THE VIETNAM SYNDROME:
POLICY AND STRATEGY SINCE 1973

Recently, Lt. Gen. Andrew Goodpaster has written that U.S. "national strategy must be credible, consistent, and rational. Only with such a strategy can we be confident as to what our military force structure should be and when and how we should be prepared to use those forces."(5) The prerequisites Goodpaster suggests stand in sharp contradiction to U.S. policy and strategy in the post-Vietnam period. This is especially true of response preparation for low intensity conflicts. During the same period, on the other hand, the Soviet conception of the geographic area where they believed their power and influence could and should be effectively extended

widened significantly. And, as W. Scott Thompson has demonstrated, in the decade of the 1970s, the Soviets aggressively
moved to project their power into these extended spheres of
influence.(6) In effect, the 1970s was characterized by an
inverse relationship marked by rapidly increasing Soviet/
rapidly decreasing American power projection.

Perhaps the most frequently cited reason for this decline
in the willingness of the United States to project its power is
due to the disillusionment resulting from our self-inflicted
defeat in Vietnam. This frustration has so blurred the
national vision that the United States has been unable to move
forward as a nation to fashion and maintain a security structure that meets its needs in a coherent and comprehensive
manner. To the contrary, what emerged was a revulsion
within the U.S. regime toward the extension of power and
employment of force in international politics,(7) coupled with
powerful antiwar/antimilitary sentiments.(8) The culmination of
these developments has been the complete dissolution of the
post-World War II U.S. foreign policy consensus. This began
with the late 1960s' "great debate" over U.S. involvement in
Vietnam, and concluded with "no more Vietnams" as the central
policy preference of the American public. The depth of this
preference has most recently manifested itself in the growing
opposition to U.S. involvement in the conflict in El Salvador.
According to a recent Gallup survey, only 2 percent of the
public thinks the United States should send troops to El Salvador to help the government, while less than one in five
mentioned providing economic assistance (19 percent), military
supplies (16 percent), or military advisers (18 percent).(9)

Not only have these developments seriously constrained
American power projection over the last decade, but from these
have emerged guidelines for future U.S. behavior in the international arena that are greatly out of step with the realities of
current world politics. It is to these "lessons of Vietnam" and
their impact on U.S. foreign and defense policy during the
1970s that we will now turn.

Political Lessons

For many American foreign policy analysts, disillusionment with
our role in Vietnam resulted in a complete reassessment of the
foundations of U.S. policy during the post-World War II period. Introspection and self-doubt led to the rejection of the
"realist" foundations that had so firmly undergirded U.S.
foreign policy until the latter half of the 1960s. This realism
held that the bipolar contest was the major cause of tension in
the international arena, and this contest was characterized by
the need to contain the Soviet imperial drive for hegemony of
the arena. Consequently, East-West conflict was a permanent

feature of international relations and its effective management constituted the linchpin of a prudent American foreign-defense policy. Central to this policy was a strong and flexible military capability that could be employed, when necessary, to parry Soviet power projections. In sum, the "utility of force" was recognized and accepted as the primary means for responding to the openly proclaimed Soviet commitment to the permanency of struggle with the West.

What were the results of this frontal assault on the foundations of American foreign policy? We would agree with Colin Gray's assessment that U.S. foreign policy has "succumbed of recent years to numerous fashionable shibboleths that do not speak to the vital interests of Western societies."(10) Specifically, this resulted in a U.S. commitment to detente that was based on the faulty assumption that the Soviet leadership was undergoing a radical transformation in its intentions and motivations. For the United States, detente signaled the end of bipolarism and, with this, the importance of the traditional calculations of military power: preparedness and the will to employ it. This was all passé, for detente signaled the emergence of an international order based on pluralism, interdependence, and the new salience of economic issues. In other words, international relations would now be characterized by the dominance of low politics (economic concerns) over high politics (security concerns).

These "new realities" were reflected in the Nixon-Kissinger doctrine's attempt to create a foreign policy based on cooperation with the Soviets. Carter, using this as his starting point, sought to fashion a more humane foreign policy that would address the multitude of interdependent problems facing all nations. For both administrations, the problem of getting the Soviets to accept this new international order was to be accomplished by providing them with economic incentives they could not refuse (i.e., grain and technology). That the Soviets were open to such persuasion was due, in good part, to the detection of "moderating" tendencies that were now apparent in the Soviet regime. These tendencies may be summarized as follows:

1. The Soviet Union may be bribed/persuaded into adopting a far less conflict-oriented framework for the conduct of its foreign relations.
2. Arms control processes speak to the real interests of both sides, and hence should provide a crucial means for defusing a major source of East-West tensions.
3. Time is on our side. Soviet foreign and defense policies will be modified benignly as the scientific-industrial revolution increases the bargaining power of technocratic elites/interest groups/pressure groups, and as a simple consequence of the aging of the regime.

4. War between the Soviet Union and the United States cannot serve Soviet interests. (11)

The fact that this moderation had already begun was evident in the Soviet acceptance, during the SALT I negotiations, of the U.S. position on parity and strategic stability. Thus, Marshall Shulman, adviser to President Carter on Soviet policy, noted that "here perhaps is the real significance of SALT I, for its most important accomplishment is to be found less in the substantive agreements reached than in the educational process." (12)

If the roots of this rejection of post-World War II foreign policy grew out of disillusionment with U.S. involvement in Vietnam, the foundation for our post-Vietnam foreign policy was derived from a variety of new theories of world politics that were proposed during the last decade. For the creators of these theories, many of whom found their way into policy circles, power politics gave way to what James O'Leary has defined as differing variations "of the universalistic interdependence vision" that has "consistently occupied an influential position in political thought since the eighteenth century." (13) While it is beyond the scope of this study to examine these in detail, we should briefly note the penetration of these ideas into the realm of the foreign policy process, especially during the Carter years.

For what O'Leary terms both radical and liberal theorists of world politics, (14) the result of this expanding economic interdependence was a restructuring of the international system. Although there are important differences between the two perspectives, they agree that a series of recent developments in international relations has signaled a decline in traditional power politics and, consequently, the need for a new basis for future U.S. foreign policy. To summarize, international politics is now characterized by: (1) the demise of superpower hegemony (bipolarism); (2) the emergence of a multipolar-pluralistic-interdependent state system; (3) the new saliency of economic issues; (4) a recognition of the limits of growth; and (5) the disutility of force as a tool of foreign policy. (15) In effect, low politics now replaces high politics. For the radicals, these developments will result in more cooperation in world politics as nations become fully cognizant of the fact that survival requires cooperation. Liberals, on the other hand, are not so optimistic. Rather than cooperation, they see economic interdependence and the emergence of the limits to growth resulting in "the return of zero-sum game strategies in international economic relationships . . . and competitive mercantilism." (16) Nevertheless, whether one sees these developments resulting in economic cooperation or conflict, the end result is the domination of low politics and the disutility of military force.

The penetration of these ideas into Carter foreign policy is readily apparent. For instance, witness the misplaced emphasis on human rights. This penetration is equally apparent in the area of post-Vietnam military policy.

Military Lessons

The political lessons the United States derived from its Vietnam involvement directly affected the military lessons it deduced. The result was a significant revision of the scope of U.S. military strategy, force structure, and contingency planning. This reflected the presumption that the projection and employment of U.S. military force was declining in utility, especially in the area of low intensity conflict. Consequently, our preparation for future conflicts centered on the U.S.-USSR strategic and NATO-Warsaw Pact theaters. In each case, the offensive side of strategy is conceded, as the former focuses exclusively on deterrence and the latter on deterrence and defense. This "relinquishing of the offensive", by the United States was nowhere more apparent than in our unwillingness to prepare for low intensity conflict in the Third World. An examination of post-Vietnam strategy and force structure will bear this out.

Following its withdrawal from Vietnam, the United States reduced its military manpower by 35 percent, altered its force planning doctrine, developed the all volunteer force, and increased its reliance on nuclear weapons.(17) Pre-Vietnam force planning had been predicated upon the assumption that the military would be prepared to fight two major wars and one minor contingency simultaneously (two and a half wars). This included extensive preparation for such irregular paramilitary contingencies as the use of guerrilla warfare skills, counter-insurgency techniques, and covert action to achieve policy goals in Third World regions. Since 1970, U.S. doctrine has been based on the assumption that we would never have to wage more than one major and one minor war at the same time (one and a half).(18) Presumably, this minor war included those types of conflict the Pentagon referred to as "limited contingencies" (requiring the deployment of irregular paramilitary forces). However, given the declining number of U.S. forces deployed abroad, its shrinking international base structure, increased reliance on weapons modernization/preparation for high intensity warfare, and domestic public opinion, the possibility of a sudden U.S. power projection into a low intensity conflict seemed increasingly remote. In fact, it was rather uncertain precisely what types of "limited contingencies" fell within the boundaries of the "one-half war" concept, thus further blurring a clear definition of the situations under which the United States would intervene. In effect, by not defining the situational contingencies concisely, the possibility of involvement is lowered for, when potential situations do arise, they can be declared outside the scope of our security interests.

How do such doctrinal shifts affect force structure and capability? According to Theodore Shackley, one of the leading experts on irregular paramilitary operations, the U.S. ability to conduct such actions "has withered into virtual uselessness."(19)

An examination of U.S. force posture and capability for conducting low intensity warfare empirically reflects the impact of this doctrinal change. To begin with, at the lowest end of potential U.S. involvement in such conflicts - security and development assistance - important cutbacks were enacted during the 1970s. Ironically, as U.S. security assistance programs were steadily decreasing, Soviet employment of such tactics was rapidly accelerating.(20) The importance of such assistance in Third World conflicts is exemplified in the Soviet sea and airlift of arms to Ethiopia in 1978. The weapons and other equipment delivered by the Soviets (nearly $1 billion worth) were effectively employed by Cuban and Ethiopian troops to swiftly drive the Somali army from the Ogaden region during the spring of 1978.(21) The United States began to seriously scale down its commitment to security assistance programs under the Nixon doctrine, and this process was accelerated as a result of the Congressional assault on these programs in the mid-1970s. Additionally, Congress began to stipulate that those who did receive such support had to conform to U.S. human rights standards. The Carter administration lent executive support to such stipulations after 1976.

The various forms of development aid the United States provided to Third World nations during the 1960s was also severely restricted in the 1970s. The 1960s was the "decade of development" in which the United States employed such assistance as an instrument of foreign policy in the struggle for the Third World, but the 1970s saw drastic revisions.(22) Foreign aid was no longer to be linked to U.S. strategic and political objectives or carefully targeted through bilateral dissemination. Instead, it was now to be channeled through such multilateral assistance agencies as the World Bank group.(23) As with security assistance, in cases where the United States was still involved with bilateral foreign aid, Congress and the Carter administration employed the human rights prerequisite.

Cuts in security assistance were accompanied by reduction in security assistance personnel. For instance, the number of Military Assistance Advisory Groups (MAAG) deployed abroad was significantly reduced. Thus, the United States gave up another important element of its power projection capability for low intensity conflicts. These were replaced by much smaller Military Training and Technical Assistance Teams. Funded entirely by Foreign Military Sales and International Military Education and Training Program funds, these lacked the scope and complexity of the MAAG units.

Reductions also affected the Special Forces, one of the units most effectively prepared for the various forms of unconventional low intensity conflict. From a high of over 9,000, the size of the Special Forces declined after their 1971 withdrawal from Vietnam to approximately 2,000 by the latter half of the 1970s.(24) Recently, the size of the Special Forces has increased to three 1,400-soldier groups stationed in the United States. However, according to one expert, serious problems remain:

> There are serious shortages . . . particularly in officers, communications personnel, and medical specialists. First term enlisted personnel are filling non-commissioned officer positions and many positions are filled one or two grades below authorizations. As a result, although this low-intensity capability is deployable, some skill levels are below those desired. Language capabilities are particularly lacking. . . .
> Two additional limitations on the capabilities of Special Forces deserve note. The first is the difficulty of attracting trained officers for second and third Special Forces assignments. . . . The second concerns training priorities for Special Forces units. Current training places top priority on the employment of Special Forces teams in unconventional warfare in a general war environment.(25)

The declining size and changing role of the Special Forces strongly reflects the post-Vietnam decision to avoid low intensity conflict. The Special Forces symbolized a commitment to respond to the new types of warfare that emerged in the post-World War II period. These imposed severe strains on both professional soldiers and conscripts. Special Forces, however, were specifically tailored to respond to these contingencies.(26)

Another valuable source of skilled personnel for irregular paramilitary operations, the Central Intelligence Agency, also experienced significant reductions. In the post-Vietnam period the attacks directed at the CIA for its involvement in such actions has had important organizational effects on the agency. For instance, Shackley notes that since 1976 over 2,800 intelligence officers, highly skilled and experienced in irregular paramilitary operations, have left the agency.(27) Additionally, budgetary constraints on the CIA affected the agency's capacity to conduct such operations. The extent of these developments is spelled out by Shackley: "Budgetary pressures, particularly under Admiral Stansfield Turner's

stewardship of the intelligence community, forced drastic
personnel reductions and maintained equipment inventories at
levels below what are necessary to sustain the third option
[irregular paramilitary operations], if it were selected for
implementation." He goes on to suggest that it would take
three years to reestablish this capability.(28)

What does all of this mean? Such military force structure and doctrinal decisions send signals to our allies and
adversaries about the extent of the U.S. commitment to respond to various contingencies. What the above clearly implies, especially when viewed in conjunction with the budget
constraints enforced upon the Pentagon in the 1970s,(29) is a
unilateral commitment by the United States to refrain from
defending its security and economic interests in those parts
of the Third World where they will be affected by low intensity conflicts. This message is clearly understood by our
allies and especially by our enemies. This latter point is
quite obvious, given accelerated Soviet power projections into
the Third World during this period of U.S. abdication. The
depth of this reluctance on the part of the U.S. government to
establish a coherent, coordinated policy for the most likely
challenges to its interests in the 1980s is reflected in the
now flawed Rapid Deployment Force (RDF). Originally tasked
to respond to a range of challenges spanning the irregular
paramilitary-limited conventional continuum, the scope of
the RDF has continually narrowed since its inception. By
February 1981, it had become obvious, according to Thomas
Etzold, "that it would be difficult if not impossible to use
elements of the R.D.F. in the Southern Hemisphere, and in
large portions of Asia, the Pacific, and even the Indian
Ocean."(30) In effect, the RDF was drastically reconceptual-
ized to fit into current U.S. military doctrine. In effect,
according to one analyst, "it appears that the suggested
military aims of the RDF are consistent with classical employment concepts, for the U.S. plans to use forces to engage
and destroy the opposing force or to seize and defend designated geographic objectives."(31) This completely ignores
nonclassical employment modes in unconventional situations. In
fact, it only deals with the most traditional conventional
conflict, a Persian Gulf version of the U.S.-USSR central front
scenario.

While these developments are potentially disastrous for
U.S. security and economic interests in the Third World, the
current political setting in the United States under the new
administration offers the opportunity for a policy and doctrine
reversal. The critical question is not whether the Reagan
administration will respond to low intensity conflicts that affect
U.S. interests, but how it will do so. It is to these issues of
doctrinal and force posture prerequisites that the concluding
portion of this study is directed. However, we must first

briefly outline, from a geopolitical perspective, the nature of these conflicts and the threats they present to U.S. interests.

GEOPOLITICAL CONFLICT ASSESSMENT FOR THE 1980s

Any appraisal of the emerging international security environment must, in our opinion, take into consideration three basic
precepts. One is that U.S. interests outside of the principal
Soviet-American areas of confrontation in Central Europe and
North-East Asia are certain to grow in importance throughout
the 1980s and may well come to exceed those which the United
States wishes to defend in the aforementioned core areas by
the end of the decade. The second is that threats to these
above interests are proliferating, while the ability of the
United States to counter those threats has declined substan-
tially over the past decade, thus exacerbating their relative
significance to this country and its allies. And the third is
that neither the quality of our current threat-perception nor
the amenability of world politics to scientific analysis allow us
to predict the time and the place when specific challenges to
U.S. interests will occur with any degree of precision.

The first of these points is, in many respects, the most
important, simply because the rational application of force in
world politics is premised on the existence of some objective
interests to be safeguarded. For many years during the Cold
War, there was a tendency to underestimate the relative importance of the Third World to U.S. security, simply because
the latter was seen to be so closely linked to the intertwined
Soviet-American strategic nuclear balance and the core theater
balances in Europe and North-East Asia.(32) Even today, it
would be inappropriate to assign too much significance to specific U.S. interests in the Third World. Indeed, nothing there
can truly be said to be a primary U.S. security interest, in
the sense that its loss would immediately threaten the very
survival of this country.(33) But it would be equally unwise
to overlook the fact that the compromise of some security
interests in the Third World might independently constitute a
grave threat to the well-being of one or more of this country's
key allies, or collectively undermine the edifice of U.S.
national security at some more distant point in the future.(34)
And it would be criminal to ignore the prevailing trends in the
diffusion of power and influence in the world, virtually all of
which point to a monotonic increase in the geopolitical role of a
number of developing countries of a variety of political per-
suasions and international affiliations.(35)

These considerations are perhaps most apparent when one
examines U.S. strategic or military interests outside of the
developed core areas. The United States has an ongoing interest in maintaining its existing system of alliances, despite

the fact that both the demise of the South-East Asia Treaty
Organization (SEATO) and the unilateral abrogation of the
Mutual Defense Pact between the United States and the Republic of China on Taiwan have been the responsibility of this
country.(36)   Even outside of issues directly related to the
Soviet-American nuclear confrontation, the United States simply
cannot "do great things alone," and the maintenance of a viable network of alliances is essential to the safeguarding of
other U.S. interests and to the ability of the United States to
project its power abroad.(37)   Closely related to that general
strategic interest is the need to ensure that the United States
has access to the naval and air bases abroad required for it to
project its power when and where necessary, or at least to
ensure that nations hostile to its interests do not acquire
access to such bases when they would constitute a direct or
indirect threat to the United States or its allies.   Nowhere else
is location as important as when a smaller number of properly
positioned bases may provide considerably more access to a
particular region (and thus greater geopolitical influence) than
a larger number of less advantageously located ones.   And
both the possession of appropriate bases by the United States
and the denial of ready access to such bases by our actual or
potential adversaries are linked directly to the third strategic
interest: keeping open both maritime lines of communication
and especially the so-called "choke points" and key strategic
waterways, such as the Panama Canal, the Cape of Good Hope,
and the Straits of Molucca.(38)   This last-named strategic
interest is of considerable significance to the United States, to
be sure; but it is of even greater importance to key U.S.
allies, such as Japan, whose survival depends on their ability
to use the seas freely.

Each of these strategic interests obviously reflects a set
of military considerations, including the impact on the ability
of the United States to apply leverage to other countries or to
preclude the Soviet Union and its various clients (as well as
third countries) applying leverage against the United States
and its allies.   But they reflect a set of economic interests as
well.   The most important of these economic interests is having
ready access to whatever strategic raw materials are needed to
maintain both the industrial base of the United States and its
allies and the military establishment which is dependent on it.
The growing dependence of the West in general, and the
United States in particular, on foreign sources of oil, tin,
chromium, manganese, and many other strategic raw materials
underscores the significance of this factor.(39)   A second
economic interest, which admittedly is of more significance to
some of its allies than it is to the United States at this time,
is ensuring both national and corporate access to stable markets in countries where there is a minimum of political
risk.(40)   A third economic interest is the promotion of moder-

nization, both to facilitate a growth in markets and to reduce the economic sources of discontent which are so often used by various movements as a pretext for insurrection.(41)

The final set of U.S. interests encompasses a number of related political considerations. One is that the United States believes as a matter of policy that the relatively few political democracies in the world must be supported, regardless of their other transgressions. This is partly a matter of national preference, and partly a function of the recognition that political democracies are likely to align themselves with the United States rather than the USSR or other authoritarian regimes on most fundamental questions. The enduring U.S. support of Israel, for example, is at least partly due to this factor. Another, but less constant, factor has been the inclination to support conservative or "rightist" authoritarian regimes over "leftist" alternatives (in or out of power), both because the former were seen to be the lesser evil and because conservative dictatorships would also be likely to support rather than oppose the United States in the international arena. And a final U.S. political interest, which clearly has economic and strategic overtones as well, is the endorsement of regional political organizations such as the Organization of American States (which includes the United States) and the Association of South-East Asian Nations (which does not), in the hope that they may serve to buttress or to create a stable balance of power in their respective parts of the world with a minimum of U.S. military assistance.(42)

Perhaps the only thing more impressive than the scope of U.S. interests in the world outside of Europe and North-East Asia is the growth in the number and the intensity of threats directed against them, coupled with the extremely uneven record of past U.S. efforts to contain those threats.(43) In the coming years, as in the recent past, some of those threats originate with the Soviet Union and its key proxies: Cuba (whose performance in Africa has been impressive, and whose role in Latin America once again appears to be growing); East Germany (a surprisingly active Soviet surrogate in Africa, as well as in other countries); and the Socialist Republic of Vietnam (whose successes in Indochina have allowed the USSR to gain access to key naval facilities in the South China Sea originally developed by the United States).(44) Direct Soviet-American military clashes, it should be noted, are unlikely to fall into the category of low intensity conflicts, if only because it is difficult to see precisely how they could be localized in scope or limited in means once they had commenced. But the clash of either great power with an ally or proxy of the other is highly likely. A second set of threats emanates from regional powers hostile to the United States or its allies, but not necessarily aligned with the Soviet Union. Iran after the accession to power of the Ayatollah Khomeni is a classic ex-

ample of such a state, as is the performance of the Organization of Petroleum Exporting Countries (OPEC) in the economic
sphere.(45)   A third   source   of   threats,   more   distant   in
magnitude but potentially more damaging over the long term to
U.S. interests, comes from internal dissention and instability
within developing countries, and terrorism in developed nations.(46)   These tend to force pro-American regimes to choose
between stability on the one hand and democracy on the other
at best, and may bring down pro-American governments in
more extreme situations.   In some instances, threats to U.S.
interests posed by hostile regional powers or by internal
insurrection originate with the USSR or its proxies; in many
other   cases,   however,   they   do   not,   although   the   USSR
certainly has demonstrated a clear willingness to capitalize on
whatever ambitions and grievances exist to the disadvantage of
the United States and its allies.   At a minimum, however, the
growth in Soviet power projection forces (including an impressive   blue-water   fleet   and   a   substantial   strategic   airlift
capability) allows the USSR a greater degree of maneuver-
ability - political and military alike - than would have been
possible a decade ago.(47)
   A perusal of the past decade also highlights a somewhat
grim development, at least from the perspective of the United
States.   This   is   that   fewer   adversaries   seem   inhibited   by
either an American presence or the threat of American intervention than was the case in the past, and that fewer allies
seem reassured by promises of American assistance than was
once the case.   Part of this may be attributable to the extremely ineffectual performance of the former Carter administration.   Part of it is certainly attributable to the shift in the
balance of power between the Soviet Union and the United
States which has taken place over the last decade.   Much of it
may well be due to the acquisition of increasingly large
quantities of increasingly sophisticated armaments by a growing
number of nations.(48)   And a major share of the responsibility for the ongoing diplomatic revolution, as we have
suggested earlier, is a function of the failure of the United
States to either define its objectives clearly or to prosecute its
war successfully in Vietnam.   Thus, the USSR and its proxies
seem increasingly predisposed to act openly against formerly
neutral or pro-American countries; regional powers are far
from awed by the United States; and internal insurrections -
especially those with a strong Marxist-Leninist component or
leadership - pursue their own objectives with the foreknowl-
edge that, in an earlier "revolutionary war," the U.S. military
machine was fought to a standstill by a far weaker nation with
a greater degree of "cost-tolerance."(49)   Indeed, the failure
of the United States to rescue its hostages in Iran during the
abortive "Operation Eagle Claw" suggested that the malaise
within the U.S. military might be even more fundamental; and

that the U.S. military was, therefore, even less of a reservoir of confidence on which threatened allies could draw than might once have been assumed to be the case.

Having outlined both the type of interests the United States has in the world at large, and the ubiquity of threats (actual and potential alike) to them which exist, the obvious question to be addressed is the likely time and place of confrontation and crisis. And here, as we indicated above, the difficulty is that predictions decrease in reliability as they increase in specificity. Five years ago, for example, few analysts would have predicted that Iran would become America's bitter adversary, that China and Vietnam (both then communist regimes) would have had a major border war, or that the United States and the Soviet Union would have found themselves shifting sides (or exchanging clients) in the war between Ethiopia and Somalia. Sadly enough, precise predictions tend to be wrong in these matters, or - when they forecast growing instability and difficulties for the United States or a U.S. client - self-fulfilling prophecies.

That caveat notwithstanding, however, some general observations can readily be made, hopefully with some reasonable prospects of accuracy. One concerns the type of conflict that is likely to threaten the stability of various parts of the world subject to low intensity conflict. The other concerns the location of such conflicts.

On the first point, the most likely type of conflict seems to be one originating within a specific country, either fomented by or capitalized upon by the Soviet Union. Although Americans became disenchanted with the notion of "counterinsurgency warfare" during Vietnam, revolutionary movements throughout the world learned precisely the opposite lesson: they learned that insurgencies or revolutions could succeed. Angola, Rhodesia, and Nicaragua reinforced that lesson - a lesson driven home by the fact that far too many of America's alliance partners (formal and informal alike) throughout the world who might be subjected to such threats possessed regimes whose character and conduct were not calculated to induce the American people to give them their wholehearted support.(50) On the other hand, the least likely form of conflict which might threaten U.S. interests, and thus raise the possibility of U.S. military intervention of the type being considered in this chapter, is one entailing the invasion of one country by another. Indeed, except for the seemingly endless string of Arab-Israeli and Indo-Pakistani wars, international wars have been fairly rare occurrences unless they have taken place as part of the Soviet-American competition, as in the case of the Korean War (1950-1953). They do seem to be becoming more frequent as the aforementioned growth of a better-armed world proceeds apace, of course; not too many years ago, conflicts such as the "Gulf War" between Iran and

Iraq and the Tanzanian invasion of Uganda would have been far more difficult. Finally, located somewhere between these two types of conflict, in terms of their probability of occurrence, are those arising from the use of Soviet proxy forces or clients against either an American ally or an ally's client.

As for the location of one or more of the above types of conflict, a distinction must be made between those which are likely to involve U.S. military forces and those which are not likely to do so, at least in a substantial and active operational role. South America is not now, and has not in the past, been particularly receptive to U.S. military intervention; and there is no reason to assume that that situation will change in the 1980s. The fact that the three largest (but not necessarily richest) nations in South America - Argentina, Brazil, and Chile - all have conservative military regimes underscores this fact. Palestine is certain to be the site of additional conflicts, if only because several of the regional powers seem predisposed to use Lebanon as a battleground and because both the Israelis and the Palestinian Arabs claim the same land as their own. The likelihood of U.S. military intervention on either side, barring the threat (or the fact) of Soviet military intervention, however, is low. And a U.S. military intervention in the South Asian subcontinent in the event that India decides to complete the reconstitution of the polity once ruled by the British Raj, or a reintervention in Indochina under any circumstances, simply do not appear at all likely in the coming decade.

On the other hand, there are certain areas where ongoing or potential conflict situations do raise the distinct possibility of conventional or subconventional military involvement of U.S. forces. Central America, and especially El Salvador and Honduras, are the most obvious candidates. It is there that "counterinsurgency" may once again be tested. But it is also there that serious consideration might more properly be given to introducing U.S. conventional forces to overwhelm an insurgency in its infancy - a plan of action that was proposed, and rejected, in Vietnam in the early 1960s. The rather high probability that a reconsideration of the situation that has evolved in Nicaragua and Panama may be necessitated cannot be overlooked, with very uncertain consequences for U.S. relations with Cuba and its Soviet protector. On the other side of the world, the situation in Thailand remains of considerable concern. In some respects, the situation in Thailand, beset with insurgencies, is similar to that which existed in Vietnam in the late 1950s. Thailand has advantages (such as an absence of a colonial past) that South Vietnam did not, but it has the disadvantage of confronting a communist Vietnam that has tasted victory and sees its support of such insurgents to be a logical continuation of its past policies. The loss of Thailand to a leftist regime, either following a successful insurgency or as a result of a lost war with Hanoi, would have far-reaching ramifications throughout Southeast Asia; yet it is by no means certain that even a conservative Republican government in Washington would be predisposed to send U.S. combat forces into another war in that part of the world, regardless of the consequences attending the defeat of another ally there. The Persian Gulf littoral, apparently the principal theater of operations assigned to the Rapid Deployment Force, is an odds-on certainty to be a tinderbox in the 1980s. Other regimes, such as that of Saudi Arabia, may be subject to the same internal stresses as those which beset Iran under the Shah. Regional disputes abound, and may easily become more intense, and another oil embargo might well raise the possibility of Western (or U.S.) military intervention, if only as a last resort. Finally, Southern Africa is certain to be the scene of the final act in the process of ending white rule in the African continent. The presence of Marxist regimes in Angola, Mozambique, and Zimbabwe and their encouragement of internal opposition to Praetoria do not suggest a commitment to restraint. South Africa will be a difficult target, to be sure, but the possibility of the loss of that key strategic country (however reprehensible its internal policies might be) in the next decade to some combination of internal and external forces is not one which the United States can consider with equanimity. Here, as elsewhere, however, the question is not whether the United States might be tempted to intervene; it is whether it will be possible to do so successfully.(51)

RESTRUCTURING FOR LOW INTENSITY CONFLICTS

Robert Osgood recently argued that the United States must either devalue the scope of its military and economic security interests or develop the appropriate limited war strategies and forces capable of defending those interests.(52) This is an accurate assessment of the choice facing the United States today. Certainly, our interests extend across the globe, and they are vulnerable to a number of threatening scenarios. Consequently, prudence dictates that the United States shed its post-Vietnam guilt, and reestablish the premise that we can and will intervene militarily in any low intensity conflicts that challenge our security interests.

Building on this premise, the United States should develop a new strategic concept based on the theme of power projection.(53) This doctrinal change would result in the development of strategies and capabilities that will provide the United States with the capacity to inject the appropriate instruments of influence and force into low intensity conflicts that threaten its security interests. While the transition from doctrine to strategies and operational capabilities would appear straightforward, the history of flexible response during the 1960s warns of the potential pitfalls involved. Consequently, in developing the capacity to effectively respond to the range of limited conventional and unconventional conflicts that may challenge U.S. security interests in the 1980s, certain procedures should be followed. To begin with, the United States must correctly assess the nature of the different low intensity conflicts it will face. While this is obviously critical, Vietnam should teach us that accurate assessment is not always forthcoming. To alleviate this problem, at the top of the executive policy system the Reagan administration should establish a permanent, senior-level organization whose responsibility it is to assess, prioritize, plan for, and direct response; to the spectrum of limited conventional-unconventional conflicts. In conjunction with this, the services and other appropriate government agencies should be coordinated into this process.

What follows is an outline of the limited conventional-unconventional capabilities the United States should develop to effectively parry the low intensity conflicts that may challenge its military and economic security interests in the 1980s.

Preparations for Unconventional Conflicts

U.S. involvement in unconventional conflicts may take various forms that would include interventions between combatants in a civil war, rural or urban insurgency, rebellion, or coup d'état to support the side that, if successful, will support our interests in the region. Such conflicts can be exceedingly complex in terms of causes, as well as with regard to the strategy and tactics employed by the combatants. If we take insurgency as an example, Bard O'Neill identifies six variations based on an examination of the goals of various movements - seccessionist, revolutionary, restorational, reactionary, conservative, and reformist. (54) By including strategy and tactics, the number of variations multiplies because of different types within each of the six categories.

In preparing for such a range of different situations, the United States will find itself involved at different times on the side of both insurgents and counterinsurgents. Too often we think of the U.S. role as primarily counterinsurgent - helping friendly regimes endure. However, given the unconventional conflict environment of the 1980s and the need to protect U.S. interests within it, we concur with Theodore Shackley that the United States must develop what he terms the "third option: the use of guerrilla warfare, counterinsurgency techniques, and covert action to achieve policy goals."(55)   Additionally,

the United States should prepare for more direct-action missions into such unconventional conflicts as the French experience in Shaba in 1978.

While we support the development of these contingencies
in principle, we would strongly caution that there are "inherent limitations in the range of contingencies one can effectively
prepare for." Commenting on the post-World War II period,
Robert Tucker has recently observed that "we are in the
throes of far-reaching change in the nation's foreign policy.
. . . A period of withdrawal . . . has come to an end. If it
is to be succeeded by a period of an American everywhere
resurgent and activist, we will only risk jeopardizing interests
that are critical to the nation's security and well-being."(56)
The area of insurgency-counterinsurgency-covert action, as
prior experience demonstrates, is particularly susceptible to
such a grandiose design. Consequently, we recommend that
those regions where U.S. military and economic security interests are threatened by such challenges be given priority
status in terms of the contingencies we prepare for. Otherwise, we shall end up with a highly generalized response
system in which we plan for all forms of conflict only to realize
once "on the ground" in a real situation that we are unprepared for specific contingencies.

While it is not the purpose of this chapter to develop this
priority list, a few examples will clarify what we have in mind.
In the Middle East, the fall of the Shah signaled the vulnera-
bility of a number of regimes to internal rebellion or revolution. However, certain of these regimes, especially Saudi
Arabia, are vitally important to the United States. Therefore,
difficulties for the Saudi Arabian regime would certainly be one
of the contingencies the United States should prepare for,
especially in light of the assault on the Grand Mosque in early
1980. In Central America, the insurgency in El Salvador
presents the Reagan administration with an important challenge. Following on the heels of the Sandinesta victory, the
insurgency in El Salvador rapidly escalated. A repeat of
Nicaragua in El Salvador, and possibly Guatemala, presents the
United States with serious security challenges. The potential
for similar problems in other regions, such as Africa, are
high. Zaire is a case in point. The Mobutu government has
been very cooperative with the United States and Western
Europe and is potentially capable of contributing to the
stability, security, and prosperity of the international trading
states. Zaire has plentiful supplies of copper and cobalt and,
when coupled with its land and population size, has real
economic potential. However, since 1975, Zaire has been a
target for covert Soviet-Cuban activity. While this has been
thwarted so far with the aid of the French, continued military
intervention by the Soviets and their proxies will present the
United States with security challenges in Zaire and elsewhere.

Since the Soviets actively stimulate insurgency and rebellion in these regions, seeking to establish dominant political influence, turnabout is fair play. For example, the tenacious Afghan resistance, employing an antiquated arsenal that includes the vintage World War I Lee-Enfield infantry rifle, has prevented the Soviets from reducing the number of troops it originally committed. Certainly, the United States could significantly upgrade this arsenal by providing the resistance with a variety of more sophisticated weapons, including precision-guided and surface-to-air missiles. The weaponry and proper instruction in its employment could be covertly provided. Likewise, similar support for the UNITA and FNLA guerrilla organizations in Angola could help them take the offensive against the MPLA and Cuban forces.

To summarize, in the area of unconventional low intensity conflict, the United States should identify those situations in which such disruptions threaten our security interests, and develop the strategies and capabilities for an effective response. Such a prioritization process will allow the United States to avoid the "flexible response" trap of the 1960s, where the range of possible contingencies was unspecified, giving the impression that the United States was prepared to intervene everywhere. Such overgeneralization of one's response capacity can result in a force structure and capability in search of missions, rather than a range of prioritized contingencies driving force structure and capability development.

In the remainder of this section, the types of force and capabilities appropriate for developing specific response packages that the United States can employ in future unconventional conflicts are identified. The primary concern at this juncture is not to outline these specific response packages, but to identify the types of forces and capabilities that would be configured for different unconventional situations. In the case of most of these elements, they have been allowed to atrophy over the last decade.

To begin with, the United States must expand its economic development assistance program. Over the last ten years, the United States has drastically reduced this program, opting instead to channel such support through international multilateral assistance agencies. As a first step in developing capabilities for responding to unconventional challenges, we suggest that foreign aid should be utilized bilaterally to ensure strategic economic interests. The objectives of such assistance include: (1) the consolidation of the position of a friendly government susceptible to internal breakdown; (2) improvement of our political position; and (3) sending a signal to other governments.(57) In sum, we concur with Secretary Haig's recently outlined position on such assistance:

> Development assistance provides the United States
> with the opportunity to influence economic, social
> and political changes abroad . . . . Over the past
> two decades, a growing percentage of U.S. official
> aid has gone to support multilateral development
> banks. We intend to meet our existing obligations to
> these institutions as we move, in an evolutionary
> way, toward a greater emphasis on bilateral rather
> than multilateral assistance.(58)

In addition to recognizing the importance of development assistance in such contingencies, the United States has to be
willing to commit technical assistance teams that provide the
expertise necessary for the implementation of such aid.

A second form of support the United States should expand for such contingencies is military security assistance.
This should take the form of special technical assistance (such
as military training) and supplies of military equipment tailored
to the specific conflict environment. Unlike the long-term
objectives of development assistance, security assistance is
specifically designed to address short-term problems in countries experiencing rapidly intensifying unconventional challenges. A case in point is the current situation in El
Salvador. Of course, such assistance should be coupled with
development aid.

Security assistance may very likely include the introduction of U.S. technical training personnel to assist friendly
armed forces or insurgents in improving maneuver and equipment skills. This will require a reemphasis and expansion of
U.S. security assistance personnel and appropriations. As we
noted previously, since Vietnam, the size and number of Military Assistance Advisory Groups (MAAG) deployed worldwide
has been decreasing. Recommitment to this capability must
include the Army's willingness to prepare individuals with the
appropriate skills for such missions. These include extensive
language and cultural education for specific situations. It
should be further noted that such MAAGs include individuals
skilled in civic action techniques. This is another area of
specialization that has been allowed to atrophy since Vietnam
and must be redeveloped.(59)

As we move across the spectrum of capabilities for unconventional response, the next step the United States must take
is a serious upgrading of its Special Forces units. To begin
with, the Special Forces mission must be refocused primarily
for organizing and advising either friendly government or
resistance forces in unconventional techniques. In order to do
this, specific steps must be taken. This means reemphasizing
specific area, cultural, and language training for those
priority situations identified. Since Vietnam, the quality and
number of individuals trained in these skills has declined.

This must be dramatically reversed. This readiness problem also manifests itself in other ways. As was noted, there remains "serious shortages . . . particularly in officers, communications personnel, and medical specialists. First-term enlisted personnel are filling non-commissioned officer positions and many positions are filled one or two grades below authorizations. As a result, although . . . easily deployed, some skill levels remain below those desired."(60) This inability to attract and keep personnel is, in large part, an organizational problem. The way up the Army's organizational ladder is through conventional unit assignments. This was true during the Vietnam war and it remains true today. Such career disincentives keep many promising individuals away from Special Forces assignments.(61) Important organizational change must be carried out in officer training so that unconventional warfare is seen as a legitimate contingency for the Army. Otherwise, Special Forces will not attract and keep officers for second and third tours, and unconventional warfare will remain outside the Army's definition of contingencies for which to be prepared.

In terms of unit structure, Special Forces should maintain its basic "A"-team model. This cellular organization, with its emphasis on multiplicity of skills, is what makes Special Forces so suited for such missions. However, in addition to training and assistance, Special Forces personnel should be prepared for a range of other paramilitary activities suited for low intensity conflicts (i.e., psychological operations, civic action, reconnaissance, counterguerrilla-guerrilla direct action operations). The expansion of the authorized strength and redefinition of the mission of Special Forces must be undertaken immediately.

In addition to military forces, prior U.S. involvement in counterinsurgent, guerrilla, and covert operations has included Central Intelligence Agency personnel. However, as was noted above, this CIA capacity was severely disrupted during the general assault carried out against the agency during the last eight years,(62) and particularly against the clandestine branch of the CIA during the early part of the Carter administration.(63) In order to effectively respond to unconventional low intensity conflicts in the 1980s, this element of the U.S. response capabilities must also be reestablished. CIA paramilitary experts made significant contributions to prior U.S. counterinsurgency and guerrilla efforts (especially in recruiting, training, logistics, and planning), and they will be equally important in the future if given the proper authority.

Finally, the U.S. capabilities for unconventional conflict should include forces for direct-action raids and attacks ranging from Entebbe to the French actions in Shaba in 1978. In the case of the former, specific units already exist.(64) However, with respect to the latter, the range of other time-urgent conflicts will require the United States to upgrade its Ranger forces. Trained for deployment into jungle, desert, mountain, and other unconventional settings, these forces are prepared for direct-assault contingencies. However, they need to be expanded and their probable missions specified. With priority missions identified, the Rangers can enhance training guidance and management.

To summarize, if the United States is to successfully parry unconventional low intensity challenges to its security interests in the Third World during the 1980s, it must initiate important changes in its military doctrine. Once this occurs, specific strategies and capabilities can be configured for response to those situations the political leadership gives priority to. The critical elements for such unconventional responses were identified. Unless the steps outlined to improve these are undertaken, doctrinal change will be meaningless.

Preparing for Limited Conventional Conflicts

A number of different criteria can be used to classify potential limited conventional conflicts, such as the number and relative strength of the combatants, the geographical location of the conflict, and the sophistication of the weaponry being employed. From our perspective, however, two sets of factors – one political, the other operational – are of primary concern with regard to the demands they would place on U.S. general purpose forces.

The political factors basically reflect the responses one makes to two questions. First, do the forces opposing the United States include either Soviet or Soviet proxy forces in more than an advisory capacity? And second, can the United States expect direct military assistance from any allied countries other than the one(s) directly involved in the conflict in the first place?

The answer to the first question has a significant effect on both the propensity of the United States to intervene and the prospects for eventual success. If Soviet (or even Soviet proxy) forces are present in strength, then much greater interests must be at stake for the United States to intervene than if they are absent, simply because their presence raises the risk of escalation and the subsequent expansion of the conflict into the central theaters of operations. The presence of Soviet or Soviet proxy forces also requires the United States to be willing to commit more forces to battle, with the likelihood that they will sustain higher losses, than if the opposite situation obtains. An affirmative answer to this question, then, has the effect of inhibiting intervention by the United States in a limited conventional conflict at the outset, and reducing the eventual likelihood of success while raising the costs to the United States of that operation whether or not it is successful.

The answer to the second question is important in precisely the same ways, although here an affirmative answer has the opposite effect. During the Indochina War, the fact that the United States fought with very few allies on its side - none of whom included its principal NATO allies - meant that it had to carry a greater military burden than would otherwise have been the case. It also meant that popular support within the United States for the prosecution of the war in Indochina was weakened by its relatively singular position in that conflict.(65) The same principles would doubtless apply in the 1980s. That is, with the firm support of other nations with which the United States had alliances, there would be, ceteris paribus, a greater willingness on the part of any given U.S. administration to intervene than if it essentially had to act alone. There would also be better prospects for maintaining political support within the United States for that intervention, and relatively less need for U.S. forces, if the intervention were seen to be part of a joint operation involving allies or (under certain carefully defined circumstances) perhaps even the United Nations.

There are obvious countervailing tendencies included in these two sets of considerations. The least favorable situation would be one in which the United States felt compelled to contemplate intervention alone against Soviet or Soviet proxy forces. The most favorable situation would involve U.S. intervention as part of a major collective effort in an area free of organized Soviet or Soviet proxy military opposition. The reality likely to dominate the 1980s, unfortunately, seems to lie much closer to the former situation than it does to the latter. The growth in Soviet conventional power projection capabilities, under the umbrella of the concurrent augmentation in Soviet strategic and theater nuclear forces, gives the USSR a growing capability to act in an increasingly wide spectrum of conflict situations. Indeed, the Soviet Union has in recent years truly become a global power in the broadest sense of the term, and the Soviet use of its own forces (e.g., in Afghanistan) and proxy forces (e.g., the Cubans throughout Africa) makes it all too clear that it is increasingly willing to use its growing military power in pursuit of its own geopolitical objectives.(66) As for the United States, it is necessary for us to realize that the prospects for collective action in defense of U.S. interests are not good. Given the composition of the UN Security Council and General Assembly, few conflicts which might prompt UN military action would seem to argue for U.S. participation in such an operation; indeed, the UN seems more predisposed as a matter of principle in recent years to act in opposition to U.S. interests and allies than in their behalf.

More to the point, it is all too clear that the United States finds itself with relatively few true allies with the capability to intervene in strength outside of their own borders in a limited conventional conflict, and even fewer who would be willing to do so in conjunction with the United States unless their own security were immediately threatened. There are many reasons for this, one of which is that the United States has pursued an alliance policy which has given this country few true allies, only a large number of clients dependent on the United States for their well-being but unable (or unwilling) to contribute much in return, and more encumbrances than we ought properly to have incorporated in our nominally impressive but practically flawed system of alliances.(67)

In addition to these political considerations, there are a number of operational factors involved in defining the type of limited conventional conflict in which the United States might become involved. These include (1) the duration of a conflict (i.e., how long the primary conflict might be expected to last, entailing in large measure an appraisal of the probability that a conflict can be kept localized); (2) its relative intensity (essentially, the rate of battlefield losses in both human and material terms likely to obtain); (3) the proximity of the potential conflict arena to the continental United States itself; and (4) the magnitude of the anticipated U.S. commitment (i.e., the absolute size of the general purpose forces which might be required to bring that conflict to a successful conclusion). From the American perspective, the most manageable conflict situation would be one in which a relatively brief and localized conflict could rationally be expected, few losses would probably be incurred, the intervention would take place relatively close to the United States, and a fairly modest commitment of U.S. forces would be necessary to win. The least manageable situation would be one in which either outside intervention or adjacent sanctuaries for hostile forces (or both) existed, anticipated long-term losses would be relatively high, the conflict was taking place at a considerable distance from the United States itself, and major general purpose ground forces would probably be needed for an extended period of time. The U.S. intervention in the Dominican Republic in 1965 is a classic example of the former (favorable) type of conflict situation; the U.S. misadventure in Indochina typifies the latter (unfavorable) concatenation of factors.(68) And the growing involvement of the United States in El Salvador in 1981 falls somewhere between these extremes; it exhibits the more favorable aspects of the above considerations in every respect except that of anticipated duration/localization.

In each of the aforementioned conflict types, moreover, any U.S. intervention in a limited conventional conflict will have to take account of the existence of one or more constraints on U.S. action independent of purely geopolitical or

military factors.   (1) By definition, what <u>can</u> constitute a
"limited" conflict involves threats that do not immediately affect
<u>vital</u> U.S. interests, regardless of their potential long-term
consequences for this country.   (2) The very waging of <u>lim-
ited</u> war runs contrary to American preferences, which clearly
prefer either <u>no</u> war or a crusade of sorts in pursuit of total
victory against a putatively evil opponent.(69)   (3) Even the
ability to use relatively small conventional forces in "surgical"
operations requires the ability both to prepare and to employ
quickly elite forces that the modern American military establishment and our political process seem less than wholly able
to do well.(70)   (4) Many of these potential conflict situations
will activate an extended version of Kenneth Boulding's classic
"loss of strength gradient,"(71) in which the factors of time
and distance combine to reduce the ability of the United States
to bring its power to bear quickly and in strength, while
simultaneously reducing the already low cost-tolerance of the
American people.   (5) Virtually any foreseeable U.S. intervention will be on behalf of a conservative regime (in many
instances, one dominated by the local country's armed forces),
and in opposition to one variant or another of leftist movements or regimes (sometimes, but not always, dominated or
influenced by local or outside communists).   This is an absolute certainty to reopen the political divisiveness of the
Vietnam war era, and prompt growing public opposition to the
intervention as time passes.(72)

Coupled with these essentially political constraints are
those of a geopolitical and economic nature.   The fact that the
United States is a global power with global interests to defend
and global commitments to maintain necessarily entails some
acceptance of risks and some choices with regard to intervention abroad that less involved nations need not make.
Similar trade-offs exist within the U.S. domestic economy
between defense and welfare outlays (defining the latter very
broadly), and internationally between what the United States
should do to strengthen its own economic position (and thereby
free resources for defense efforts) and what it must do to
support a functioning international economic order (and thereby further strengthen, or at least not weaken, it allies
abroad).   In both instances, anything short of the creation of
a militarized "garrison state" committed to the creation of a
global "American Empire" is always likely to find security
<u>obligations</u> exceeding security <u>assets</u>.   And both the unlike-
lihood and the undesirability of such a garrison state taking
shape in the 1980s suggest the need for greater care with
regard to the sizing, deployment, and utilization of U.S.
general purpose forces in preparation for intervention in
limited conventional wars than might have been required in a
more favorable geopolitical environment, or with a more militarized American society.(73)

In all instances, of course, the broad set of missions which those forces must be able to carry out can be defined in similar terms, although the relative importance of specific missions (and variants on them) will differ depending on the precise operational and political characteristics attending a given conflict. One is that U.S. forces must be able to localize a conflict, precluding external involvement by Soviet or Soviet proxy forces, and terminate either existing outside intervention or adjacent sanctuaries. The second is to concentrate on the destruction of the opponent's organized military potential within the country in the shortest possible time with a minimum involvement of U.S. ground forces, both to reduce U.S. casualties and to minimize the impression that the United States is waging another imperial war, with all of the attendant political liabilities within the United States itself. The third is to provide the local government being supported with sufficient time to upgrade the quality of its own security forces. And the fourth is to conduct operations within the local country in a way that minimizes both the destruction certain to occur as part of the conflict, and the overall U.S impact on that economy and society.

The test of U.S. general purpose forces, then, will be in their ability to carry out these missions in any of the possible conflict situations in which they might become involved, taking full account of the domestic political and economic constraints on the United States and the international security environment within which the United States must necessarily act. A number of possible measures to provide the capacity to act effectively in limited conventional conflicts can be identified, ranging from broad strategic issues to the recruitment of personnel for the armed forces.

Perhaps the most fundamental considerations are strategic in the broad sense of the term. Potential conflict situations must be monitored closely, with the actual commitment of U.S. forces to battle preceding rather than following the deterioration of a situation to the point where only direct and massive U.S. military involvement can avert disaster. Preventive action is always preferable to corrective action, if only because fewer U.S. forces will be required for a shorter period of time, and will sustain fewer losses, if preemptive measures can be implemented. Effective deterrence at all points of the conflict continuum is predicated, it must be remembered, on a general perception that a country has both the capacity to act and the will to do so promptly. A determination to regain the strategic initiative will do much to enhance deterrence even in the case of potential limited conventional conflict situations, and to increase the prospects for success if deterrence fails. And here, as elsewhere, the adage that the best defense is a good offense applies with particular force.

Once it is decided to take the initiative and intervene militarily in any type of a limited conventional conflict situation, two operational precepts must be followed: sanctuaries must be attacked and terminated at the outset as a source of military assistance to an opponent; and the actual conduct of ground warfare in the country being assisted must be kept to an absolute minimum. To wage any type of conventional war on the territory of any nation will be disruptive at best, and destructive of its society and economy at worst. And if any country is to be ravaged by war, it should be the one(s) against which the battle is being waged, and not the country being assisted; a policy which accepts the occasional need to destroy part of a country in order to "save" it is little more than a criminal misjudgment. Thus, for instance, the decision to employ U.S. ground forces in Indochina should only have been made if the United States was willing to simultaneously close off the Cambodian and Laotian sanctuaries with U.S. ground forces, and to bring the ground war to North Vietnam (especially in the area south of Vinh near the 17th parallel). Similarly, in the event of, for example, a Nicaraguan invasion of El Salvador, with Nicaraguan forces supplied by Cuba, the U.S. response should be to intervene with ground forces in Nicaragua rather than in El Salvador, and to impose an absolute air and sea blockade against Cuban air and sea traffic to that part of the world. If the forces available for such action are not available, if the costs of such action are seen to be militarily prohibitive, and if the political consequences (especially regarding relations with the USSR) are seen to outweigh the political gains that would be associated with a successful intervention, then intervention ought not to take place at all. We have had enough of well-orchestrated interventions in which (reversing the classic British experience) we won most of the battles and lost the war.(74)

The United States must recast its general purpose forces to give greater emphasis to those elements required to project U.S. power abroad and to allow U.S. ground forces to operate effectively within the designated target area. This means far more resources devoted to air and naval general purpose forces and to strategic mobility forces (especially strategic airlift) than is now the case, and far less attention to maintaining a large army oriented toward a protracted conventional war against the Soviet Union in Central Europe - a conflict whose likelihood can be envisioned only if one utterly ignores both Soviet and NATO doctrine.(75) Under some limited conventional conflict situations, to be sure, a long-term need for large U.S. general purpose ground forces can be envisioned, at least if the United States defers acting until the time for decisive intervention with minimum forces has passed. But there is no reason why a revitalized reserve system that truly integrates the active, Selected Reserve (including National Guard), and Individual Ready Reserve components of the "Total Force" into an establishment capable of rapid mobilization and prompt deployment overseas cannot be created. And, if such a system were created, the United States could concentrate its efforts on the truly essential conventional force balances while retaining a "surge" general purpose ground force capability should the need for it arise.

A very hard look must be taken at the Rapid Deployment Force. It has become all too apparent that the RDF is a gerrymandered force with far more nominal strength than its actual organization and resources would warrant. It is, in fact, the classic example of an entity designed by a committee whose members were primarily interested in ensuring that each of their parent organizations had a "piece of the action" than they were in creating a maximally effective force. To be effective, the RDF must be composed wholly of tactical air and ground forces from one service - that is, the Marine Corps - whose component formations must be immediately available to the RDF commander without the need to "request" their release from other commands. And the RDF must have sufficient mobility to be able to deploy rapidly when and where needed to avoid running afoul of the classic "too little, too late" syndrome all too characteristic of U.S. military operations in recent years. It goes without saying that increased naval gunfire support and light tactical air support are essential to its successful employment.

We must have much better economy of force with regard to the deployment of those forces assigned to limited conventional conflict deterrence and suppression missions, whether or not they are actually part of the RDF.(76) On the one hand, the "forward strategy"(77) of large overseas deployments may have some value in the core theaters of Central Europe and Northeast Asia. When it comes to maintaining adequate intervention forces for the host of possible limited conventional conflict situations that might arise, however, the demand for such forces in various theaters would surely exceed available resources by a wide margin. Similarly, except for Caribbean/Central American contingencies, it would place an equally excessive demand on strategic mobility forces to concentrate the majority of the intervention forces (especially in the RDF) within the continental United States. What one gains by having a central reserve on which to draw, one loses in terms of time and distance from the threatened areas. The decision to deploy prepackaged materiel forward and to "marry" it up with personnel from the continental United States is intriguing, but has a number of difficulties in terms of consummating that particular marriage in time of an actual conflict. Perhaps a suitable intermediate measure would be to deploy a friendly nation in each of the principal regions where limited conventional conflicts could occur (again with the exception of the Caribbean/Central American region) a major RDF element in divisional strength, with supporting units, which would be primarily responsible for the initial response to a conventional threat in that region.

There is the problem of providing whatever forces are created with sufficient numbers of well-qualified, well-trained, and well-disciplined personnel. The difficulties attending the current all volunteer force (AVF) and the debate over the various forms of conscription which might serve as useful alternatives to it are well known and need not be dealt with at length here.(78) Whatever the objective merits of the various manpower procurement systems might be, however, especially with regard to the armed forces as a whole, volunteers are clearly preferable for the components of the Rapid Deployment Force or whatever elements might be tasked for involvement in limited conventional conflicts. Those conflicts, as indicated earlier, are far from compatible with the American "way of war" (to use Russell Weigley's term); and political democracies in general do not wage protracted conventional wars well, at least in political terms, in the modern world. The involvement and death of conscripts in limited wars necessarily politicizes the war within the United States, and provides a basis for domestic opposition to that intervention, to a far greater degree than is the case when only volunteers are involved. Even in the latter case, of course, the failure to achieve a clearly defined and persuasively articulated set of political-military objectives will eventually produce domestic opposition to a continuation of U.S. involvement in a conflict, regardless of how the soldiers are procured. But volunteers buy time for those objectives to be achieved and, in limited conventional conflicts, time is an extraordinarily precious commodity.

Finally, once committed to battle, the United States must assume full command over all operations (including those of the local country's forces), and must proceed with the understanding that political success is predicated on military success. The parallel command structures which existed in Vietnam were a prescription for disaster, and we cannot allow a repetition of that disaster simply to assuage the sensibilities of local political and military leaders whose survival has become dependent on American political steadfastness and military prowess. Further, an adversary cannot be brought to the negotiating table unless it is clear that the alternative to negotiation is disaster, and that a breach of whatever settlement is reached will simply make that disaster a reality. The world in general has never thought much of good intentions when questions of the national interest were involved, and the addition of an ideological component to that definition has exacerbated matters still further. Victory is a two-way street, even in the low intensity conflicts of the modern era;

and, if others against whom the United States is fighting can walk it, so can the United States. All that is required is a realistic understanding of the type of war being fought, a careful definition of objectives and interests, and - one committed to battle - a determination to use the forces necessary to achieve those objectives rather than to bring an opponent to a negotiating table for a brief respite. These requirements are well within our reach, and it is up to us to realize them.

IN THE FINAL ANALYSIS - A POLITICAL DECISION

The decade of the 1970s was one of U.S. foreign policy retrenchment in which we convinced ourselves that military force as an instrument of policy was declining. This resulted in our subsequent unwillingness to employ military power to ensure security interests. During this period of uncertainty and moral introspection, the Soviets operated under no similar self-imposed restraints. In fact, as we have noted, they either directly or indirectly expanded their power projection into the spectrum of Third World conflicts that we have labeled as "low intensity."

As the United States moves into the 1980s, the challenges to our security interests will continue to occur in these limited conflicts. And yet, as we have demonstrated, the United States remains the least prepared for the most probable types of challenges. To this end, we have presented a detailed outline of the steps that must be taken if the United States is to parry these challenges and protect its military and economic security interests in Third World regions.

However, in the final analysis, if these recommendations are to be converted into operational policy and strategy, the impetus must come directly and forcefully from the top of the Reagan administration. It must articulate to the public and Congress the compelling reasons for developing and employing such forces, and then it must ensure that the U.S. military and other pertinent agencies develop the appropriate strategies and capabilities to parry the low intensity challenges.

NOTES

(1) George Osborn and William Taylor, "Low Intensity Conflict and U.S. Policy: Political Military Considerations," unpublished manuscript, p. 6.

(2) Samual Francis, The Soviet Strategy of Terror (Washington, D.C.: The Heritage Foundation, 1981), pp. 5-6, 22-23.

(3) Donald Vought, "Preparing for the Wrong War," Military Review (May 1977), pp. 28-29, 33.

(4) Harold Rood, Kingdoms of the Blind (Durham, N.C.: Carolina Academic Press, 1980), pp. 268, 272.

(5) Andrew Goodpaster, "Development of a Coherent American Strategy: An Approach," Parameters (March 1981), p. 2.

(6) W. Scott Thompson, Power Projection (New York: National Strategy Information Center, 1978). Thompson identifies two components of power projection: (1) the "capacity to develop an infrastructure of influence ranging from 'treaties of friendship' . . . to an active alliance system . . . the prepositioning of forces and equipment, the deployment of a worldwide naval support system, the development of reconnaissance capabilities, and the expansion of command and control communications"; (2) the "capacity to inject appropriate instruments of influence and force over distances into rapidly changing violent (or potentially violent) situations in order to protect or further develop the major power's infrastructure" (pp. 7-8).

(7) See David Tarr, "The Strategic Environment, U.S. National Security, and the Nature of Low Intensity Conflict," in Non-Nuclear Conflicts in the Nuclear Age, edited by Sam Sarkesian (New York: Praeger, 1980).

(8) See Samuel Huntington, "The Soldier and the State in the 1970s," in The Changing World of the American Military, edited by Franklin Margiotta (Boulder, Colorado: Westview Press, 1978).

(9) Washington Post (March 26, 1981), p. 2.

(10) Colin Gray, The Geopolitics of the Nuclear Era (New York: National Strategy Information Center, 1977), ch. 1.

(11) Ibid., p. 9.

(12) Marshall Shulman, "SALT and the Soviet Union," in SALT: The Moscow Agreements and Beyond, edited by Mason Willrich and John Rhinelander (New York: The Free Press, 1974), p. 121.

(13) James O'Leary, "Envisioning Interdependence: Perspectives on Future World Orders," Orbis (Fall 1978), p. 503.

(14) Ibid., pp. 505-22.

(15) Ibid.

(16) Ibid., p. 519.

(17) Lawrence Korb, The Fall and the Rise of the Pentagon (Westport, Conn.: Greenwood Press, 1979), ch. 2.

(18) National Security Decision, memorandum 3, printed in John Leacocos, "Kissinger's Apparat," Foreign Policy (Winter 1971), p. 25.

(19) Theodore Shackley, The Third Option (New York: Reader's Digest Press, 1981), p. 19.

(20) See Thompson, Power Projection; and Brian Crozier, Strategy of Survival (New Rochelle, N.Y.: Arlington House, 1978).

(21) See Steven David, "Realignment in the Horn: The Soviet Advantage," International Security (Fall 1979), pp. 69-90.

(22) For a useful discussion of the use of aid in such a manner, see Klaus Knorr, The Power of Nations (New York: Basic Books, 1975), ch. 7.

(23) See Robert Koehane and Joseph Nye, Power and Interdependence: World Politics in Transition (Boston, Mass.: Little, Brown, 1977).

(24) Eliot Cohen, Commandos and Politicians (Cambridge, Mass.: Harvard University, The Center for International Affairs, 1978), p. 25.

(25) Howard Graves, "U.S. Capabilities for Military Intervention," unpublished manuscript, pp. 9-10.

(26) Cohen, Cammandos and Politicians, ch. 3.

(27) Shackley, The Third Option, p. ix.

(28) Ibid., pp. 19-20.

(29) Korb, The Fall and the Rise of the Pentagon.

(30) Thomas Etzold, "Happy Birthday, RDF-and No Happy Returns," Washington Post (February 22, 1981).

(31) Thomas Fabyanic, "Conceptual Planning and the Rapid Deployment Joint Force," unpublished manuscript, p. 5.

(32) W.R. Schilling, T.R. Fox, Catherine M. Kelleher, and Donald J. Puchala, American Arms and a Changing Europe (New York: Columbia University Press, 1973).

(33) See the basic discussion of what constitutes vital and nonvital national interests in Donald E. Neuchterlein, National Interests and Presidential Leadership: The Setting of Priorities (Boulder, Colo.: Westview 1978), esp. chs. 1-2.

(34) It is worth noting that the political leaders of many countries do not have the same inclination to consider such interests worth preserving as they do lesser threats to lesser interests which may have a more immediate effect on their own

political careers. The behavior of former Senator Frank
Church (D-Idaho) during the furor over the presence of a
Soviet brigade in Cuba is a case in point.

(35) See the discussion of these trends in Alan Ned Sabrosky's "America's Choices in the Emerging World Order," International Security Review 4/3 (Fall 1979).

(36) Both events, it should be noted, occurred as the United
States groped to find a new role in the post-Vietnam era, and
need not constitute a harbinger of things to come.

(37) See, for example, Robert E. Osgood, Alliances and
American Foreign Policy (Baltimore: Johns Hopkins University
Press 1968), for a classic statement on this point.

(38) For a brief discussion of these issues, as well as the
specific role of sea power therein, see Charles D. Allen, Jr.,
The Uses of Navies in Peacetime (Washington: American Enterprise Institute 1980).

(39) Steven D. Symms and Marianne Winston, "Resource De-
pendency and American Security," International Security Review, 4/4 (Winter 1979-80).

(40) For a discussion of this concept, see Dan Handel, Gerald
T. West, and Robert G. Meadow, Overseas Investment and
Political Risk (Philadelphia: Foreign Policy Research Institute
1975).

(41) There is all too often a solid basis for domestic discontent and revolution which is overlooked by those enamored
with some of the less admirable pro-U.S. regimes in the developing world.

(42) Many regional organizations, such as the Organization of
African Unity (OAU), obviously are not supportive of U.S.
interests, and others, such as the Organization of American
States (OAS), are far less comfortable "homes" for the United
States than was once the case.

(43) General Sir Walter Walker, The Next Domino? (London:
Covenant Publishers 1980), presents an unusually interesting
appraisal of this phenomenon from a different point of view
than most Americans tend to encounter.

(44) The subject area of "proxy war" is one which deserves
extremely careful attention, as the Soviet reliance of proxies
seems to be growing in direct proportion to the Soviet ability
to transport and supply such forces in various parts of the
Third World.

(45) That there may exist countervailing economic and strategic interests is worth noting. The Shah of Iran, for example, was one of this country's principal military clients in
that part of the world, but he had also encouraged oil price

policies within OPEC that were not supportive of U.S. economic well-being.

(46) Insurgents necessarily make use of such instability to further their own causes. See Bard O'Neill, "Insurgent Strategies: An Examination of Four Approaches," in American Defense Policy, 4th ed. (Baltimore: Johns Hopkins University Press 1977).

(47) For an appraisal of one key aspect of this pattern, see Elmo R. Zumwalt, Jr., "Gorshkov and His Navy," Orbis (Fall 1980).

(48) Both the growth in the international arms trade and the misapprehension of its role in foreign policy are examined in Stephen P. Gibert, "Arsenal Diplomacy: Problems and Prospects," International Security Review 5/3 (Fall 1980).

(49) The notion of "cost-tolerance" was coined by Steven Rosen. It essentially refers to the relative ability of a particular nation to absorb human and material losses in pursuit of political, military, or economic objectives.

(50) Far too often, the United States defined among its so-called "Free World" coalition nations whose regimes were internally repressive and corrupt, and which professed a measure of anticommunism in order to gain U.S. support against those who would overthrow them. Nations such as Haiti, the Dominican Republic, Nicaragua, and others scattered throughout the world fall - or fell - into this category. Ironically, having provided that aid, the United States usually declined (in the name of national sovereignty) to induce such regimes to eliminate the root causes of discontent.

(51) See James L. Payne, The American Threat: National Security and Foreign Policy (College Station, Texas: Texas A&M University Press 1981).

(52) Robert Osgood, Limited War Revisited (Boulder, Colo.: Westview Press, 1979), p. 85.

(53) The concept is borrowed from Thompson, Power Projection.

(54) Bard O'Neill, William Heaton, and Donald Albert, Political Violence and Insurgency: A Comparative Approach (Boulder, Colo.: Westview, 1980).

(55) Shackley, The Third Option, pp. 17-18.

(56) Robert Tucker, "The Purposes of American Power," Foreign Affairs (Winter 1980/1981), pp. 241, 274.

(57) For an informative discussion see Knorr, The Power of Nations, ch. 7.

(58) Alexander Haig, Security and Development Assistance (Washington, D.C.: U.S. Department of State Bureau of Public Affairs, 1981), p. 3.

(59) For the background on civic action see Edward Glick, Peaceful Conflict (Harrisburg, Penn.: Stackpole Books, 1967).

(60) Graves, "U.S. Capabilities for Military Intervention," p. 9.

(61) See Vought, "Preparing for the Wrong War."
(62) See Ernest Lefever and Roy Godson, The CIA and the American Ethic (Washington, D.C.: Ethics and Public Policy Center of Georgetown University, 1979), ch. 2.

(63) Shackley, The Third Option, pp. 158-60.

(64) See Richard Shultz and Stephen Sloan, Responding to the Terrorist Threat (New York: Pergamon Press, 1980) pp. 33-37.

(65) U.S. allies in that war included (in widely varying strength) South Korea, Australia, New Zealand, Thailand, and the Philippines. Virtually all of America's other allies either outspokenly opposed the U.S. role in Vietnam, or maintained a posture of "studied neutrality."

(66) See, for example, Lord Saint Brides, "The Empire Plays to Win," Orbis (Fall 1980).

(67) See Alan Ned Sabrosky's, "Allies, Clients, and Encumbrances," International Security Review 5/2 (Summer 1980).

(68) For a good postmortem on the latter, see W. Scott Thompson and Donaldson Frizzel (eds), The Lessons of Vietnam (New York: Crane Russak, 1977).

(69) See Russell Weigley, The American Way of War (Bloomington, Ind.: Indiana University Press, 1973).

(70) Alan Ned Sabrosky, James Clay Thompson, and Karen A. McPherson, "Organized Anarchies: Military Bureaucracy in the 1980s," Journal of Applied Behavioral Sciences (forthcoming).

(71) Kenneth Boulding, Conflict and Defense (New York: Harper & Row 1962) discusses this concept, but only from the perspective of distance.

(72) The rise of early opposition to a very limited U.S. involvement in El Salvador in early 1981 exemplifies this process. Much of the radical movement of the Vietnam war era has remained dormant; it has not disappeared.

(73) For a full discussion of the role of general purpose forces in American strategy, see Alan Ned Sabrosky's "U.S. General Purpose Forces: Four Essential Reforms," Orbis (Fall 1980).

(74) It is this situation that obtained in Vietnam. See Richard Shultz, "Reassessing U.S. Strategy in Vietnam: Past Lessons and Future Planning," International Security Review 5/4 (Winter 1980-81).

(75) See the discussions in Joseph D. Douglass, Jr., "NATO Theater Nuclear Modernization," International Security Review 5/1 (Spring 1980); and Walter F. Hahn, "Does NATO Have a Future?" International Security Review 5/2 (Summer 1980).

(76) A classic appraisal of the paramount importance of the principle of "economy of force" appears in Edward Luttwak, The Grand Strategy of the Roman Empire (Baltimore: Johns Hopkins University Press 1976).

(77) See Robert Strausz-Hupé, William R. Kintner, and Stefan Possony, A Forward Strategy For America (New York: Harper & Row 1961).

(78) For a concise overview, see Alan Ned Sabrosky, Military Manpower and Military Power (Chicago: Chicago Council on Foreign Relations, 1980).

Index

Abrams, General Creighton W.,
43-44, 54, 118
Accelerated Pacification Pro-
gram, 34, 145
Agency for International De-
velopment (AID), 24, 39
American military, profession-
alism of, 164-168
American values, 159-168
Army of the Republic of Viet-
nam (ARVN), 28
aim of, 24, 25
American military and, 146
attrition and, 126
Hau Nghia and, 35
Long An and, 39
Long Huu and, 41
Vietnamization and, 55-56
Attrition strategy, 23, 28,
43-44, 124-130, 135
See also Abrams, General
Creighton W.; Hau Nghia;
Long An; Viet Cong; West-
moreland, General William

"Big Unit War." See Attrition
strategy
British Advisory Mission, 4,
18
See also Thompson, Robert G.

Carter, President Jimmy, 177,
187, 195, 197, 204
Casualties, 123
Chieu Hoi (Open Arms) Pro-
gram, 39, 41, 57, 103-104,
147
Chinh-Hunnicutt affair, 42
CIA, 24, 29, 199-200, 212
Civil Guard. See Regional
Forces
Civil Operations and Revolu-
tionary Development Support
(CORDS), 55, 58, 59, 92
Communist strategy 1965-1966,
43
"Control," 30-32, 56-57, 107.
See also was Hau Nghia; Long
An; Vietnamization-Pacifica-
tion, qualitative examina-
tion, quantitative examina-
tion
Conventional military thought,
29, 42-43, 156
"The Counterinsurgency Plan
for Viet-Nam," 3, 18
Counterinsurgency warfare,
144, 156-157
County Fair operations, 29, 31

Democratic Republic of Vietnam
(DRV), 121-123, 129-130,
135

About the Editors
and Contributors

DOUGLAS S. BLAUFARB, author of The Counterinsurgency Era, served with the U.S. government for over 25 years. Most of his service was with the CIA in various posts around the world, including Vietnam and Laos. Since his retirement in 1970, he has served as a consultant for the National Security Council and as a Policy Analyst for the Rand Corporation.

JAMES W. DUNN is a Colonel in the U.S. Army and currently Chief of the Histories Division of the U.S. Army Center of Military History. He served two tours in Vietnam: in 1965 he was an adviser in Hau Nghia Province, and in 1971 he was an adviser in the Phoenix directorate of CORDS. Col. Dunn holds a Ph.D. in American Studies from the University of Hawaii and has taught at West Point and St. Bonaventure University.

LAWRENCE E. GRINTER is currently Professor of International Affairs at the Air War College. He earned his Ph.D. in Political Science from the University of North Carolina and served as a researcher for the Simulmatics Corporation in Saigon. He has taught at Haverford College, the National War College, and the School of Foreign Service at Georgetown University. He is the author of articles, reviews, monographs, and book chapters on Vietnam.

RICHARD A. HUNT, a historian at the U.S. Army Center of Military History, earned a doctorate in History from the University of Pennsylvania. While serving with the U.S. Army, he was assigned to the faculty of the Institute for Military Assistance at Fort Bragg and was a staff officer in MACV headquarters. Author of several articles on the Vietnam war, he is writing a comprehensive two-volume history of the pacification program for the Center.

ALAN NED SABROSKY (Ph.D., University of Michigan) is Director and Vice-President of the Foreign Policy Research Institute and Editor of Orbis: A Quarterly Journal of World Affairs. A former Marine, he has taught at Middlebury College, the United States Military Academy at West Point, and the Catholic University of America. His published work includes Blue-Collar Soldiers? Unionization and the U.S. Military, Defense Manpower Policy: A Critical Reappraisal, Military Manpower and Military Power, The Eagle's Brood: American Civil-Military Relations in the 1980s, and over forty articles and book reviews in numerous anthologies and professional journals.

RICHARD SHULTZ received his Ph.D. from Miami University and is currently Assistant Professor of Politics at the Catholic University of America where he conducts courses on National Security Policy, Strategic Analysis, Military Strategy, Foreign Policy, and Intelligence. He is also a Research Associate of the National Strategy Information Center in Washington, D.C. In addition to numerous articles and book reviews in professional journals and anthologies, he is co-author of Responding to the Terrorist Threat: Security and Crises Management.

DONALD B. VOUGHT is a retired Colonel, United States Army. He served in Vietnam with the Military Assistance Advisory Group. Colonel Vought holds an M.A. in Political Science from the University of Louisville and is also a USACGSC graduate. The author of numerous articles in professional journals and anthologies, Colonel Vought has served as a consultant to the Department of the Army since his retirement.